ROAN MOUNTAIN

ROAN MOUNTAIN

HISTORY OF AN APPALACHIAN TREASURE

JENNIFER A. BAUER

natural
HISTORY
PRESS

Published by Natural History Press
An imprint of The History Press
Charleston, SC 29403
www.historypress.net

Front cover: View of North Carolina from the top of Roan Mountain. *Photo by Carrie Maye Sullins.*

First published 2011
Second printing 2013

Manufactured in the United States

ISBN 978.1.60949.401.8

Library of Congress Cataloging-in-Publication Data

Bauer, Jennifer A.
Roan Mountain : history of an Appalachian treasure / Jennifer A. Bauer.
p. cm.
Includes bibliographical references and index.
ISBN 978-1-60949-401-8
1. Roan Mountain (N.C. and Tenn.)--History. 2. Roan Mountain (N.C. and Tenn.)--Description and travel. 3. Natural history--Roan Mountain (N.C. and Tenn.) I. Title.
F262.R39B38 2011
975.6'8--dc23
2011042384

Lovingly dedicated to the girls in my life, Carrie, Julia, Abigail and Madison; all bright and shining hopes for the future.

Contents

Preface

During an especially lush spring in the mid-1970s, I found myself headed for a totally new and refreshing environment. I was nineteen years old, and the upcoming summer was mine to spend at my heart's desire. My destination was Great Smoky Mountains National Park.

Still quite unsure of what the years ahead might hold, I was hoping that this mountain adventure would provide me with the perfect escape to help me decide just what it was I wanted to do with my life. The southern Appalachians certainly offered a strikingly different atmosphere from that of my home, Baltimore, Maryland.

Loaded down with backpack, sleeping bag, camping equipment and a small library of university catalogues, I made my way to an obscure campground in the Smokies. Reading and rereading my catalogues, I kept coming back to the sections on elementary education, and I began to get a feeling that I had chosen a career path. Still, I wasn't quite sure.

One warm, breezy day as I sat reading course descriptions, never expecting to see a soul in such isolated surroundings, I was quite surprised when a fellow in a park service uniform appeared out of nowhere. His name was Troy Brown, and he was the ranger assigned to the particular area where I was staying. After some brief introductions, he offered to show me some special places—spots deep in the mountains where few had ever visited. It seemed a great opportunity to learn about an area that was entirely new to me, so we set off on a daylong exploration.

Every step of our trip presented something different from anything I had ever experienced growing up in a city. We traveled over slick, mossy logs, through rushing creeks and deep into the woods, discovering old, abandoned dwellings that seemed to call forth images of the families who had long since deserted them. There is no doubt that the places and images from that day made a profound impression on me. But more than that, I was touched by Troy's love for the environment and his commitment to doing whatever he could to protect mountain resources. I even began to share his sense of insult at those moments when we happened upon the assorted trash left by careless campers. As our hike was drawing to a close and we crossed the last bridge to the campground, we stumbled upon a pile of dirty diapers stacked against a tall, graceful hemlock. Apparently, the strain had been too great to carry them to a trash can located just ten feet away! It was as if the perpetrators had littered Troy's personal home; mine, too. From that day onward, I knew what sort of career I wanted to pursue.

That brief summer interlude in the outdoors was just the beginning, creating in me a desire to learn everything I possibly could about plants, animals and all other subjects having to do with the natural world. That fall, I enrolled at East Tennessee State University as a biology major. After a couple of quarters, it came time to choose an area of concentration within the Biology Department. The decision was an easy one for me, as I was more interested in botany than in any other field. Before long, I was a student worker for the botany professors, and I was taking as many field courses in botany as I could handle.

I had yet to find my way to Roan Mountain. It took a very special teacher and friend to introduce me to this place so far removed from my native Baltimore. John Warden, a professor in the Biology Department, had years earlier discovered the Roan and its magnificent and unusual flora and fauna. Anyone who met him knew immediately that Roan Mountain must be a wonderful place, for John easily communicated his love and enthusiasm to students and friends alike. He took me to the Roan many times, generously sharing his vast knowledge of the mountain's plants and history. Each trip seemed to leave me wanting more, so upon the completion of my undergraduate coursework, I immediately enrolled in the master's program.

My master's thesis was initially intended to follow up work done by Dr. D.M. Brown on the Roan in the 1930s. Dr. Brown had provided some of the first scientifically documented material on the botany of the mountain. Now, fifty years later, I was hoping to revisit the areas he had photographed, capturing on film the changes that had taken place over the course of half a century. Yet one thing led to another. I came to understand that the plants on the Roan were just one small component of the ecosystem and that even documenting the entire ecosystem would fall far short of capturing the essence of the place. As I dug deeper and deeper in the literature, I found the human history of the Roan to be especially interesting. The mountain's earliest inhabited years were quickly being forgotten as memories faded and important documentation was stored in attics or relegated to library collections.

Something made me want to preserve the stories, the facts and the lost histories of the Roan, for the mountain's past was anything but ordinary. I spent every spare moment I could find immersed in library microfilm, microfiche and rare book collections. Every old paper and text I discovered seemed to refer me to other early writers, turning my research into a scavenger hunt through time. It was amazing how much history on the Roan had been written and filed away through the years, even if it was in bits and pieces. Still, there were gaps in the story of Roan Mountain that could only be filled in by local people themselves. I began searching for those people born before the turn of the twentieth century, people with personal knowledge of earlier days, and then I broadened my hunt to include those whose elders had at least left memories and tales with them. Again, I found that each of my contacts sent me to others. Some I reached by mail and some in person. All were more than eager to share their experiences and recollections. An unexpected blessing was the great number of old photographs documenting earlier times on Roan Mountain that many of my contacts were willing to pass along.

In the midst of all this work, and while I was still trying to complete my degree, an odd twist of fate occurred. John Warden informed me that an interview committee from the Tennessee State Parks system was coming to East Tennessee State. They were hiring seasonal naturalists for three-month positions. I decided to give it a try and was lucky enough to be hired to work that summer in a park in Kingsport. The following summer, I was transferred to the Roan, and before long I was working full time as a ranger naturalist at Roan Mountain State Park. Opportunities for meeting area people and for conducting my own research into the history of the Roan then became abundant. A chronicle of the mountain and the people who have called it their home began to fall into place.

Warm thanks are due to the many people who shared their knowledge and enthusiasm of Roan Mountain with me. Words cannot express just how much I appreciate your help; your love of this special place makes it possible to continue to add to our knowledge of Roan Mountain and document it for generations to come.

A special thank you goes to Ruth Kerley and Jo Buchanan, who went "above and beyond" to help with this story. Also to a dear friend, Jo Ann

Cordell, who inspired me, and all who knew her, to learn, share and remember the old ways.

My mentor and botany instructor, John Warden, and General John Thomas Wilder's great-grandson, Thomas O. Maher, have both encouraged me for over three decades to move forward and to stay focused on the importance of documenting Roan's stories, ecology and unique attributes. Most importantly, I would not have made it to the end of this labor of love without the strength and teachings of my mother, Sylvia, and the support of my husband, Bob, and my family. They all cheered me on as I researched and wrote, while they took care of the daily chores of life.

The final product is a book that attempts to impose a sense of order on a random collection of misplaced photographs, notes, partial histories, scientific data, oral interviews and local tales. It is hoped that the end result will be judged worthy of its subject, one of the most popular places in the Southeast today.

Introduction

The pages to follow begin an adventure laced with discovery of a place beloved by untold numbers resting along some of the highest ridges of the southern Appalachian Mountains. This place provided a home, nourishment and refuge to native peoples on the North American continent. In later years, as explorers from foreign lands found their way to what was considered the New World, intrigue developed in regards to this place where natural resources abounded and huge expanses of unsettled land appeared endless.

Primarily along the eastern coast of North America, settlers from Spain, France, Sweden, Holland and England claimed land during the seventeenth century. Between 1754 and 1763, the French and Indian War, fought by England, France and the Indians of North America, ended with an English victory. By this time, thirteen British-ruled colonies had grown along the eastern seaboard under the rule of King George III, but there were those who wanted a new life outside British control. These were the people who crossed the Proclamation Line of 1763 and settled on the western side of the Appalachian Mountains.

The mountains, hollers and coves that we now call Roan Mountain became one of many gateways into areas of new settlement, alive with numerous possibilities and hopes for the future. Those folks who first settled in the wilderness were strong and hardworking, held true to their beliefs and were devoted to family and neighbors and willing to risk all for a new life. These very traits hold true today in families whose ancestries go back to the people who first settled outside the British colonies—love of home, family, friends and this wonderful place called the Roan.

Introduction

Roan Mountain captures the hearts of those who visit, for a trip to the highlands is much like a visit to Canada. The elevation, climate and associated ecosystems combine to present one of the most biologically diverse places on our planet. Lush red spruce and Fraser fir forests, open grass and shrub balds and dramatic cliffs drop off into valleys below. The fourteen mile Appalachian Trail corridor across the Roan boasts the highest concentration of rare species along the entire 2,180-mile-long Appalachian Trail. Spring comes late, and winter arrives early at 6,285 feet, creating a very special ecosystem boasting a host of nationally and globally threatened and endangered plants and animals.

It is no wonder that biologists, conservation organizations and citizens consider the protection of the Roan an extremely high priority. Many devote their entire lives to this very task.

Like an island rising high above the valleys below, the Roan is home to an incredible diversity of life. Enjoy the journey that follows into the history of the place, the natural world and the people blended together to create a story full of personality and unforgettable memories.

I
Ecology

Geography

The southern section of the Appalachians is divided into two major mountain ranges, the Unaka Mountains to the west and the Blue Ridge Mountains to the east. The two ranges run roughly parallel to each other, extending northeast and southwest. A number of cross ranges are oriented southward from the Unakas to the Blue Ridge. Located at a latitude of eighty-two degrees west and a longitude of thirty-six degrees north, Roan Mountain is one of the highest of those cross ranges.

There are a variety of explanations that attempt to account for Roan Mountain's name, none of which has gained wide acceptance. Some people claim that the mountain appears a distinct roan color when its trademark Catawba rhododendron is in full bloom in late June, thus the name. Others say that Daniel Boone was a frequent visitor to the mountain on his excursions in the high country and that the mountain received its name as a tribute to Boone's roan-colored horse. Another theory involves the local population of mountain ash trees, whose vibrant red berries make the forests come alive during the autumn. The mountain ash was known as the rowan tree in days past, and that name eventually came to be applied to the entire mountain, with the "w" dropped over the course of time. One popular legend has it that André Michaux, a famous French botanist and one of the earliest men to document the southern Appalachians, was inspired to name the mountain after his native Rhone Valley while gazing upon its scenery one particularly lovely day. The spelling was later altered from Rhone because early settlers thought Michaux must have been referring to the mountain's roan color and

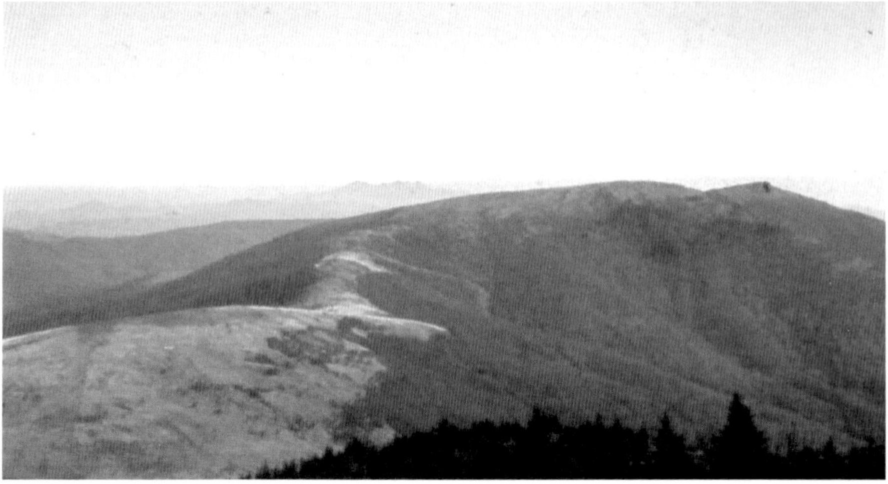

Round Bald (bottom left) across Engine Gap, Jane Bald and Grassy Ridge Bald. 1900.

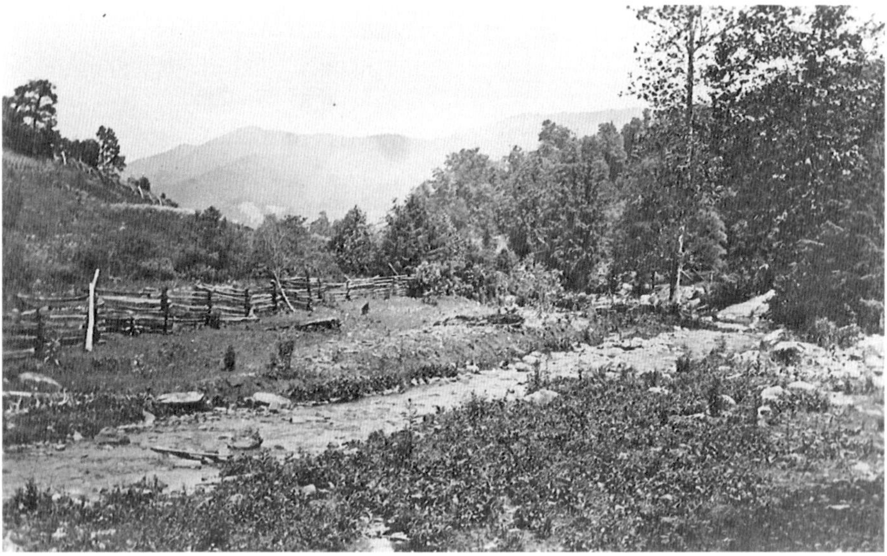

Water flows everywhere through the high mountains as seen along a local creek lined with a split rail fence. 1880s. *Courtesy of Thomas O. Maher.*

misspelling the name himself. It should be noted, however, that Michaux was not a native of the Rhone Valley.

It is every bit as difficult to categorize the Roan as it is to account for the origin of its name. I had visited a number of peaks in the southern

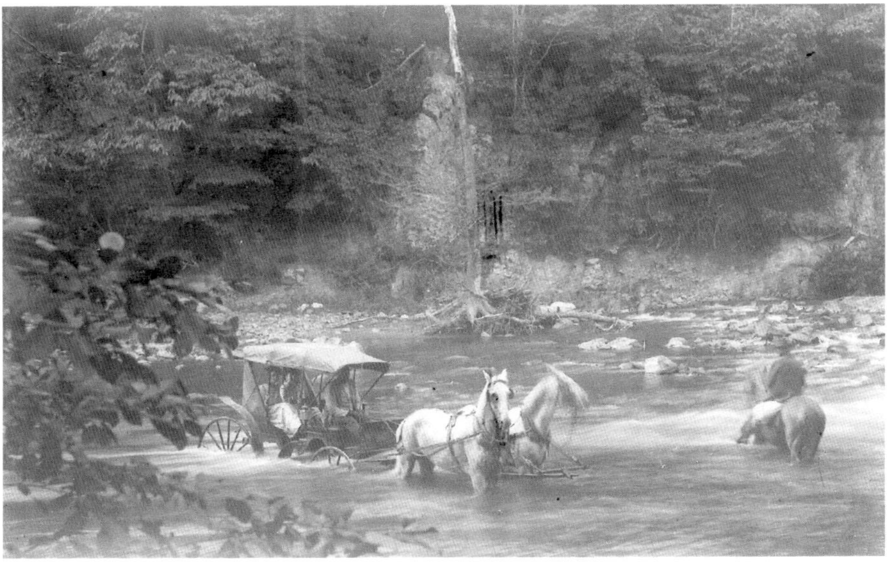

Wilder's horses, Comet and Jupiter, traversing the Doe. 1880s. *Courtesy of Thomas O. Maher.*

Appalachians before I made my first trip to Roan Mountain, and I noticed that most of the other summits rose to a high peak, often topped with a fire tower or an overlook. Once you'd climbed the tower or partaken of the view, you'd seen pretty much everything there was to be seen.

Such is not the case with Roan Mountain, and I suppose that is part of the reason why it continues to impress me to this day. The Roan does not simply end at a high peak. Rather, its long, high ridge—or summit—spreads in waves for more than five miles. Roan Mountain proper encompasses approximately twelve square miles, but if the entire surface area created by the mountain mass is taken into consideration, then that total area is more like fifty square miles. The altitude at the base of the Roan is approximately 2,500 feet. The ridgeline, or summit, ranges from a high of 6,285 feet at Roan High Knob to a low of 5,500 feet at Carver's Gap. Rounded spurs and broad, V-shaped valleys are situated on either side of the ridgeline. To the west, the area is drained by the Doe River, while to the east, it is drained by the Toe River, both of which empty into the Tennessee River.

The easy confusion between the Doe and the Toe and the fact that Roan Mountain is not a single peak but a long, high ridge make things difficult enough for the first-time visitor, but matters are further complicated by the fact that the Tennessee–North Carolina boundary runs along the ridgeline.

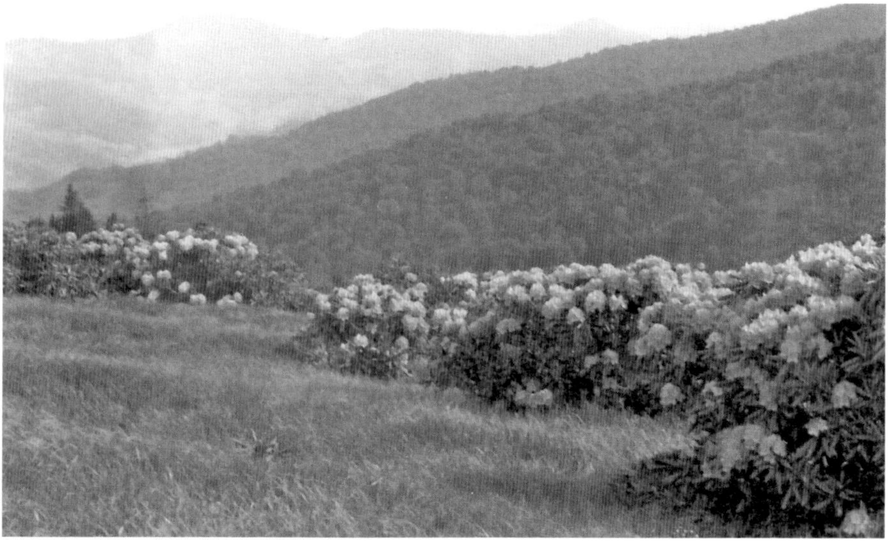

Rhododendron on Round Bald. 1930s. *D.M. Brown Collection.*

Many newcomers have been left to ponder whether particular overlooks give a view into the Volunteer State or Tar Heel country. They are sometimes uncertain where points of interest near the ridgeline are located in relation to the border, or even whether they themselves are standing or driving in Tennessee or North Carolina at a given time.

To put things in perspective, it might be said that most of the commerce and human activity in the immediate area is concentrated on the Tennessee side, while many of the notable natural features of the Roan itself are to be found on the North Carolina side.

The closest sizable town in either state is Johnson City, Tennessee. Most visitors approaching Roan Mountain from the Tennessee side take Highway 19E from Elizabethton, a road that climbs through the small communities of Valley Forge, Hampton and Crabtree to the village of Roan Mountain, Tennessee, situated at the base of the mountain. The village of Roan Mountain is a pleasant mixture of the old and the new. Historic buildings dating back to the nineteenth century line the old Main Street. For example, the S.B. Woods Pharmacy, dating to 1898, still operates on Highway 19E. Directly across from it are two antique shops located in buildings that date to the same period. Along the old Main Street, which intersects Highway 19E across from the Carter County Bank, the old theater and early stores are mixed in with renovated nineteenth-century homes. The newer eateries and grocery stores are clear signs of changing times.

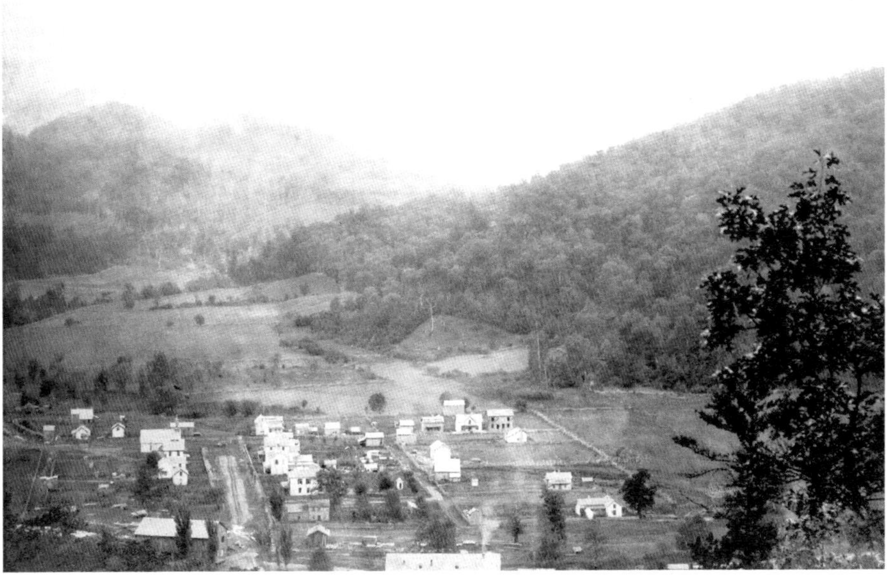

The town of Roan Mountain with the roof of Roan Mountain Inn in the foreground. 1888. *Courtesy of Thomas O. Maher.*

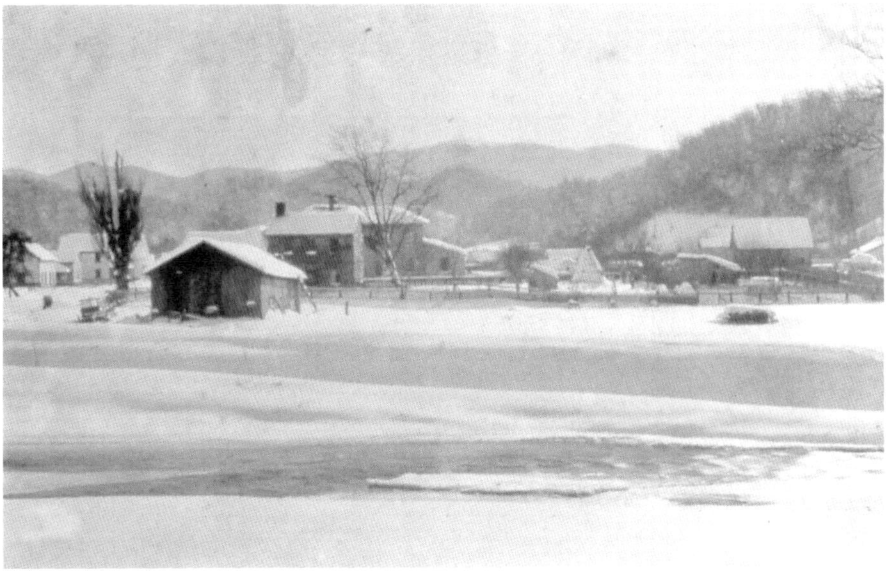

Looking across the Doe River toward General Wilder's home. 1880s. *Courtesy of Thomas O. Maher.*

Travelers who continue on Highway 19E reach the North Carolina border after only five miles, but those who wish to proceed the twenty-two miles to the top of the mountain should follow the prominent signs for Roan Mountain State Park and the Rhododendron Gardens visible at the main intersection in the village of Roan Mountain.

After turning onto Tennessee Highway 143, it is approximately four miles to the entrance of Roan Mountain State Park, a resort park created in the 1950s and developed in the 1970s. Park visitors can enjoy camping and a variety of recreational activities. Cabins are also available for rent.

Leaving the park, the climb up begins in earnest. As the road winds its way upward, the views open up to reveal astonishing vistas back into Tennessee, primarily toward Johnson City. On clear nights, it is easy to see car lights around Johnson City on I-26. At the top of Roan Mountain, there is an intersection named Carver's Gap. The road to the right, maintained by the United States Forest Service, stretches for three miles along the crest of the ridge.

The original road to the top, the Hack Line Road, was built in the 1870s by General John T. Wilder to transport his guests from the Roan Mountain Inn, located at the Roan Mountain railroad depot, to the Cloudland Hotel on top of the Roan. He advertised "a ride of twelve miles up a new and beautiful road, winding up the sides of the mountain, passing the most

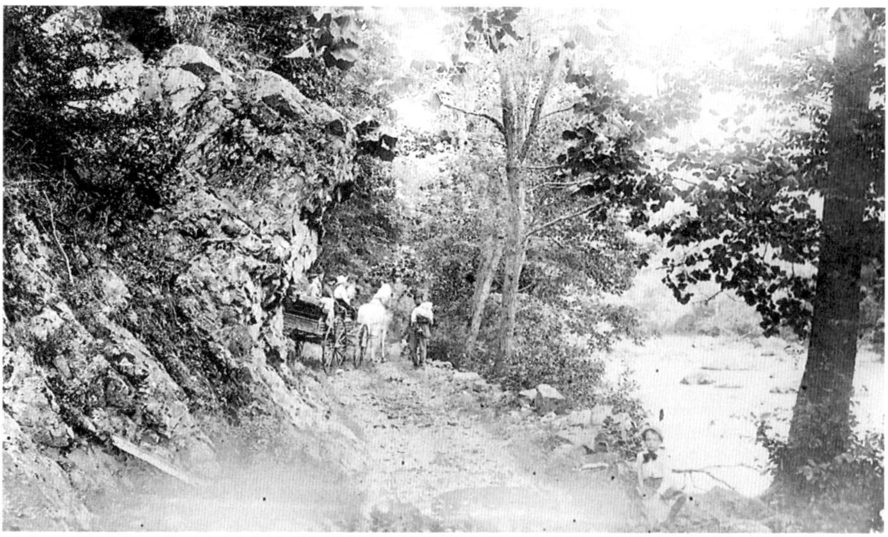

Along the old road, a buggy carrying the Wilder family is seen beside the Doe River. 1880s. *Courtesy of Thomas O. Maher.*

magnificent scenery at every turn." Aptly named, a buggy called a "hack" was used to transport the visitors up the road to the hotel.

After the hotel closed, businessmen from Johnson City bought control of the road and turned it into a toll road, which opened about 1931. A tollgate was installed near the home of John Greer, who was employed by the road company for fifteen years. John, or his wife and children, would take the one-dollar toll per car and driver, asking twenty-five cents for additional passengers. His family provided other services as well, selling milk and food products to travelers, providing a place to stay and standing ready with a hose to cool down overheated cars. At Carver's Gap, another toll station was constructed, so John and Harrison Street, the tollgate keeper at the Gap, would stay in contact via telephone to manage the direction of traffic up and down the narrow road.

Today, the Hack Line Road Trail is an officially designated trail in Cherokee National Forest. Hikers can access the trail just below Carver's Gap on the Tennessee side and walk down the mountain through some of the most impressive forests in the Southern Appalachians.

Boone, Banner Elk, Blowing Rock and Grandfather Mountain are some of the main attractions in North Carolina within an hour east of Roan Mountain. This area of the mountains is popular among tourists in the summer and skiers in the winter. Visitors approaching Roan Mountain from the east and northeast generally find their way to Elk Park, North Carolina, and then follow Highway 19E across the Tennessee line to the village of Roan Mountain, where they proceed up to the crest of Tennessee Highway 143. Those approaching from farther south in the Tar Heel State make the climb through a portion of the Pisgah National Forest on North Carolina Highway 261 from Bakersville, the closest community on the North Carolina side. North Carolina Highway 261 meets Tennessee Highway 143 and the United States Forest Service road at the state border at the crest of Roan Mountain.

That intersection is an important one. It falls near the center of what is known as "the highlands of the Roan," with a roughly equal number of the mountain's principal attractions to the southwest and the northeast. It also marks an intersection with the Appalachian Trail, which rides the Tennessee–North Carolina border through that section of the mountains. The Appalachian Trail is the longest continuous marked trail in the world, stretching some two thousand miles from Georgia's Springer Mountain to Maine's Mount Katahdin. En route, it traverses some of the finest country east of the Mississippi, including eight national forests, two national parks, a number of state parks and a good deal of private land as well. The place

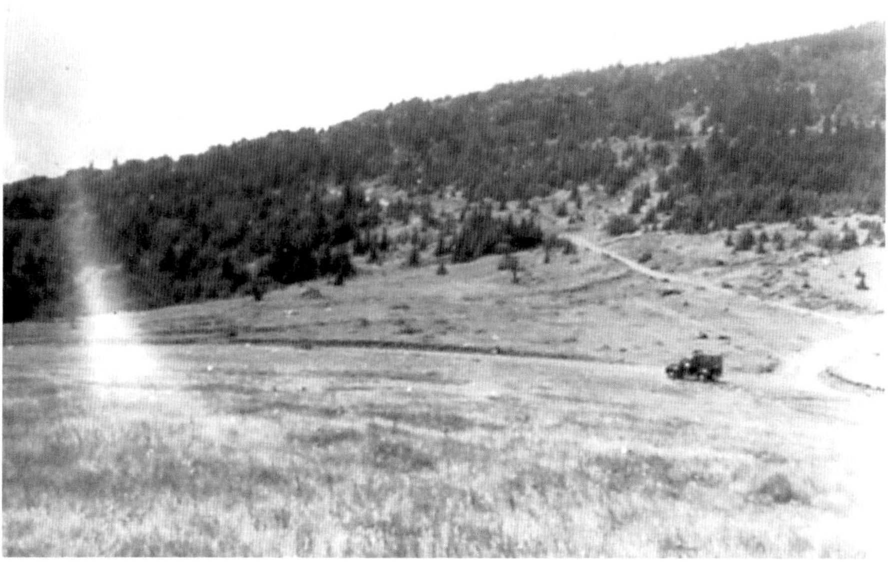

Early traffic traveling into North Carolina via Carver's Gap. 1930s. *D.M. Brown Collection.*

where the state highways and the Forest Service road converge is known as Carver's Gap, named for John Carver. Carver was a familiar figure in the gap in days gone by, as it was his favorite site for grazing his flocks of sheep and cattle.

Visitors who turn onto the Forest Service road at Carver's Gap pass through a lush forest of spruce and fir that covers Roan High Knob, the highest point on the mountain. Along the road, clearings and small grassy areas provide places for picnics and great views into the North Carolina mountains. Occasional trails lead from the gravel pull-offs back into the forest. Farther along, the road forks. The right fork leads to a parking lot that overlooks Tennessee and to the former site of the Cloudland Hotel, the spectacular edifice that brought Roan Mountain its greatest fame back around the turn of the twentieth century. The left fork leads to the Rhododendron Gardens, perhaps the most popular natural feature of the Roan today. The gardens offer more than two hundred acres of Catawba rhododendron, the largest such expanse in the United States. Visitors flock to see the beautiful crimson-red colors in mid- to late June.

Past the Rhododendron Gardens, there is a loop in the road, and at the far end of the loop is the start of a foot trail that leads to Roan High Bluff. Roan High Bluff marks the beginning of a series of high rock cliffs and

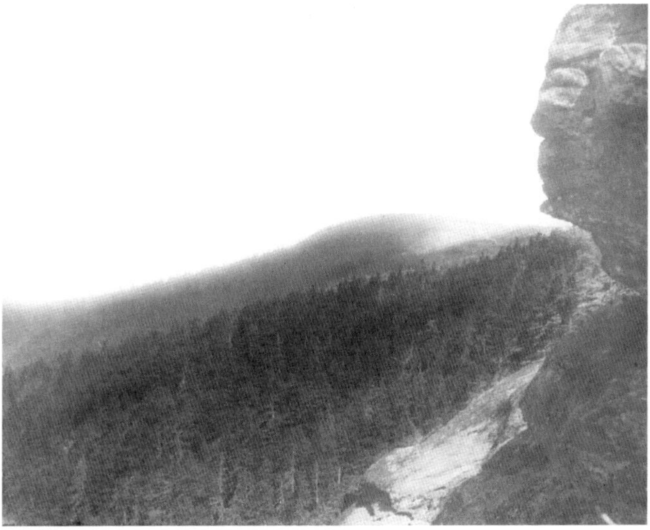

Roan High Bluff, once called Profile Rock or the Roan Sphinx. Some said it resembled William McKinley. 1930s. *D.M. Brown Collection.*

ridges that highlight the southwest end of the Roan. Charles Lanman visited the mountain in the middle part of the nineteenth century and recorded his impression of Roan High Bluff in *Letters from the Alleghany Mountains*: "The ascent to the top of this peak is gradual from all directions except one, but on the north it is quite perpendicular, and to one standing near the brow of the mighty cliff the scene is exceedingly imposing and fearful." Both the Rhododendron Gardens and Roan High Bluff fall on the North Carolina side of the border.

Roan Mountain is famous partly because of its large balds areas that remain free of trees for no apparent reason. The Roan's principal balds lie northeast of the place where the state highways and the Forest Service road converge, and they are accessible from Carver's Gap only by trail. In fact, it is a hike of about fourteen miles from Carver's Gap before another road is reached.

The first bald past Carver's Gap is Round Bald, which sits above Engine Gap, named for the steam engine based there in the early part of this century that transported cherry lumber from Tennessee to the Champion company's paper mill in Canton, North Carolina. Past Engine Gap is Jane Bald, which boasts abundant rock outcroppings and rhododendron.

The story of the naming of Jane Bald comes from a journey that ended sadly for Jane's sister, Harriett Cook. In 1999, Michael Joslin wrote a wonderful story for the *Johnson City Press*, written from an interview with Elsie Yelton, Harriett's granddaughter. Jane and Harriett Cook decided to make a trek from North Carolina into Tennessee to visit their two sisters whom they had not seen in some time. Another sister, Judy, tried to convince them not to go, for Harriett had just recovered from milk sickness, a disease brought on by drinking milk from cattle that had been poisoned by eating certain kinds of snakeroot. Though Harriett seemed well, Judy feared the milk sickness might recur during the strenuous trip over the mountain.

The girls arrived safely and enjoyed a good visit with their Carter County sisters, starting back across the Roan on November 16, 1870. Harriett became very weak as she tried to make her way back, and to worsen the situation, the weather turned cloudy and cold. She just made it to the bald when she fell ill from the milk sickness again. Jane sat devotedly by her sister's side through the dark, cold night, and as soon as the morning light broke, Jane rushed down the mountain in search of help.

Charley Young did not live far from Carver's Gap, and he came quickly to their aid, bringing a wagon and supplies up the mountain as far as he could go. It had turned terribly cold, and Jane thought she would freeze on the return wagon trip. Luckily, they found Harriett, still alive, and carried her to a featherbed in the back of the wagon. They made it home and got her settled in, but shortly after Harriett died at the age of twenty-four years. Jane, whose name was given to the mountain bald, enjoyed a long life into the 1940s.

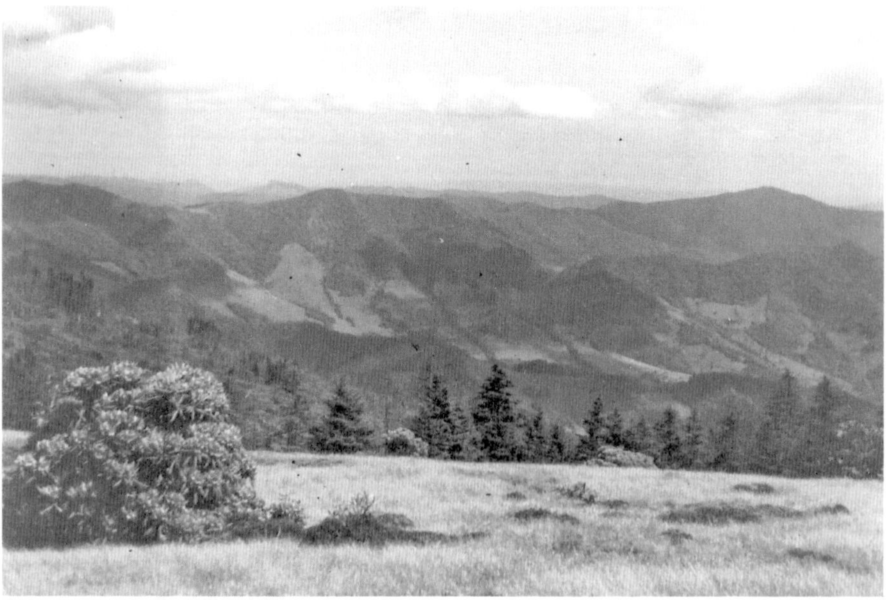

Looking into the North Carolina mountains. 1930s. *D.M. Brown Collection.*

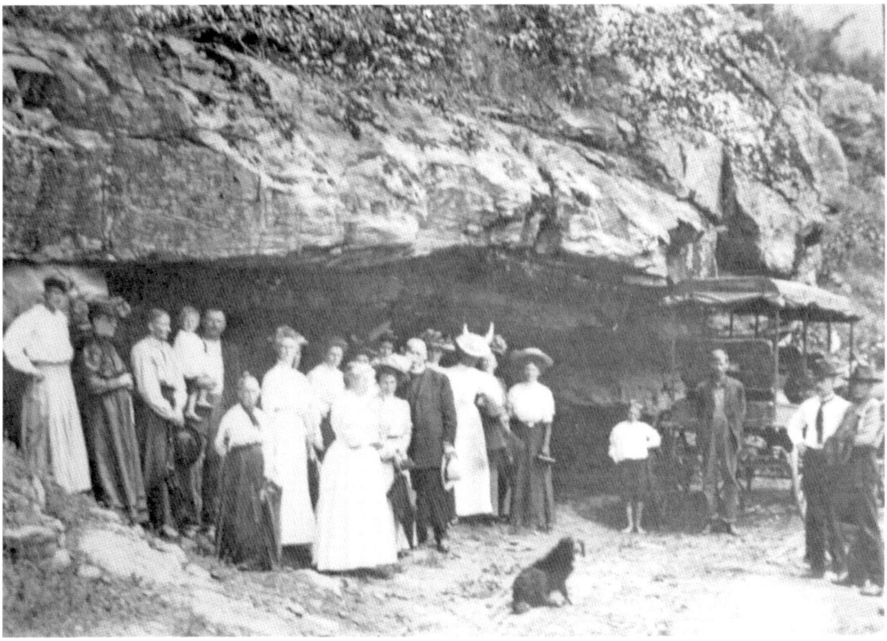

In 1905, the Daughters of the American Revolution placed a plaque at the Sheltering Rock, also called the Resting Place, honoring the efforts of the Overmountain Men. *Courtesy of Mel McKay.*

Beyond Jane Bald is Grassy Ridge Bald—formerly known as Chair Rock Bald—and then Yellow Mountain and Hump Mountain, which are not considered part of Roan Mountain proper, though they are part of the general area called "the highlands of the Roan." During the American Revolution, the Overmountain Men who mustered at Sycamore Shoals on September 25, 1780, came through Roan Mountain on their march to defeat the British at Kings Mountain, South Carolina. They spent the night of September 26 at the Sheltering Rock, a place that provided a dry location for storing their black powder. The following morning, they traversed between Yellow Mountain and Hump Mountain on their historic march. Past Hump Mountain, Appalachian Trail hikers finally begin their descent to Highway 19E just above the village of Roan Mountain.

Roan Mountain is a uniquely interesting place, as the great majority of its visitors will attest. Shared by Tennessee and North Carolina, it attracts guests from well beyond the boundaries of those two states. People come to hike the balds, to see the rhododendron in bloom, to enjoy the fall colors and to camp and picnic at the state park. Though it is easily accessible, the

Roan is really a world unto itself. For example, the mountain is less than fifty miles from Johnson City, yet the growing season in the highlands is more than a month shorter than Johnson City's, and during a good winter season, the Roan may boast a two-foot base of natural snow. Whatever the reasons for their initial visits, people who make the trek to Roan Mountain generally come back again and again.

FLORA AND FAUNA

The Appalachian Mountains were formed approximately 400 million years ago, when the moving continental plates of North America and Africa collided along what is now the eastern coast of the United States. The entire process of buckling, fracturing and uplifting is believed to have taken about 50 million years.

The rocks that make up Roan Mountain actually predate the formation of the Appalachians. The oldest variety is called Cranberry gneiss. Dated at more than 1 billion years, it is among the oldest rocks to be found in the United States. As a point of reference, it is believed by many scientists that

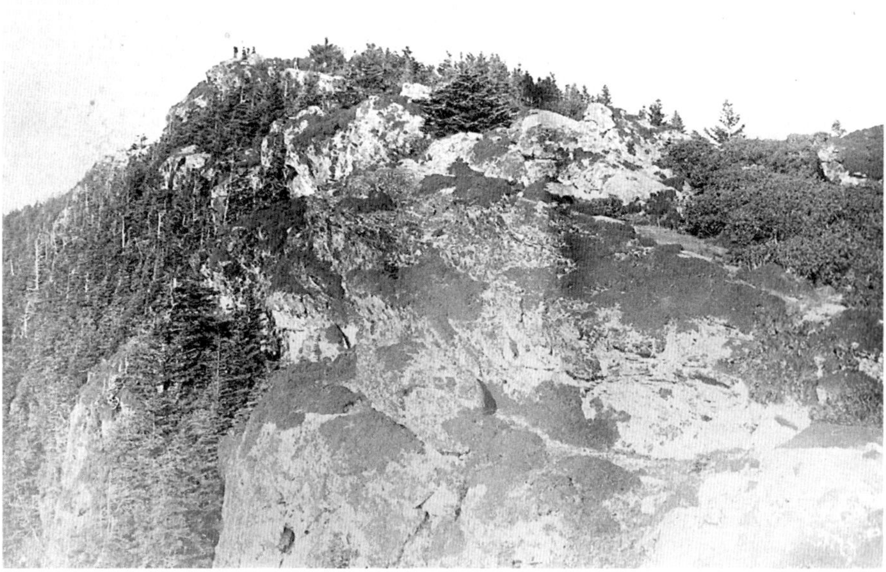

An impressive and rare look at Roan High Bluff in the 1880s before it became covered with trees. The sphagnum moss visible on the rocks is evidence of the effects of glaciers. *Courtesy of Thomas O. Maher.*

the most advanced forms of life on earth at the time of the rock's formation were sponges, coral and jellyfish. Cranberry gneiss consists of pink feldspar layered with thin bands of dark mica. Another of the dominant rocks on the mountain is Roan gneiss, dated at about 800 million years. Like Cranberry gneiss, it is classified as a metamorphic rock. Roan gneiss is a green-black hornblende rock with thin bands of dark gray mica. The variety of igneous rock known as beech granite, a reddish-colored rock dated at 700 million years, is also much in evidence.

Geologists believe that the peaks in the vicinity of Roan Mountain may have been as high as twenty to thirty thousand feet before the slow processes of glaciations and erosion brought them to their present height over the course of many millions of years.

It is glaciation that is given a large share of the credit for the Roan's unique flora. Oak-hickory forests dominate the mountain below thirty-five hundred feet, with beech-maple forests gaining preeminence between thirty-five hundred and five thousand feet. The glaciers exerted their principal impact in the spruce-fir forests that are found above five thousand feet, giving rise to an area of unusual vegetation known as the "Canadian zone."

During the geological time period called the Wisconsin Glaciation, glaciers reached their farthest point south before warming weather made them begin to retreat northward. With the movement of ice through and beyond Tennessee and the Carolinas, arctic and Canadian plant and animal species migrated southward as the southern climate began to mimic that of lands far to the north. Before the retreat, the Fraser fir, a soft evergreen most common today in the far northeastern United States and Canada, was thriving as far south as Florida. With the coming of warmer weather, the retreating glaciers left behind remnants of their travels—a number of rare and endangered plants that are considered to be Canadian species. Isolated atop the Roan and other mountains of similar height, they are unable to spread because of their need for high elevation, a cool climate and a short growing season.

John Strother, a member of the team that surveyed the Tennessee–North Carolina state line in 1799, commented on the visual effect of the Canadian zone: "As one ascends…the size of all the trees perceptibly diminish, especially near the 6,000 foot line, to be succeeded, generally, on the less precipitous slope, by miniature beech trees, perfect in shape, but resembling the so called dwarf trees of the Japanese. They really seem to be toy trees."

First-time visitors to the Roan are likely to be pleasantly surprised at the Canadian zone's cool climate during the summer months. It is

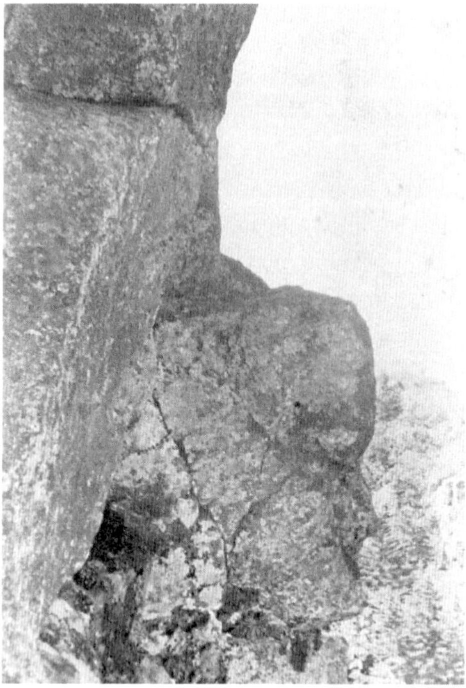

Roan High Bluff in the 1880s. *Courtesy of the Archives of Appalachia, East Tennessee State University, Murrell Family Collection.*

not unusual for the temperature to drop thirty degrees as a midsummer thunderstorm approaches. The surprise may not be so pleasant if they happen to visit during the harsh, unforgiving winters, when temperatures may reach twenty-five degrees below zero. The growing season on the high reaches of the mountain is limited to a little more than three months of the year. Moisture level and winds are higher and snows are deeper than at lower elevations.

The plant communities of the Canadian zone attracted some of the most important botanists in the world to Roan Mountain in the eighteenth and nineteenth centuries, and they continue to attract both professional and amateur plant lovers today. Above five thousand feet, the beech-maple forests give way to spruce-fir forests. Inexperienced hikers on the Roan often find it astonishing that the composition of the forest should change so completely over the course of a half mile's walking distance or even less on steep slopes. From certain lookout points at high altitudes, visitors can see the transitional areas where deciduous trees become dwarfed and finally disappear, only to be replaced by the spruce and fir. Some scientists have attempted to ascribe the hardiness of the spruce and fir to the presence of a high content of fatty substances manufactured by their leaves. Fatty materials, the theory goes, depress the freezing point, and they also help cells retain their water when it would otherwise be drawn out by the presence of ice.

Red spruce trees, distinguished by their four-sided, sharp-pointed needles, are growing more numerous than firs in the Canadian-zone forests. The Fraser fir is distinguished by its flat, soft, two-sided needles, which have a whitish underside. Firs were once more numerous than spruce trees on the Roan, but they have died off considerably in recent years due to infestation by an insect called the woolly balsam aphid, or adelgid. Still, the forest floor is a testament to the firs' ability to survive; their seedlings are as thick as a carpet as they try to regain their rightful place in the spruce-fir zone.

Purple wood sorrel is a small clover-like herb whose flowers illuminate the deep shade during midsummer. It is among the many notable species present in the high forests. Clinton's lily, with its wide leaves and soft yellow blooms, grows in thick patches in places where filtered sunlight reaches the ground. On warm, damp summer days, hikers in the forests may happen upon an array of mushrooms that boasts every color in the rainbow.

The other notable feature of the Canadian zone is the Rhododendron Gardens, located past Roan High Knob toward the southwest part of the Roan. News of the gardens' beauty has spread far and wide so that now

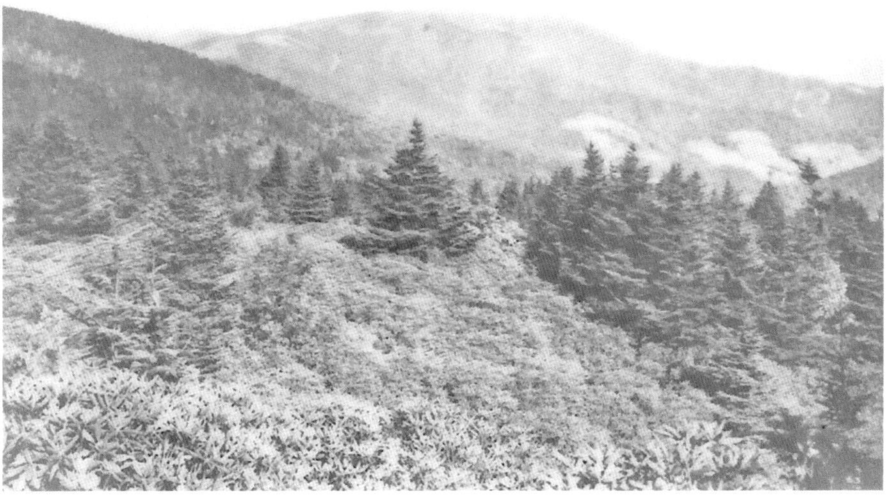

Fraser fir and red spruce trees begin their lives popping up amongst the shrubs. 1930s. *D.M. Brown Collection.*

thousands upon thousands of people flock to the mountain at the peak bloom period during the summer. In a good year, a single bush might boast over one hundred clusters of flowers, while hundreds of bushes spread out over the mountainside. Catawba rhododendron shrubs are so plump and round that it appears they must have been pruned by the hand of man to achieve their perfect shape, yet the only sculpture at work on Roan Mountain is that of Mother Nature. At first, visitors are captivated by the broad panorama of beautiful crimson, but if they care to look closely enough, they may find the close examination of an individual rhododendron flower just as fascinating. Each petal is sprinkled with an intricate pattern of tiny spots along its lip that acts as a kind of runway for pollinators circling and looking for a flower to achieve their mission of fertilization, thus creating new seeds. Rhododendron bushes also spread via their root systems.

It takes a keen eye to pick out some of the tinier species in the Rhododendron Gardens, but the rewards are great. As small as the tip of a baby's finger, the flower of the rare plant dwarf enchanter's nightshade must be seen nose to nose to be appreciated. The plant's leaves, which cover the ground beneath the rhododendron, appear to be quilted. Gray's lily is a rare, beautiful red flower with a black-spotted throat. Mountain ash, elderberry, gooseberry, mountain avens, Michaux's saxifrage and many other plants also make their home in the Rhododendron Gardens. Special areas of transition occur in places where the older rhododendron shrubs are being overtaken by evergreens. With the rhododendron bent into bizarre, twisted shapes, the aura is much like the enchanted forest of children's storybooks.

No discussion of the vegetation on Roan Mountain can be complete without an attempt to unravel the mystery of the balds, areas whose lack of forest growth defies explanation. Such areas speckle the Roan and the rest of the southern Appalachians rather liberally, but they are exceedingly uncommon elsewhere.

There are two basic types of balds, with numerous variations. Areas populated only by grasses, sedges, herbs and wildflowers are known as grass balds. Areas that support the growth of shrubs are called shrub balds or heath balds. The Rhododendron Gardens constitute the major shrub bald on Roan Mountain, followed closely by the Green Alder Bald. The six grass balds are more extensive, and they are all situated east of Carver's Gap—Round Bald, Jane Bald, Grassy Ridge Bald, Big Yellow Mountain and Hump Mountain, or "the Hump," as it is popularly known. Green, or Mountain Alder (*Alnus viridis var. crispa*), is found more commonly on rock outcrops, but also in Carvers Gap and various spots along the highlands. Its presence here is extremely unusual, as Roan has the only population south of Pennsylvania of a species that is a more common resident of eastern Canada north to Greenland.

The Roan's balds are located on long, broad ridges above fifty-five hundred feet in altitude. They cover an area of more than one thousand acres, mostly with a southern exposure. Of special note is the fact that the Roan's continuous stretch of grass balds is the *longest in the world.*

Early visitors to Roan Mountain commented on its prominent balds. In fact, the unusual vegetation on the balds played a large part in making the Roan a haven for the botanist-explorers of the eighteenth and nineteenth centuries. Botanist Asa Gray, for example, wrote of being able to ride his horse for several miles along the crest without encountering a tree to obstruct his view.

Balds are not entirely static; plant succession does occur on them. Old photographs reveal that Roan High Knob was once an open meadow with rhododendron thickets on the side. Photos taken over the course of the past one hundred years show that the tree line was substantially lower on the mountain in years gone by, especially on the North Carolina side. This suggests that that the balds are slowly being encroached upon by larger plant

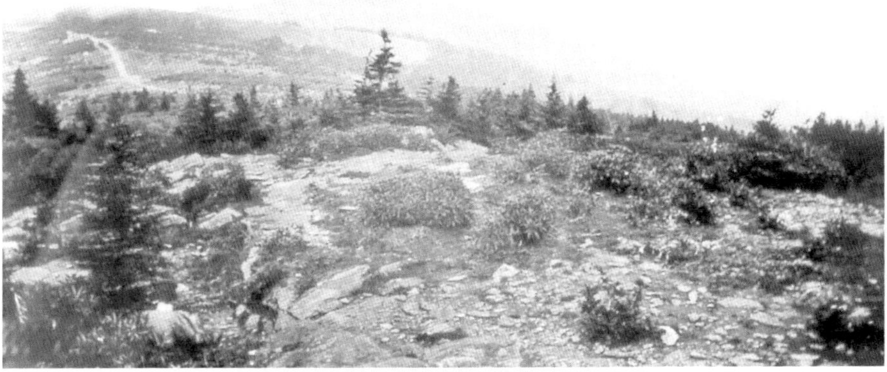

The openness of the Ridgeline Road in 1897 illustrates the absence of forest along the highest ridges of the Roan. The high knob can be seen in the distance. *Courtesy of Thomas O. Maher.*

species and that prudent management of the fragile, beautiful ecosystem will become increasingly necessary as the years pass.

The Cherokee Indians have a legend that accounts for the origin of the balds. They say that there was once a giant yellow jacket known as Ulagu that terrorized a particular Cherokee village by swooping down, carrying off young children and flying away faster than the village's warriors could follow. After much anguish, the Indians hit upon the idea of posting sentinels along the tops of mountains as a means of tracking Ulagu's flight to its home. That accomplished, the Cherokees prayed to the Great Spirit for aid, and the Great Spirit obliged by sending a bolt of lightning to split open the mountain where Ulagu lived. The warriors then proceeded to hunt down the beast and kill it. So pleased was the Great Spirit by the Cherokees' resourcefulness, by their piety in beseeching him for help and by their bravery in finally killing Ulagu that he rewarded them by keeping the tops of the mountains bare of trees so they could serve as sentry posts should the need ever arise again.

Early white settlers in the mountains had their own legends about the origin of the balds, many of them centering on the devil. It was said that balds came about whenever the devil went walking in the mountains, with each of his footsteps causing the growth to be permanently stunted.

Scientific theories have ranged from the mundane to the preposterous. Scientists have long lined up to offer their pet explanations or to take turns

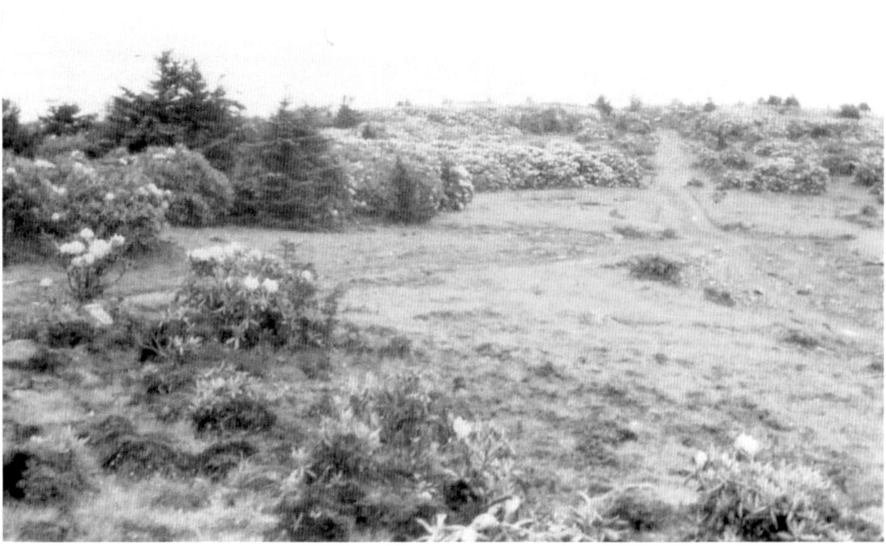

The prominence and expanse of the balds can be seen along the Ridgeline Road.

poking holes in one another's theories. In *The Natural Gardens of North Carolina*, Bertram Whittier Wells summed up the scientific community's frustration in trying to account for the origin of the balds: "Why this hesitancy to go back to forest when forests are all around them? In all the rest of the state when a treeless area is left undisturbed it is but a matter of from five to twenty years until the pines begin to take it, and on most sites, if no fire comes, the oak-hickory or oak-chestnut forest will follow the pines. It may thus be seen that the balds are all out of joint with the rest of our vegetation: they ought to disappear but they don't." Despite the best efforts of a good many bright minds, no completely satisfactory theory has ever been offered.

One school of scientific thought favored natural causes. Helen R. Edson was among the very first to try to explain the balds. Mrs. Edson, a New Yorker, was surely one of the hardiest visitors ever on the Roan. One year in the 1880s, she stayed through the winter in a small cabin atop the mountain so she could document the effects of cold and moisture at high altitude. At the end of her study, she published an article entitled "Frost Forms on Roan Mountain," complete with photographs showing frost buildup on the vegetation. In a 1903 paper entitled "An Ecological Study of the Mountainous North Carolina," J.C. Harshberger summarized her findings:

> *Mrs. Edson describes the action of a winter storm upon the vegetation. The factor in the production of the frost forms, which weigh down the limbs of*

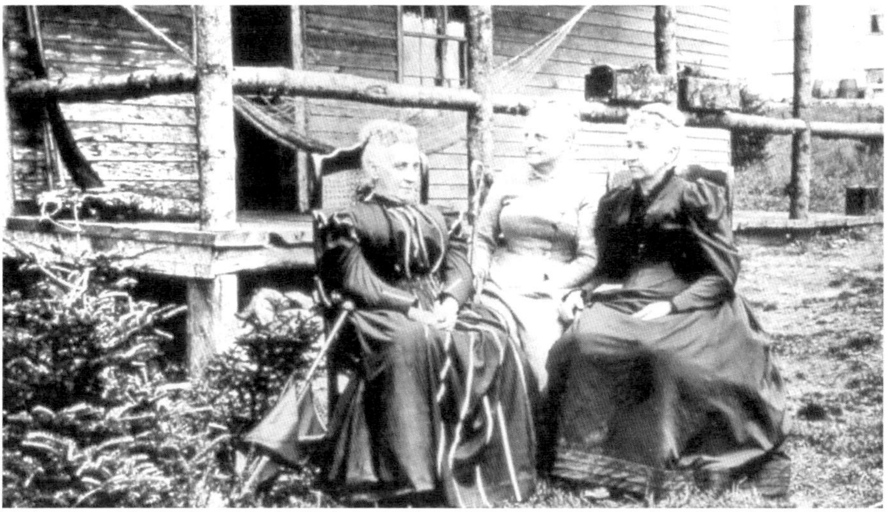

Helen R. Edson (center) conducted a scientific study while at a cabin in front of the Cloudland Hotel. 1880s. *Courtesy of Thomas O. Maher.*

> *trees and snap them off, is the frozen vapor of the wind and rain. The lower the temperature, the denser the cloud becomes; the velocity of the wind and the exposure determine the growth on the frost forms. Hence the absence of trees is due to the effect of the ice and snow of winter.*

Harshberger went on to add that "wherever the topography is such as to permit the full force of the ice storm, there tree vegetation is scanty or altogether wanting, and its place is taken by grassy stretches, or by thickets of alder and rhododendron, plants which are adapted to withstand ice storms." Subsequent research has failed to find a direct causal connection between harsh weather and the balds, however.

Other natural cause theories have ascribed the balds to soil acidity or fires, but they have failed to address the issue of how either could bring about the sharp demarcation that characterizes the balds. The forest does not thin at the edge of a bald; rather, the line between a bald and the surrounding forest is as distinct as if it were the product of human clearing. Extensive soil acidity tests have failed to prove that balds are infertile.

In 1957, W.D. Billings and A.F. Mark of Duke University proposed a theory that natural balds occur only in forest margins. Every tree species has an upper and lower altitude limit, and it was Billings and Mark's contention that balds arise at the edge of the tolerance range of the dominant tree in a particular forest. While their theory may have been a good starting point, it did not address why balds fail to develop in marginal zones where the conditions of soil, climate, altitude and forest composition are identical to those at the site of the existing balds.

William H. Gates of Louisiana State University proposed an elaborate theory. Gates's research was concentrated on and around Wine Spring Bald and Wayah Bald, eighteen miles west of Franklin, North Carolina—or about one hundred miles from Roan Mountain—but so confident was he that he sought to extrapolate his findings to account for balds throughout the southern Appalachians.

During the course of his camping vacations on Wine Spring Bald over the course of eight consecutive summers, Gates observed the infestation of a local population of red oaks by an insect identified as the twig-gall wasp. During the larval stage of their development, the wasps pushed their way through the bark and twigs of the oaks in such numbers that the trees were effectively girdled and killed. Gates observed that the infestation had a very sharply defined border visible at a distance of two or three miles and that all trees within the affected area were victims. And it just so happened that the twig-gall wasp's altitude range corresponded fairly closely to the high and low altitudes between which balds throughout the southern Appalachians are generally found—from three thousand to six thousand feet.

Gates could not seem to emphasize the destructive power of the wasps strongly enough. "It is impossible to describe the attack of these wasps adequately," he wrote. "Practically *every* twig of *every* oak was infested... When one considers the thousands of oaks involved, the total number of insects becomes incalculable." Later, he noted, "It is utterly impossible to give any conception of the almost infinite number of gall larvae that were to be found on Wayah Bald and Wine Spring Bald." Indeed, so impressed was Gates that he refused to let contrary observations stand in the way of what he knew in his heart was good theory. When he failed to find evidence of twig-ball wasps on any other balds, he speculated that it was precisely the insect's tendency to hit-and-run that left other balds free of damning proof; in a case of circular reasoning, what should have been a fly in his theory's ointment became instead further proof of its correctness. A more important point that Gates missed was that wasp infestation could not cause the permanent absence of trees on balds.

Another school of thought ascribed the balds to human activity. In 1936, B.W. Wells theorized that they were the sites of old Indian campgrounds used during the summertime. As evidence, he cited the facts that Indians preferred ridge trails for travel and hunting and that good sources of drinking water are commonly found at the lower margins of balds. However, Wells's argument failed to address why the balds should remain long after their use as Indian campsites was ended. He also neglected to consider the variety of Indian legends that seek to explain the origin of the balds; the balds were a mystery to the Indians, too, and they obviously predated the Indians' presence in the mountains.

A related theory suggested that the balds were cleared by humans—whether Indians or white settlers—as game lures. While such lures may have had some utility in the hunting of some animals, like wild turkeys, the fact remains that most balds are situated above the altitude range of the white-tailed deer, one of the principal game animals in the southern Appalachians. Many deer are to be found in valleys and on the lower slopes of the mountains, but seldom will one venture as high as the balds.

Burning and grazing certainly contributed to the presence of the balds even if they could not have caused them in the first place. A great deal of burning occurred on the Roan throughout the nineteenth century and up to about 1930. "I can still see the black spring smokes arisin' from the

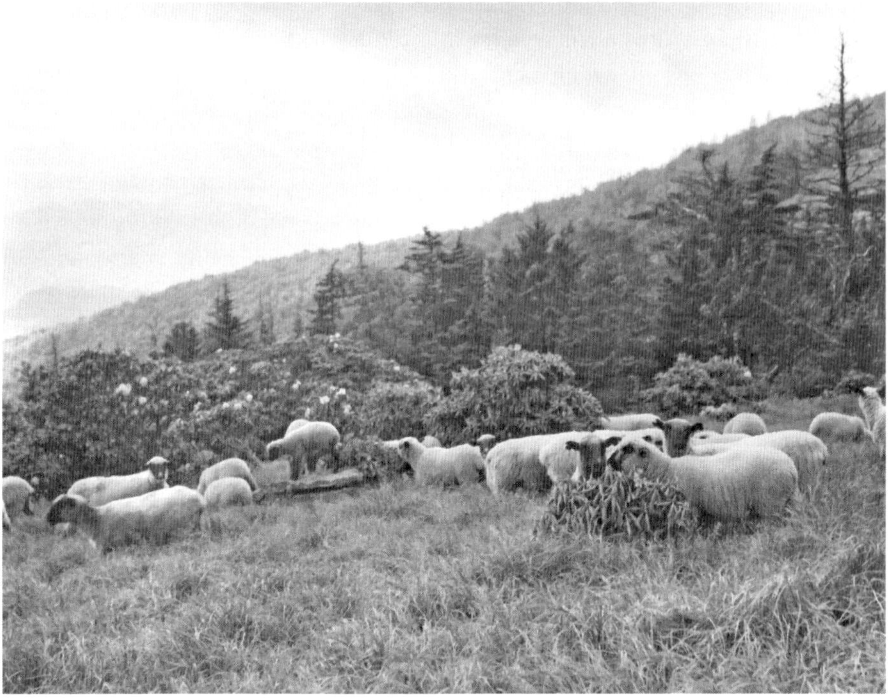

Sheep grazing in a grass and shrub bald. 1930s. *D.M. Brown Collection.*

top of the mountain," recalled one old-timer from the North Carolina side who went on to explain that burning was intended to thicken up the grass for grazing.

Old photographs document the grazing of sheep on the Roan. The grazing areas were widely scattered from the Rhododendron Gardens clear across the balds to Grassy Ridge. Grazing did have a positive side. It kept the balds and their magnificent views open and clear, since livestock prevented beech trees, blackberries and other small trees and shrubs from gaining a foothold in their pasture area. Yet at the same time, erosion and trampling became a problem. Holes and ditches formed along the ridges. Small, delicate tundra species were damaged or destroyed by the constant trampling. J.H. Redfield noted in 1879 that "much of the summit prairie flora has doubtless been destroyed by the large herds of cattle, horses, and sheep which are every summer sent to the mountain top for pasture." The welfare of the Roan's supply of Gray's lily was of particular concern. This rare plant was especially vulnerable because it grows in open bald meadows. J.W. Chickering noted in 1880 that "the persistent and careful search of all the botanists, with efficient help from many others, brought to light only ten specimens (of Gray's lily); all growing in clumps of Alder or Rhododendron, and thus protected against cattle, sheep, and goats, those enemies of all botanists, who bid that in distant time to exterminate it from the Roan."

The effects of grazing were still much in evidence on Roan Mountain fifty years after Chickering's day. Paul Fink mentioned in *Backpacking Was the Only Way* that "the whole top of the mountain was a veritable maze of sheep and cattle paths." Again, it should be noted that burning and grazing could not have *caused* the balds, since the balds were in existence before human habitation.

One of the most comprehensive and believable theories on the balds takes both natural and human influences into consideration. During the time when glaciers covered the southern Appalachians, many tundra and Canadian species found their way to the high mountains in the area, species typically found only many hundreds of miles to the north. Only the tallest of the Appalachian peaks could continue supporting the new species after the glaciers retreated, and they thus became isolated in pockets. With the coming of humans, the pockets containing northern vegetation became the logical places to instigate the practices of burning and grazing, since those areas were more sparsely populated by plant life than the surrounding country. Burning and grazing then played a role in keeping the balds open

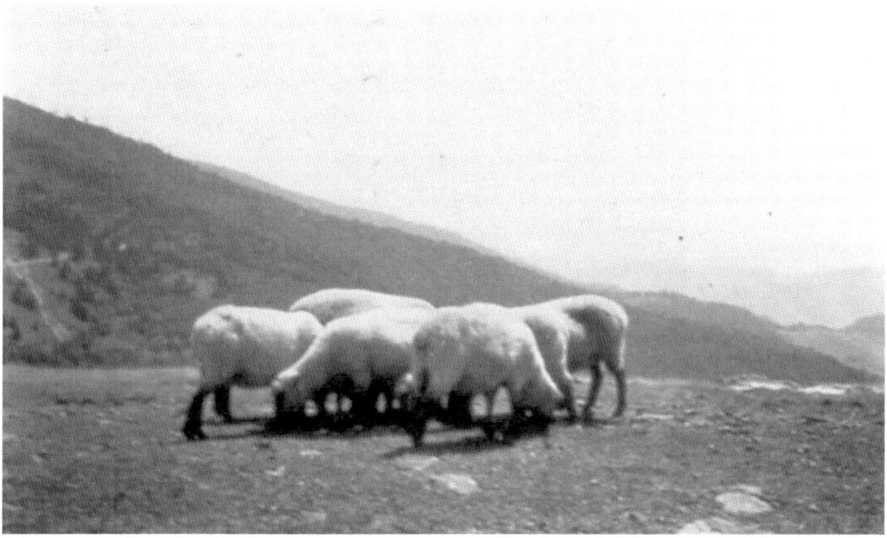

Those "enemies of all botanists," grazing the vegetation down to a nub. 1930s. *D.M. Brown Collection.*

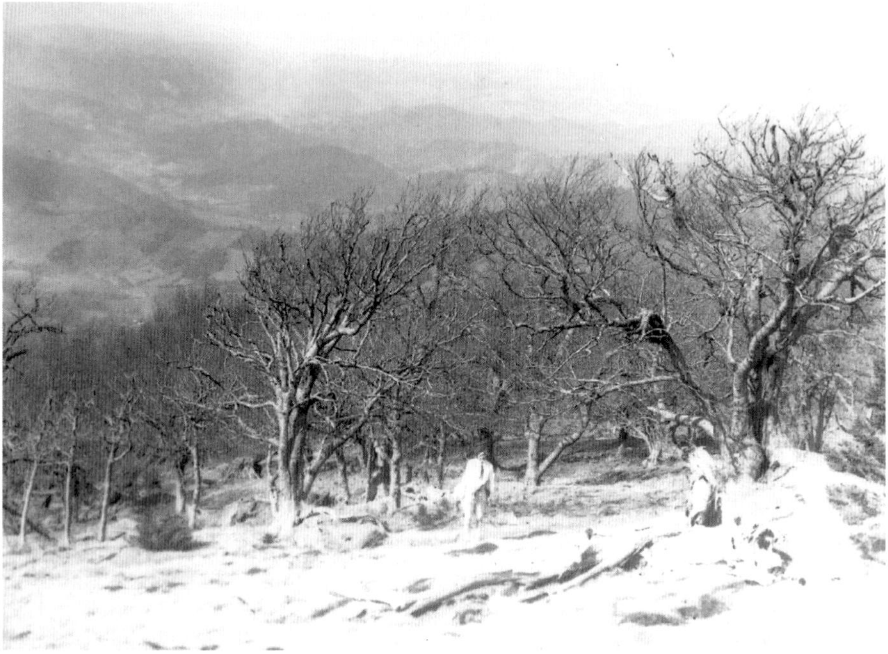

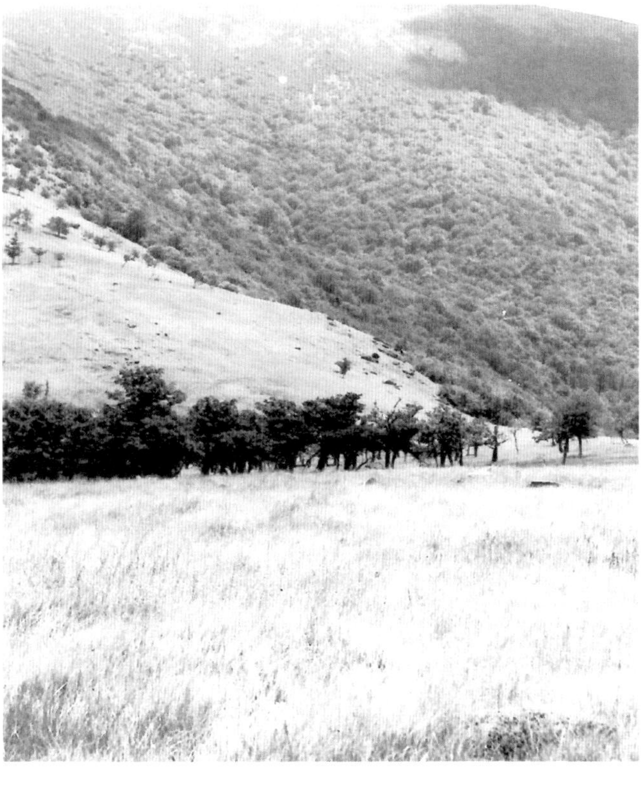

Above: Thelma Brown at Buckeye Gap, also called Engine Gap, in the 1930s. *D.M. Brown Collection.*

Left: Buckeye Gap looking toward Grassy Ridge. 1930s. *D.M. Brown Collection.*

until the present. Still, it remains to be explained why some balds are located at lower elevations and in warmer local climates than are some areas that are heavily forested. Taken as a whole, the balds are random dots on the high peaks of the southern Appalachians, with no particular rhyme or reason to their placement. Perhaps the only definite thing that can be said about the balds is that their cause will remain a mystery for many years to come.

Though the plant life on the Roan has been studied considerably over the years, Roan Mountain's fauna is equally of interest. There are many unique animal species in residence, ranging from snow fleas to bobcats. Several small mammals considered endangered have found the Roan the perfect place to survive. Among them are the least weasel, the woodland jumping mouse, the Smokey shrew and the southern bog lemming. The elusive eastern spotted skunk may also be sighted infrequently, as may the northern flying squirrel, a resident of the spruce-fir forests. The tiniest of owls, the saw-whet, can reproduce only in those high forests.

During the late nineteenth and early twentieth centuries there were several prominent ornithologists who visited the Roan and examined the birdlife. Their recorded observations have been invaluable to ornithologists studying the composition of species on the Roan today.

In 1886, George B. Sennett, an Ohio businessman and well-traveled amateur ornithologist, visited the Roan and subsequently published his sightings. Between April 15 and 29, and again from June 26 to September 4, he spent time in Mitchell County, North Carolina, visiting Bakersville, Cranberry and Roan Mountain. His writings indicate that his observations on the summit of Roan Mountain took place between April 24 and 29 and June and July. It is interesting to note that he evidently visited the Cloudland Hotel, for he mentions hearing the songs of the winter wren while standing on the "hotel balcony" atop the Roan.

His noteworthy sightings on Roan Mountain were the American woodcock and red crossbill. While in Cranberry on August 9, he collected an immature lark sparrow, which is possibly still the only record of this species from that area.

While conducting a statewide survey of the birds of Tennessee in 1895, Samuel N. Rhoads came to the Roan at the conclusion of this survey. Affiliated with the Academy of Natural Sciences of Philadelphia, his more notable sightings included chimney swifts nesting in the chimneys of the Cloudland Hotel, olive-sided flycatcher, common raven, red crossbill and yellow-bellied sapsucker. The yellow-bellied sapsucker observation was the first indication that this species nested in Tennessee.

Stephen C. Bruner and Alexander L. Field were the next known ornithologists to visit the Roan during the summer of 1911 as part of a month-long trip in western North Carolina. They arrived at Roan Mountain Station via the East Tennessee & Western North Carolina Railroad in late June and ascended the Roan, camping in the "balsam" forest at sixty-one hundred feet. Traveling with packs weighing about thirty-five pounds per man, they were also equipped with a shotgun and rifle. From the summit, they recorded thirty-two species of avian life on the Roan. After a ten-day stay, they departed on July 9.

The dean of Tennessee ornithology spanning the first two-thirds of the twentieth century was Albert F. Ganier, born in Vicksburg, Mississippi, in 1883. During his successful career, he became one the founders of the Tennessee Ornithological Society, editor of the *Migrant*, curator of birds at the Nashville Children's Museum and president of the Tennessee Academy of Science in 1926 and inaugurated the journal of the Tennessee Academy of Science that same year. For these, and many other lifetime accomplishments, he was honored as Tennessee's Conservationist of the Year for 1966, receiving the Governor's Award presented by James Bailey of the Department of Conservation.

From June 15 to 20, 1936, Ganier led twelve bird students on a trip to Roan Mountain. Of the thirty-two species found above five thousand feet, the most interesting were a peregrine falcon, horned lark and vesper sparrow on Round Bald.

In 1934, Bruce Tyler and Bob Lyle visited Roan and published their sightings in the *Migrant*. Three years later, a significant statewide bird survey was conducted by the U.S. National Museum under the guidance of ornithologist Alexander Wetmore. This survey was accomplished using teams of birders throughout the state. From September 10 to 25, the team of Watson Perrygo and Henry Schaeffer worked the upper slopes of the Roan. Their excursion began as a camping trip and quickly converted into a stay in a small cabin due to the excessive rain and fog. Some of their interesting observations included the golden eagle, peregrine falcon and olive-sided flycatcher. They noticed "much migration movement among the smaller birds," which follows course with the observations of birders today.

Face-to-face encounters with wildlife can sometimes be a little too thrilling, which may help explain why some of us naturalists lean toward botany. I remember one late summer day on the Roan several years ago when the weather had turned as cool and crisp as fall. It seemed a perfect day for a little adventuring, so I headed out with a friend and her dog to

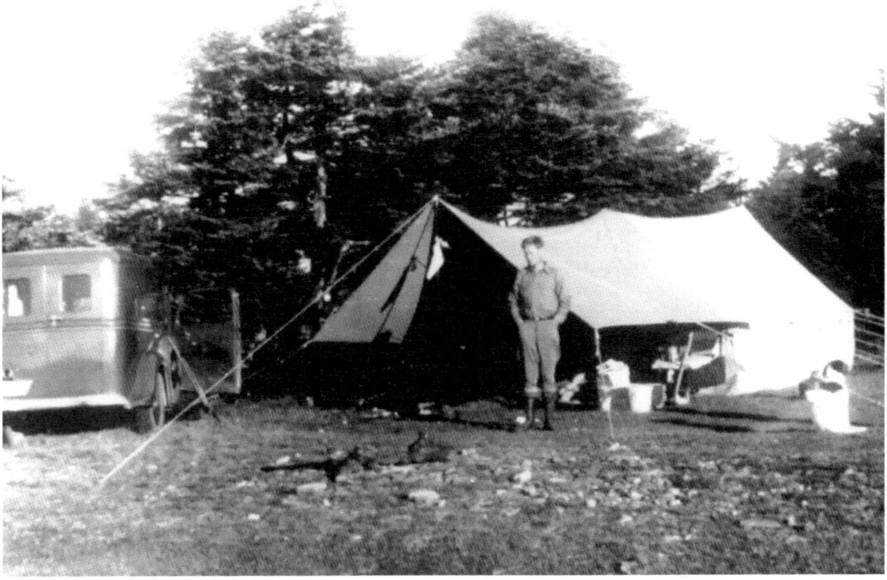

Ornithologist and taxidermist Henry Robert Schaeffer pictured at his camp on Roan Mountain. 1937.

an area of high cliffs rich in beautiful plants—one of my favorite places for exploring and relaxing. Getting there was a real challenge. The first part of the hike was an easy walk along a gravel road, but once the road ended it was necessary to follow the high ridgeline, which was completely overgrown and piled high with downed trees; winds at the top of the Roan are so strong and the soil layer so thin that trees sometimes drop as if they were no more substantial than blades of grass. It took us a full forty-five minutes to crawl through a painful seventy-five feet of trees, briers and the like. The rest of the hike was relatively easy, as the ridge top was lined with huge rocks and rock shelters. What stood out in my mind more than anything else was an odd odor that overcame us at one point in our travels—it was musky and a little like a wet dog. My friend and I commented on it and plodded onward.

Once we reached our destination, we spent the day basking in the sun, snacking and watching the ravens circling above us. As daylight began to wane, we realized we'd better start scrambling back if we wanted to get through the overgrown areas before dark.

The walk back was quiet, especially since we were too tired and lazy to feel obliged to move quickly. An evening breeze began to stir, and I suddenly noticed the strange odor again. I asked my companion if she, too, smelled it, but before she could answer, we found ourselves face to face with her dog—closely followed by a mother bear and her cub! In a flash, I recalled my wildlife lessons. Lesson number one said that a hiker should never run from a bear since bears can outrun humans. Yet before I could come up with a reasonable alternative to running, my friend yelled, "Let's get out of here!" and was off at top speed. Wildlife lessons to the contrary, I was instantly hot on her trail.

How we managed to negotiate our way through the trees and briers I will never know, but I do know that we whittled our precious time of forty-five minutes down to ten minutes. And I never felt a single brier, either. When we finally paused to assess the situation, we were joined by my friend's dog, none the worse for wear, and fortunately *without* his fan club.

I'm confident I will remember that musky, wet-dog odor if there ever is a next time. With hunting pressures and so many communities and homes occupying the black bear's old range, those magnificent animals sometimes find it difficult to hold their own. It is thrilling to know that they are still living in the mountains, managing quite well in the more secluded areas of the Roan.

The special environment on Roan Mountain is one that is able to sustain some of the most rare and interesting plant and animal species to be found anywhere. Even those visitors who have come to the mountain time and again still find ample opportunities for discovery whenever they look closely enough to see them.

STUDYING THE NATURAL WORLD

As we move into the twenty-first century, the biological uniqueness of the Roan continues to call out to those people who possess an interest in researching, exploring and developing a deeper understanding of the natural interactions and populations that occur on Roan Mountain. Research is constantly taking place with respect to the identification and knowledge of the plants, birds, insects, forest types, successional changes, climate and other animals that inhabit the mountain. Exciting pieces of information are discovered on a regular basis, making the Roan a continually intriguing "living laboratory" for biologists, naturalists and visitors interested in learning more.

The natural communities on Roan Mountain consist of different types of balds, high-elevation cliffs, the spruce-fir forest and their related flora. Each area possesses its own unique attributes that enhance the survival of different species.

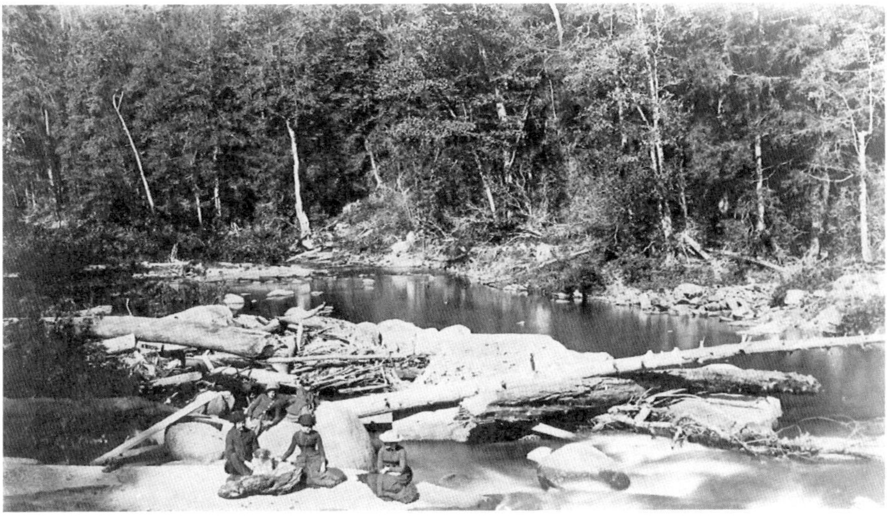

The Appalachian Mountain environment provides ample opportunities for discovery; these ladies are seen at the base of Elk River Falls. 1880s. *Courtesy of Thomas O. Maher.*

Twenty-seven rare natural communities and nearly eight hundred species of plants make up the ecosystem of the Roan. Of these many species, six are federally listed: the Roan Mountain bluet, spreading avens, Blue Ridge goldenrod, rock gnome lichen, Carolina northern flying squirrel and the spruce fir moss spider. In addition, what is considered the richest repository of temperate zone biodiversity on earth is represented by over eighty regionally rare or southern Appalachian endemic species.

The National Partners in Flight Bird Conservation Plans list 31 bird species in high-priority categories from over 180 avian species recorded on the Roan. Rare-breeding species are of special interest and include the alder flycatcher, golden-winged warbler and northern saw-whet owl. In addition, Roan Mountain serves as a migratory route for several species that are struggling to hold their own in breeding and wintering grounds, as well as changing habitats along their migratory routes.

The red spruce and Fraser fir forest is one of the most endangered communities in North America with its global significance making it a candidate for federal listing. Stands of trees are dying off, due partially to the infestation of the woolly balsam adelgid, an aphid with no natural predators in this country. The adelgid was introduced into Brunswick, Maine, in 1908 and made its way to the southern Appalachian mountains by the 1950s. The Fraser fir has a normal life span of up to 150 years. However, the trees began dying 5 to 10 years after aphid infestation, showing the predator's deadly effects. Before the trees begin their sudden decline and imminent mortality, they may produce one or two seed crops, but this early decline of Fraser fir has continued to be quite devastating to the production of mature stands.

A study conducted by C.W. Dull and others in 1988 in the Great Smoky Mountains National Park showed that in 1976, only twenty-five acres of fir showed heavy mortality. Yet in 1985, areas of dead fir rose to forty-six hundred acres, and by 1988, 91 percent of the mature Fraser firs were dead in the Great Smoky Mountains. Other factors have come into play with regard to the firs' decline, including the effects of acid rain, air pollution and increased recreational use.

The profound effects of air pollution have been recently studied with alarming results. As the high mountains of the Southeast are heavily exposed to industrial pollutants, evidence of the presence of various pollutants is seen in high amounts of cadmium, mercury and lead that are found in the soil. Exceptionally sensitive plants, such as the endangered rock gnome lichen, are particularly susceptible to death from pollution. Lichens act as air filters and are very intolerant of pollutants. Thus, due to the interaction of these factors, estimates indicate that the spruce/fir forests in the southern Appalachians have been depleted up to 90 percent since the turn of the century.

The spruce/fir forest and balds of the highest mountains in the southern Appalachians are extremely specialized ecosystems. Each high elevation habitat has been described as an island since its communities are isolated from others like them. The elevation, climate and environmental conditions are so unique that many of the plants and animals found on Roan are considered endemic, meaning they live solely in that habitat or on that particular mountain.

An invertebrate of special interest to Roan Mountain is one that is so tiny that it can only be seen in great detail under a scanning electron microscope but can be observed under a dissecting microscope if magnified thirty times or greater. The tardigrade was first observed in 1773 by J.A.E. Goeze and has adopted the common names of "slow stepper" and "water bear." There are approximately 750 known species worldwide of this fascinating creature, which possesses four pairs of legs with claws, has a bear-like appearance and moves with a slow, lumbering gait. They are described as either "armoured" or "naked," depending on the appearance of the cuticle—the outer body covering.

All tardigrades are aquatic, even if they live on land, as they require a film of water around them to remain active. One of their more unusual traits is their ability to adjust their biological activity in response to environmental conditions. When external conditions become unfavorable, the tardigrade enters a latent state called cryptobiosis. Low oxygen in the water, low temperatures and evaporative water loss are a few of the factors that induce them to enter this state.

The ability to adjust and slow their metabolism enables them to survive what would normally be deadly conditions. Dried herbarium specimens of mosses have been found to contain tardigrades that have been in this low metabolic state for up to 120 years! The average life of active tardigrades is estimated to range from three to thirty months, yet their actual life span can be much longer if they go in and out of these latent states.

On the Roan, the water bear is most commonly found in moss, lichens or leaf litter. The first recorded tardigrades on Roan Mountain were found in 1962 by G. Riggin, who at that time reported three species in mosses in the spruce-fir forest. Years later, in 1987, W. Maucci also collected mosses in the spruce-fir forest and reported ten species in five genera.

The most extensive study conducted on the Roan was undertaken by Dr. Diane R. Nelson of East Tennessee State University in 1973, when she identified twenty-one species from mosses on beech trees. At that time, she discovered three new species, but they were not named. On September 8, 1988, Karen McGlothlin, Dr. Nelson's graduate student, returned to the sites where they were previously collected and, together with Dr. Nelson in 1993, redescribed and named the first new species, *Hypsibius roanensis*, which was named after Roan Mountain. The second new species was named

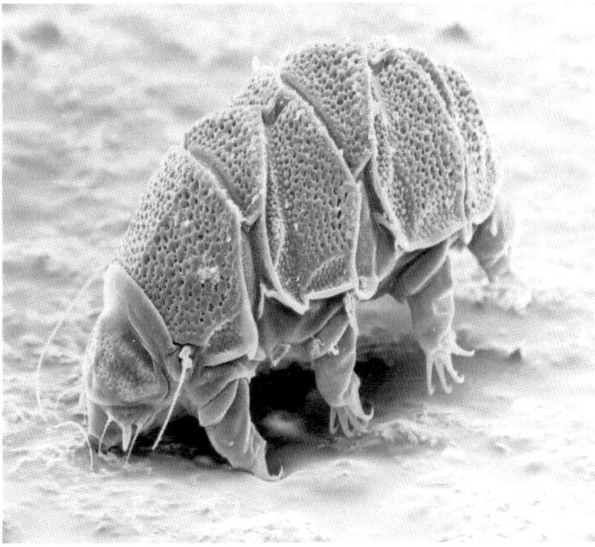

One of the many tardigrades found on Roan Mountain, *Echiniscus manccii. Courtesy of Diane R. Nelson.*

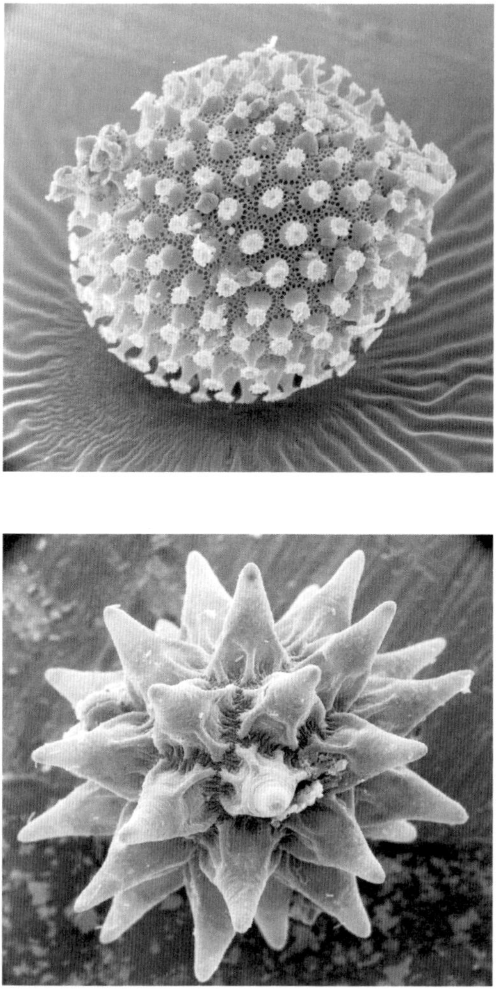

Scanning electron micrographs show the intricate beauty of the tardigrade eggs. *Courtesy of Diane R. Nelson.*

Calohypsibius schusteri sp. Nov. in 1996 in honor of Dr. Nelson's mentor, Robert O. Schuster, at the University of California–Davis.

Continuing the studies of Dr. Nelson and Karen McGlothlin, Roberto Guidetti of the University of Modena, Italy, described two additional species from the Roan that live in the leaf litter. The first was named *Macrobiotus nelsonae,* in honor of Dr. Nelson, who sponsored his yearlong research at East Tennessee State University. *Murrayon stellatus* was also found in a similar habitat and named for the star-like dots on the cuticle.

There is much to learn about the tardigrade, making it an ideal subject for future biologists. The intricate detail of this animal is impressive considering the magnification needed to see it. Though you don't see them readily on a walk in the woods, they are all around us living in their own, minute world.

Also highly dependent on the spruce-fir forest is the northern saw-whet owl. Its range was much more extensive during the height of the last glaciations, eighteen thousand years ago, when the spruce-fir forests were more broadly distributed in the Southeast. As temperatures warmed and the glaciers retreated, these forests, which need cool climates, became restricted to the tops of our highest mountains. Isolated populations of saw-whets also remained in the high elevation spruce-fir forests in which they bred.

The southern saw-whets are seemingly smaller and slightly different in appearance than their northern relatives, with an estimated five hundred pairs of birds now living in western North Carolina and upper East Tennessee. Saw-whet owls nest in natural tree cavities or woodpecker holes and prefer old-growth forests containing a mixture of spruce, fir and some hardwood. When hunting, they will perch four to ten feet above the ground, looking and listening for their favorite prey: deer mice, shrews and voles. They sometimes eat only the front half of their prey first, leaving the remaining portion, which is either eaten later or taken to the nest to feed the young. The female incubates the eggs and cares for the nestlings while the male provides most of the food for the family. If the female leaves the nest before the young are able to survive, the male will remain to continue feeding. They have been known to leave nests in areas where hikers and campers become prevalent.

Little was known about the saw-whet owl on Roan and associated spruce-fir peaks until two professors and their graduate students began to study the birds independently: Dr. Fred Alsop, biology professor at East Tennessee State University in Johnson City, Tennessee, and Dr. Matt Rowe, biology professor at Appalachian State University in Boone, North Carolina. Both have worked diligently to identify the factors necessary for the owl's continued survival in a diminishing habitat.

Dr. Matt Rowe arrived at Appalachian State in 1984 after working with burrowing owls. As he had an interest in the study of owls, it was exciting to have the opportunity to be in an area with which the saw-whet owl was associated.

His previous studies, with graduate student Chet Tomlinson, included work on Grandfather Mountain and Mount Rogers. By playing a tape of the saw-whet's advertisement call, they confirmed that the birds were mostly restricted to high-elevation spruce-fir forests mixed with northern hardwoods.

In 1993, joined by graduate students Timothy C. Milling and Bennie Cockerel, he began a study of saw-whets on Roan Mountain, the Black Mountains (including Mount Mitchell) and the Great Balsam Mountains. Surveys were conducted during the breeding season in hopes of confirming the presence and nesting habits of the owl. As birds were located, transmitters were placed on them to track their location, migration habits and preferred forest types. Between 1993 and 1996, transmitters were placed on approximately twenty-five birds, confirming the owls' preference for high-elevation spruce-fir forests. In addition, there were five nesting pairs of saw-whets found on the Roan in the areas surveyed.

Simultaneously, Dana Ann A. Tamashiro, another of Dr. Rowe's graduate students, was beginning studies to see if the saw-whet owl in the southern

Appalachians was genetically different from its relatives in the North. By capturing owls with mesh mist nets, she would collect physical data, band the birds and draw a small blood sample for genetic analysis. She felt that these southern birds represented a "genetic reservoir," unlikely to breed or mix with northern populations.

In the North, saw-whets will migrate south in the winter in search of food, but in the southern Appalachians it is believed that these populations migrate altitudinally, moving farther down the mountains to lower elevations. Protecting their wintering grounds is of high importance to ensure their survival year round. Future plans are to determine where these tiny birds go in the winter. Since the saw-whet can hunt for prey in three feet of snow, it might stay at the high elevations until the snow is too deep to enable successful hunting, at which time it would migrate down the mountain until the conditions improved in the spruce-fir zone.

During the late 1960s, Dr. Fred Alsop was a graduate student at the University of Tennessee in Knoxville. It was at this time that he began studying the saw-whets' use of nest boxes in the Great Smoky Mountains National Park. In the 1990s, his graduate students continued this work with him in the areas of Unaka and Roan Mountains. In 1992, graduate student Rad Mayfield set out nest boxes on the Unaka Mountains and discovered the first nesting record of a saw-whet owl known for this area.

Dr. Alsop's work continued on the Roan in 1993–95 by studying the owls' nesting and reproductive habits with graduate student Mark Barb, who set sixteen nest boxes on Roan Mountain, which produced five confirmed nests. They determined that the saw-whet laid five eggs per clutch, average eggs staggered two days apart, with four or five birds surviving to fledge the nest. Of special interest was the fact that the first eggs were laid in mid-March, much earlier than the mid-April lay of their northern relatives.

The saw-whet's story is one that cries out for preservation of the spruce-fir forest. Its significance is emphasized by Dr. Alsop's comment:

> *Maintaining stable populations of a top predator such as the Northern saw-whet owl in an ecosystem can only be accomplished if the ecosystem itself is maintained in a healthy state and in "islands" large enough to allow metapopulations to exist.*

There are many questions still to be answered, but it's reassuring to know that so many biologists are intently interested in furthering our knowledge

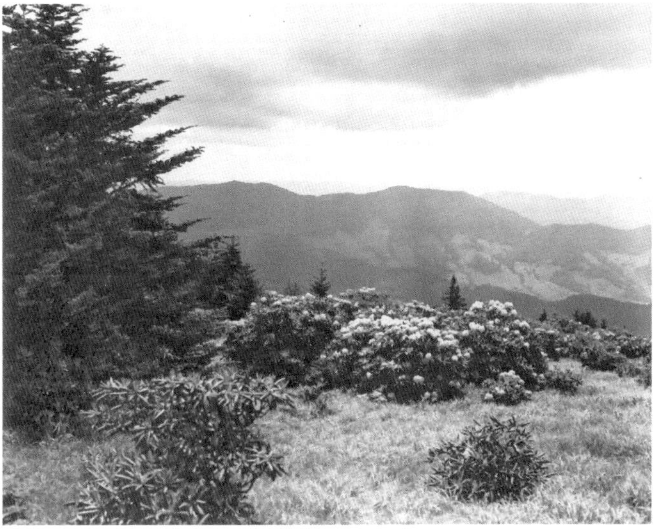

Unique Canadian zone communities provide habitat to a host of rare plants and animals. 1930s. *D.M. Brown Collection.*

of the bird to help ensure its conservation. In looking for the future of the saw-whet, Dr. Matt Rowe states:

> *Southern Appalachian saw-whet owls are probably the most endangered of all our endemic birds. With fewer than 500 breeding pairs in the southern Blue Ridge…given that logging, logging induced fires, and the balsam woolly adelgid have caused the loss of up to 90% of our high elevation spruce-fir forests in the last 100 years…extrapolation suggests there were as many as 5,000 pair of saw-whets in the southern Appalachians just a century ago. It therefore seems reasonable to use 5,000 breeding pairs as the goal for our conservation efforts. Protection of our spruce/fir forests, and of mid-elevation older growth hemlock, will be required if we hope to prevent the regional extinction of these owls…More information is also required on the basic natural history of this owl, especially regarding juvenile dispersal and overwintering ecology.*

The northern flying squirrel is a mammal that has been the subject of extensive study for many years. Dr. Peter Weigl of Wake Forest University has devoted a great portion of his career to monitoring their numbers and habitats. In addition, Dr. Weigl continues to hold an interest in the grass balds and the early impacts of the mega-fauna that once roamed their ridges.

The northern flying squirrel is a small, dark brown squirrel with a white belly, ranging in weight from forty-five to seventy grams. By its name, one would think that the squirrel might flap its little legs to fly, but this perception is not accurate. In reality, it stretches its legs and uses a fold of skin, which lies between the foreleg and hind leg, using it as a sail of sorts. This adaptation allows the squirrel to travel up to eighty yards or more from the trees to the ground.

They are nocturnal animals that feed on nuts, seeds, occasional insects and an underground hypogenous fungus, commonly called the truffle and false-truffle. It is believed that after ingestion of the fungus, the sporocarps spend about a month in the body and then are released as pellets. These pellets contain spores that could spread the beneficial fungus throughout the forest.

The fungus has an interesting symbiotic relationship with the red spruce trees. Enzymes produced from the mychorrhizae enable it to feed on carbon sources from the tree. To help the tree, bacteria associated with the fungus capture nitrogen from the air and make it available to the tree's roots.

Dr. Coleman McCleneghan, professor at Appalachian State University, and graduate student Claire Bird have been studying the relationship between the squirrel and the truffle. Their hopes are to find information that will help us understand what role the flying squirrels might have in the dispersal of the fungi.

In the early spring of 2001, an unexpected need to understand the pine bark beetle and its relationship with the red spruce became necessary. Don Duer, entomologist for the U.S. Forest Service, became quickly involved in the study of this insect, as its presence was negatively affecting red spruce trees—thus, flying squirrels and truffles!

The beetle's primary host is loblolly and short-leaf pine, but over several years, infestations spread in the lower elevations into the white pine forests, killing large numbers of trees very quickly.

It was believed that recent drought, preceded by mild winters, created conditions conducive to pine bark beetle success. Many of the white pine stands were composed of overly mature trees, which were more susceptible to attack.

After wiping out their lower-elevation food source, the beetles moved rapidly up to the top of the Roan. Within two weeks they had killed a small stand of red spruce at Carver's Gap and had infested several other areas across the highlands of the Roan.

Needless to say, this rapid die off created a great deal of concern for the future of the red spruce on Roan Mountain. After several meetings, traps with chemical attractants were set to aid in their study of the pine bark beetle and its natural predator, the checkered beetle. High numbers of both species were found in the traps.

The infestation in the southern Appalachians was so severe that the pine bark beetle had exhausted its common hosts. They have also been known to move into hemlock, red spruce and other conifers in these types of extreme conditions.

Though it can only be surmised as to how the beetle got to the top of the Roan, it is possible that the adults were present in loblolly and short-leaf pine stands that had been planted near Roan Mountain. The adults will travel on wind currents, and it is assumed that high numbers of beetles arrived on the Roan at the same time. Though uncommon, the pine bark beetle may engage in swarming activity where hundreds may colonize to search for a new food source. Normally, a few adults will search for food and send out pheromones, a scent that travels by air that will attract others to the new location.

Since these infestations come in cycles, the Roan and the southern Appalachian mountains would most likely be safe from such destruction for many years. The beetle had reached its peak for this cycle and would die off for possibly seven to ten years.

The endangered spruce-fir moss spider (*Microhexura montivaga*) is another organism whose survival depends very heavily on the Fraser fir trees atop the Roan. It is one of only two spider species on the federal list of endangered species. Until recently, it was not thought to be on Roan Mountain, even though the conditions were right.

The spider is considered an evolutionary relic, being the only member of a primitive and primarily tropical tarantula-like family in North America. The only other species of *Microhexura* lives in the Pacific Northwest, with other related genera being strictly or primarily tropical.

On September 25, 1998, Dr. Frederick Coyle and one of his students from Western Carolina University came to Roan Mountain to search for this spider, previously unknown to the Roan. Suitable microhabitats were known to exist, yet as of that date, the species had not been found. Dr. Coyle arrived just three hours prior to a gathering on Round Bald in which over one hundred folks were to be photographed in commemoration of John Muir's visit to Roan Mountain exactly one hundred years ago. The timing was exceptional, adding an extra thrill to the already exciting day, as word quickly swept through the crowd on the bald that the rare spider had been found on the Roan by Dr. Coyle. Assisting him was his graduate student Robert Edwards and Jamey Donaldson, a superb botanist who guided them through areas of rare plants.

During their six-day survey of Roan Mountain, they discovered thirty-one spruce-fir moss spiders, all in areas receiving very little human visitation.

The spider was discovered in 1925 by Cyrus R. Crosby and Sherman C. Bishop during a collecting trip to Mount Mitchell. Its discovery on the Roan took it to the most northern extent of its range, requiring its adaptation to colder, high-elevation climates. Its range is of particular interest, as most unusual plant and animal species found on the Roan are at the *southernmost* extent of their range.

This small spider is less than one-eighth of an inch long. This is very unique, as most of its known relatives, including tarantulas, are much larger. It thrives under moss and lichen mats, growing on rock and boulder outcroppings protected by the shading branches of mature stands of primarily Fraser fir trees. With fir trees dying off, the moss spiders' habitat is being destroyed by the heat and drying effects of the sun. Their populations have dwindled to very small pockets of surviving old Fraser firs on north-facing rock outcrops. Eggs are laid in June, with spiderlings emerging in September. Maturity is not reached for two to three years after hatching.

Again, discovery, uniqueness, biodiversity and habitat preservation prevail in this story. Dr. Coyle's thoughts on this subject perfectly state why his discoveries, and others like it, are so vastly important:

> *Our discovery of the spider on Roan Mountain added hope that the species may be able to recover if the decline of the fir forest can be halted. Maintaining adequate genetic diversity is a crucial factor in the battle against extinction. The discovery of an additional population increases the possibility that the species is still genetically viable.*

Another species of extreme interest is the golden-winged warbler (*Vermivora chrysoptera*). Like many species that are struggling to hold on in our ever-changing world, this colorful bird is declining in numbers due to many factors. Roan Mountain and select habitats in the southern Appalachians provide good breeding areas for this species. In the Tennessee/North Carolina mountains, researchers estimate that there are about one thousand nesting pairs of golden-winged warblers on the southern edge of their nesting range.

This species is declining rapidly—so quickly that it has been named a Species of Global Concern on the Audubon Society's species watch list, and the U.S. Fish and Wildlife Service has deemed it a national Bird of Management Concern. Yet none of these "titles" gives the bird any legal protection.

The most important step in protection came on June 6, 2011, when the U.S. Fish and Wildlife Service issued a "90-day Finding on a Petition to

List the Golden-Winged Warbler as Endangered or Threatened" under the Endangered Species Act of 1973.

During this ninety-day period, scientific information and comments "solely based on the best scientific and commercial data available" are received by the Fish and Wildlife Service (FWS). If substantial scientific or commercial information is presented, that would lead a reasonable person to believe that the measure proposed in the request, to list the species as endangered or threatened, is warranted. Next, the FWS would be required to promptly conduct a species status review, which would be summarized in its twelve-month finding. If the process ends with a species acquiring the designation of endangered or threatened, it is legally protected on a national level.

One concern related to golden-wing survival is the loss of appropriate nesting habitat. The golden-winged warbler is what Curtis Smalling of Audubon North Carolina deems an "early successional habitat specialist," a species that requires a habitat mix of grasses, flowering herbaceous plants, small shrubs and a sparse selection of small trees. Around the Roan, these types of plant combinations are most commonly seen in boreal, wetland or old farm field reclaimed environments. Each of these provides plenty of cover for nesting and easily attainable food for this ground-nesting species, often found near blackberry briars. As a matter of fact, the cover is usually so dense that most birders are more likely to know a golden-wing is nearby when they hear it singing, not because they saw it first.

On first reading, it would not seem like this would be an uncommon habitat in the southern Appalachians, but in reality, we are speaking of a transitional situation. For in the midst of grasses and small herbs come shrubs and small trees, and finally, this field would mature into a forest. The early successional habitats were maintained historically through natural disturbances such as fire, wind and flooding. Conservation in the twenty-first century involves planned, active management in which these natural disturbances are mimicked to stop the normal succession to forest.

There are other factors that affect populations of this species. Golden-winged warblers can hybridize with blue-winged warblers, thus reducing the number of "pure" individuals through genetic mixing. In some areas, parasitism by brown-headed cowbirds is a concern, as the cowbird will use the warblers' nest, thus reducing the survival of the young warblers. During migration, birds die from flying into high buildings, towers and other man-made obstacles. Over the past one hundred years, the breeding range of the golden-wing has shifted to the north and to higher elevations, possibly as a result of climate change.

We must not forget that this tiny bird is also referred to as a neotropical migrant, meaning that it will breed in North America but spend the winter in Mexico, the Caribbean and/or Central and South America. Overall, there are more than two hundred species of neotropical migrants with the golden-wing overwintering in portions of Latin America. Thus, great challenges arrive when trying to save migratory species in peril when they winter in countries outside North America. Loss of habitat, clear-cutting, use of chemicals and human actions often severely harm, if not destroy, wintering grounds for many species.

Presently, much needs to be learned about the needs of the golden-winged warbler. All aspects of its management and conservation are being actively studied by the Golden-Winged Warbler Working Group. This is a unique group of American ornithologists, conservationists and managers from academia, federal and state agencies, industry and international nongovernmental organizations. Their mission is to ensure the conservation of golden-winged warbler populations through sound science, education and management.

Surprisingly, this story is even larger than that of this specific warbler. There are other declining migratory bird species that require the same habitat as the golden-winged warbler. Conservation practices that will benefit one species most likely will benefit others that have the same needs.

Rick Knight has become somewhat of a legend on Roan Mountain, particularly during the cool days of fall when he could be reliably found sitting by the fence at Carver's Gap meticulously banding birds during migration. It seemed that every person who saw him sitting there working would wander over in curiosity. Patiently, he would continue his task, reaching down into the next brown lunch bag in line and gently removing a small bird. As he took measurements and identified his find, he would graciously explain to the crowd that had gathered to watch exactly what he was doing and why. Finally, he would place a tiny band on the bird's leg, and the folks would watch the unharmed creature fly away. His devotion to his research is quite remarkable, for Rick collected data from mid-August through October for ten years, ending in 2007.

His curiosity was first peaked as he noticed daytime movement of migrant birds at the gap. Since actual migratory movement usually takes place during the nighttime hours, he wondered what species might be traveling through Carver's Gap and in what numbers. Of particular interest were the neotropical migrants that nest in North America and winter in the tropics. So as a licensed bird bander, he obtained the proper permits and began his data collection.

His process involved running mist nets in shrubby areas to catch the birds. Mist nets are nearly invisible, made of a soft nylon and are commonly used by scientists who study flying animals. They are safe, and injury is uncommon, while their usage provides quality scientific information on species that are not easily observable. During these ten years, Rick banded 6,590 birds representing seventy-seven species.

Rick's studies and observations strongly suggested that Carver's Gap is an important site for a broad group of migrants. In additional to birds, dragonflies, damselflies and butterflies are commonly seen moving through the gap during the same period of time. In 2010, he published a fine article in the *Migrant* entitled "Summer Birds of the Roan Mountain Highlands," an excellent read for anyone interested in birding in a very unique environment.

It is important to note that ornithologists have continued their studies and observations on Roan Mountain en mass since the first noted early explorers visited between 1886 and 1937. Jim Tanner, of ivory-billed woodpecker fame, was a professor at East Tennessee State College prior to World War II. While here in May 1942, he found an American woodcock nest in the Rhododendron Gardens. Fred Behrend and Lee Herndon, both from Elizabethton, began birding on the Roan in the 1940s. Fred was credited with finding the first snow buntings on the grass balds in November 1954. The present Lee and Lois Herndon Chapter of the Tennessee Ornithological Society was formed in 1944 in honor of Dr. and Mrs. Herndon. Then, in 1978, the first nesting alder flycatchers in Tennessee were discovered by Richard Lura, Ed Schell and Gary Wallace.

The late John Warden, botany professor from East Tennessee State University, devoted his teaching career to encouraging students to study and

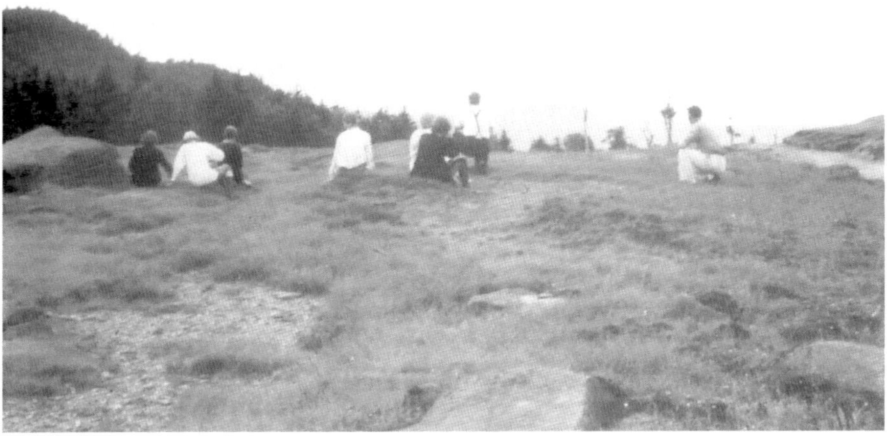

Dr. D.M. Brown, who conducted the first scientific botanical studies on Roan, is pictured with his class at Sunset Gap. 1930s. *D.M. Brown Collection.*

document the plants and their ecology on the Roan. Following the work of Dr. D.M. Brown and Dr. Frank Barclay of ETSU, John contributed a wealth of information to the knowledge base of Roan Mountain's flora; subsequently, the John C. Warden Herbarium at ETSU was named in his honor. Many of the following studies build on John's inspiration.

Jamey Donaldson is also a highly committed and devoted researcher on the Roan who is actively engaged in several projects. The most intriguing to those who visit the balds is the Baatany Goat Project. First begun in 2008, the goat project is a Grassy and Alder Bald restoration program using goats as an experimental management tool.

The Roan boasts the world's only southern Appalachian Green Alder Bald (*Alnus viridis ssp. crispa*) and the world's best example of the southern Appalachian Grassy Balds. The Green Alder is generally restricted to the three miles along the main ridge from Carver's Gap to Grassy Ridge, along the Appalachian Trail, with the highest concentration from Jane to Grassy Ridge Bald.

These plant communities are globally rare and threatened by encroachment of woody plants, a process of succession that could result in conversion back to a forest habitat. Different approaches have been tried or considered in regards to bald management, but no one has taken on the demands of the constant care of animals to conduct a scientific study, until now.

After the crowds of the rhododendron season come and go, Jamey and an able-bodied group of volunteers herd the Angora goats to a predetermined location on the balds. This place becomes the goat's home, and Jamey's home, for the summer. The goats are an excellent choice, for, as browsers, they selectively remove the woody plants that are undesirable in a bald environment. Their main target: Canada blackberry. Another plus is the fact that this species of goat gleans a good portion of its fluid requirements directly from the vegetation it is browsing on, thus lightening the heavy load of carry-water up and down the mountain.

A complicated endeavor at best, Jamey is aided in the "lowlands" by Todd Eastin, Anne Whittemore, Julie Judkins, Frosty Levy, Nora Murdock, Russell Ingram and Joe Powell.

Jamey's study is sponsored by Friends of Roan Mountain, who assist in putting goats "up for adoption." Those who adopt goats will name their goat, will receive a photo of their goat and, most importantly, are helping to save unique ecosystems by enabling the study to continue. The ultimate goal will be the development of a refined model and protocol for using goats in Grassy Bald restoration. The projects motto says it all: "Why MOW when you can EAT it?"

In his spare time, Donaldson is doing fieldwork and compiling data for the Roan Biodiversity Lists. The final product of this study will be an invaluable tool for naturalists, biologists and scientists now and into the future.

Moni Bates, botanist for the North Carolina Plant Conservation Program, has spent several years working with the beautiful and showy Gray's lily (*Lilium grayii*). This rare lily is an eye-catcher, with dark spots lining the throat of a red flower, often making it an unexpected "guest" on a picnic table or in a bouquet. Her work involves understanding why populations of this rare plant are declining across its range. Fungal infection, habitat destruction, illegal collecting, canopy shading, low seed capsule production and early senescence of flowering plants prior to capsule production have all played a role in lowering the numbers of this showy lily.

Presently, Dr. Frosty Levy, East Tennessee State University, along with graduate students Joseph Powell and Russell Ingram, are actively involved in continued studies surrounding the Gray's lily. Their work centers on the effects of goat browsing coupled with disease attributed to a pathogenic fungus.

Melissa Aikens, who is working on her PhD at the University of Virginia, is striving to develop an understanding of the life history of Roan rattlesnake root (*Prenanthes roanensis*). This species was discovered and named by John White Chickering in 1880 and is now considered rare or threatened throughout its range.

Philip White's dendroecology project in the red spruce and Fraser fir forest is the first of its kind. He studied tree ring evidence, which indicated that historic and modern forests were very different from each other. In addition, he studied factors related to logging, climate, the balsam woolly adelgid infestation, acid rain and human action.

Actively involved in understanding the delicate interactions of the Roan is Nora Schubert, who has worked for many years as the Southern Appalachian Highlands Conservancy's seasonal ecologist. Her studies include the golden-winged warbler, Roan Mountain Biodiversity animal lists, Grassy Balds Restoration and, as an educator, the More Kids in the Woods initiative.

Tyler Smith, as part of his PhD dissertation at McGill University, studied the Roan Mountain sedge (*Carex roanensis*). This species was originally collected by D.M. Brown in 1936, first described in 1947 and then thought to be extinct for forty-nine years. It was later collected in 1985 by Dr. John A. Churchill of Johnson City, Tennessee. Dr. Churchill was a neurologist and a botanist, devoting his life to seeking out rare and unusual plants in the Appalachians. He was actively involved in writing a book on the plant life he studied when he died at the age of eighty.

By the end of his project, Tyler found additional populations of Roan Mountain sedge. This rare endemic is now found only in southwest Virginia, northeastern Tennessee and northwestern North Carolina.

We mustn't forget the small and delicate federally endangered mountain bluet (*Houstonia Montana*) and the summer bluet (*Houstonia purpurea*). Dr. Sherri Church investigated the phylogeny of bluets (*Houstonia genus*) while working on her PhD at the University of Virginia. Later, Dr. Kelsey Glennon studied under Dr. Church, working specifically with hybridization and polyploidy factors between the two species occurring on Roan Mountain.

Dr. Tim McDowell, botanist from East Tennessee State University, along with student Dee Medford, has worked with the rare plant species *Geum radiatum* and *Houstonia Montana*, comparing morphological variation among different populations on the Roan.

Though many focus on the rare and unique beauties of the mountain, attention to the invasive exotic species is of the utmost importance. Lisa C. Huff, East Tennessee Region natural areas manager for the Department of Environment and Conservation, does just that. She realizes the profound negative effects that invasive species have on native plant populations. Wondering what "invasive" means? Just think about the success of kudzu! Those are the types of plants that Lisa tracks—and, subsequently, tries to eradicate from Roan Mountain.

In the 1980s, when I was a student of botany professor John Warden of East Tennessee State University, I was quite intrigued with his concern over a few dandelions he had found on the roadside going up to the top of Roan Mountain. Over the years, he continued to track and mark the unwanted progress of this plant as it got closer and closer to Carver's Gap.

Now, over twenty years later, Lisa is tracking the unwanted progress of many more exotics as they spread and continue to thrive at higher and higher elevations. The most recent invader on Roan, garlic mustard, was first observed in 2007 and rapidly moved up the Tennessee side. In 2011, it was found at Carver's Gap.

The numbers of projects and the variety of subjects studied on Roan Mountain are astounding. In order to do justice to the efforts that individuals and university programs have given to their research, one could devote the pages of an entire book. Just as early explorers found the ecology of Roan Mountain especially unique, so do our scientists and biologists of today. The sustained interest and efforts put forth by researchers are a testament to the importance of understanding the complexities of the Roan and thus finding ways to protect its numerous, unique habitats.

II
Making a Living

Logging

The forests on Roan Mountain once boasted grandeur seldom, if ever, seen today. As recently as the 1880s, botanists were still attesting to a level of growth that seems difficult to believe. "It was not uncommon to find logs whose diameter was nearly five feet," E.G. Britton wrote in 1886. "Between 3,000 or 4,000 feet of altitude," J.W. Chickering noted in 1880, "we notice the enormous chestnuts, *Castanea visca*, one measuring 24 feet in circumference and hundreds of others five and seven feet around and running seventy or eighty feet without a limb." Chickering wrote elsewhere that "one specimen of *Prunus serotina* [black cherry] was measured, which was 19 feet in circumference and probably 70 feet without a limb and straight as a pine."

For one reason or another, the Roan's trees have been felled since the early days of settlement. The kind of mighty specimens seen by the likes of Britton and Chickering have long passed from existence. The hardships of living back in the hills and hollows of Roan Mountain in times gone by were many. Travel was difficult. Winter weather was harsh. Survival was a daily task undertaken by all the members of a family. Crops had to be grown, money had to be raised and livestock had to be fed. Settlers' efforts at meeting those goals brought a great deal of suffering to the forests and the land itself.

Farmland was first cleared in the bottoms and then successively higher and higher up the ridges. Trees were killed by girdling, thus eliminating unwanted shade and invasive root systems. Most trees were left to fall before being rolled into heaps and burned. Settlers also burned woodland to create pasturage—a process known as "greening the grass"—and they turned their

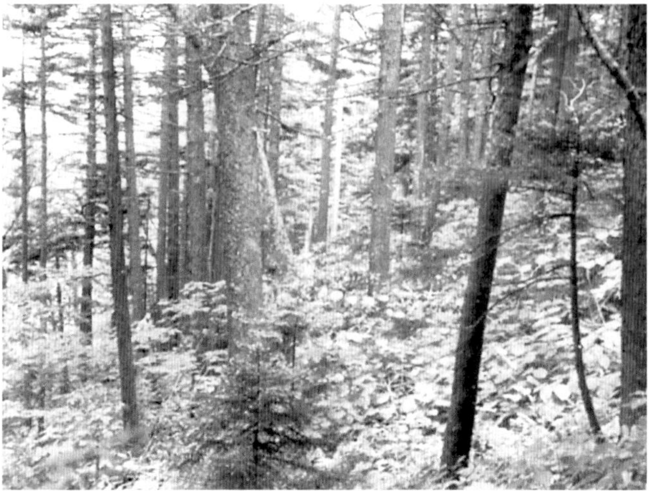

Virgin timber on Roan in the mid-1930s. *D.M. Brown Collection.*

cattle and pigs loose on the forests, leading to the trampling of countless young trees.

The soil on Roan Mountain and in the surrounding area was uncommonly rich. It boasted a layer of humus several inches thick above a base that was black and porous, thanks to the large percentage of decayed vegetable matter it contained. But the effects of being exposed to sun and rain were devastating, and the soil was quickly depleted and eroded upon being cultivated. Once the humus layer was carried away, the soil lost much of its capacity for holding water, and when soil cannot hold water, it is ripe for further erosion. Rainfall of eight inches in the span of eleven hours has been recorded in the Roan Mountain area. Such a quantity of water will have an impact on any kind of terrain, but that impact is most pronounced on steep, bare slopes. As a 1902 Department of Agriculture report on conditions in the southern Appalachian region states:

> *The effect of exposing mountain lands to the full power of rain, running water, and frost is not generally appreciated. The greater part of our population lives on level land and does not see how the hills erode, and even in the hills nearly all the people go indoors when it rains and therefore do not half understand what is going on. In the dashing, cutting rains of these mountains the earth of freshly burned or freshly plowed land melts away like sugar. The streams from such lands are often more than half earth and the amount of best soil thus eroded every year is enormous.*

The first year after clearing, most mountain fields were planted in corn or buckwheat. One or two more years of cultivation in corn followed, and then a year or two of wheat, rye or oats and then the fields went to grass. It wasn't long before weeds and gullies took the fields and destroyed their worth. More and more fields had to be cleared to replace those that had died so quickly. And the forests had a difficult, if not impossible, time reestablishing themselves on the depleted soil.

Settlers used their timber to supplement the difficult living they made from farming. They turned a fair profit by selling cherry, black walnut, hickory and tulip poplar for fuel and fencing, but they further harmed the land in the process. They tended to fell trees wastefully high on the stump, and they gave little consideration to cutting them in the direction where they would do the least damage in crushing younger trees. In retrospect, it was also shortsighted that they cut black walnut and other prime species for use in fencing and the like simply because oak and pine were not so close at hand. In fairness, early settlers could not be expected to be fully aware of the consequences of their land management, and the damage they caused was nothing in comparison to what followed when commercial lumbering firms moved into the area.

The difficult access to the forests of the southern Appalachians meant that lumber companies were rather slow in exploiting them. Naval stores were

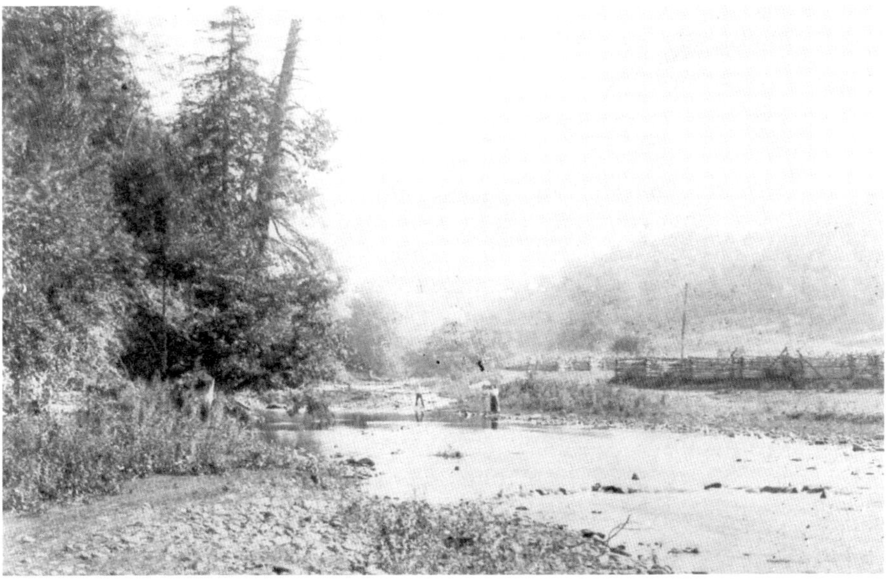

Mountain land was cleared from top to bottom for agriculture and lumber interests. 1880s. *Courtesy of Thomas O. Maher.*

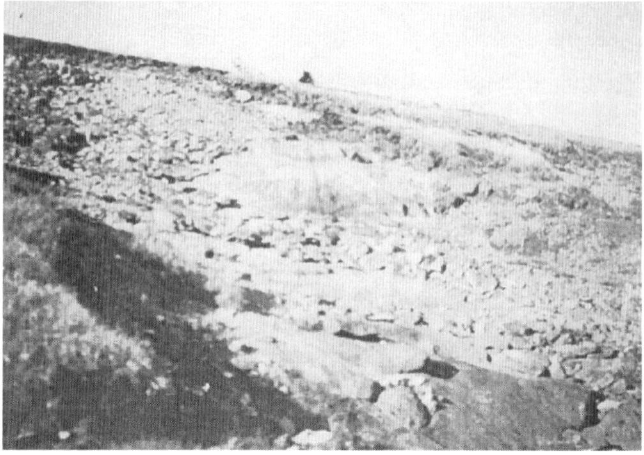

After much abuse, the rich soil easily washed away without vegetation to hold it in place. 1902.

produced from the pine forests of colonial North Carolina, but big-time logging in the United States really began in Maine and the rest of New England. It was the development of the steam-powered circular saw in the 1820s that made the move westward and southward possible. After the hardwood stock in Pennsylvania, Ohio, Indiana and Illinois was picked over, timber scouts made their way to the southern Appalachians. They were looking for cabinet woods like walnut, cherry, birch, ash and hickory, and they also hoped to find construction timber like tulip poplar, white pine and basswood. Caleb Trentham set up a sawmill on the Little Pigeon River near Gatlinburg, Tennessee, in 1868, and other firms followed soon afterward. Logging practices were fairly conservative in the early days. Timber was cut selectively, as mills did not want logs less than twenty inches thick at the small end. Few fires were built in the forests, and natural reproduction was not interrupted.

Roan Mountain was ripe for exploitation. It is believed that approximately three million board feet of cherry were shipped to the mills via Engine Gap, the low area between Round Bald and Jane Bald. The transportation system used at Engine Gap was an ingenious one. An incline railway was constructed through the gap from Burbank, Tennessee, to Roan Valley in North Carolina. That arrangement was unusual, as timber is customarily funneled *down* a mountain, not *up* it. There was a wire running from the Tennessee side up the Roan to Engine Gap, where a bell was tied. When lumber collected in the Volunteer State was ready for shipment, the bell was rung, and the operator of the stationary steam engine located at Engine Gap set about pulling the load up the mountain and sending it over the top and down to the mills in North Carolina.

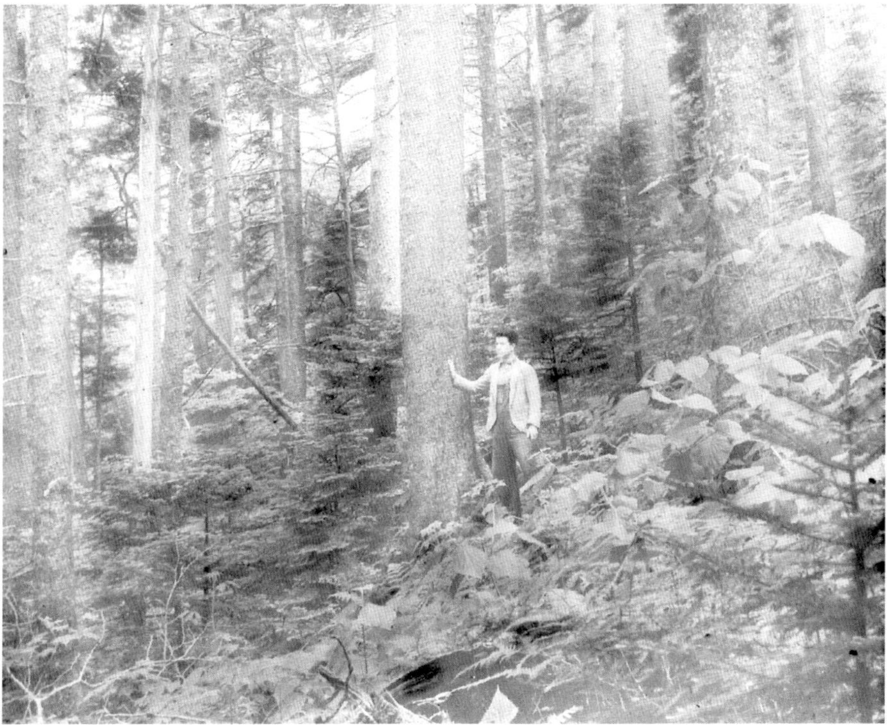

Lowell Ellis, a student of Dr. Brown's, beside virgin timber on the Roan. 1930s. *D.M. Brown Collection.*

There were other logging operations in the area, too. Up and down the hills and hollows, water wheels were set up to power sawmills, and flumes were constructed to move cut timber from higher to lower elevations. The flume system, in which water running through a long chute helped propel the logs downhill, was certainly more practical than dragging timber up a mountain.

One of the more talked-about flumes in the area ran from Burbank, just above the current site of Roan Mountain State Park, down to the village of Roan Mountain. Local residents liked to use the flume for many pastimes outside the realm of lumbering. Walking the high beams of the structure was popular among young and old alike. One man, remembering his boyhood days, remarked, "We used to walk clear from Burbank to town on top of the flume. I remember folks a-floatin' all kinds of stuff down it, too. They'd float pigs and chickens and whatever else they could get their hands on. Once someone nailed a duck by its feet to an old board and sent it down."

Another fellow recounted a wild and woolly tale that is hard to believe, though he swore it was the truth. It seems that while cutting timber above

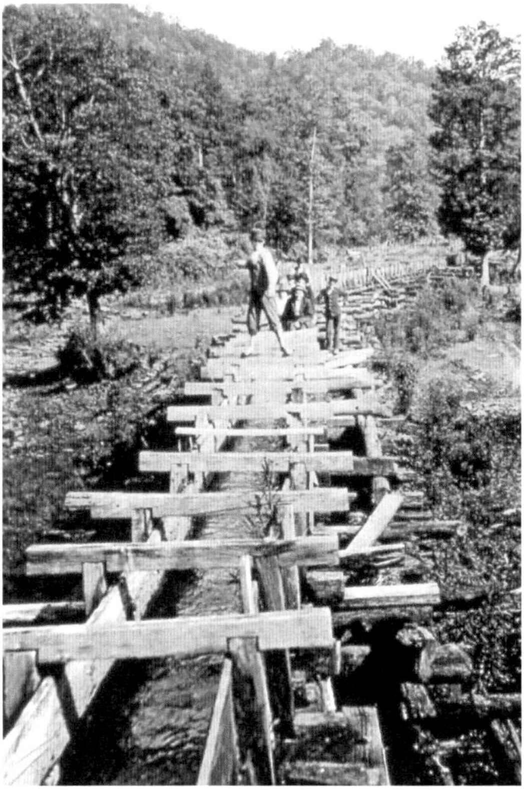

A logging flume running from Burbank toward the present-day state park. 1880s. *Courtesy of Thomas O. Maher.*

Burbank during the winter, some poor soul was killed when a tree fell on him. "The snow was too deep to ever get him down to the village for a decent burial," my source said, "so he was wrapped up real good and put in the flume. When he popped out the other end, he was tended to proper-like." The reaction of the men at the bottom end of the flume is difficult to guess, especially if they knew the victim but hadn't heard of his passing. When the flume from Burbank to the village of Roan Mountain was torn down, its lumber was used by local residents in the building of barns, boxes and the like.

Early logging efforts, though considerably smaller in scope than what was to follow, were a prelude to disaster. There were indications that trouble was coming. Scattered here and there on the steep slopes of the southern Appalachians was evidence of landslides in times of heavy rainfall; evidence that whole sections of forest had been uprooted and sent downhill, only to be stopped yards later by stands of trees on firmer footing. And many of those instances were in virgin forest, where the humus layer was deep and the soil was in excellent condition. The potential for landslides was infinitely greater where lumbering had taken place.

In 1901, from May 20 to May 23, the southern Appalachians saw rain and floodwater unlike any in memory. The people who lived though it christened it the "May Flood" or the "May Tide," and for years afterward they told tales of pigs and cattle washing away; of neighbors going downstream on the roofs of their homes, never to be seen again; and of everything communities and families had worked for being totally destroyed. The losses associated with the flood were incredible. Compared to the Great Flood of 1867, the water in Carter County was reported as being eight feet higher.

Along the Catawba River, farmland was swept away for more than two hundred miles. Erosion was so severe that it was reported that *all* the soil in many creeks had been removed, leaving only large stones and rocks. Almost all the dwellings and farms in the flood plain were destroyed, along with railroad bridges, roadbeds and culverts. Mountains of lumber from destroyed buildings in Mitchell County, North Carolina, were found on the Nolichucky River near Greeneville, Tennessee.

From Elk Park to Hampton, there were a total of sixty-two locations where railroad track belonging to the Forge Mining Company was completely gone. In Roan Mountain alone, the narrow-gauge railroad was devastated, its track washed out in thirty-nine places. All the bridges in the Doe River Gorge were destroyed, with one train being trapped there for three weeks before a crew could reach it. Damage was so great within the confines of the gorge that train service was not restored until August.

A letter from James A. Maher to General Wilder, his father-in-law, contains one of the best accounts of the flood scene. Maher and his wife,

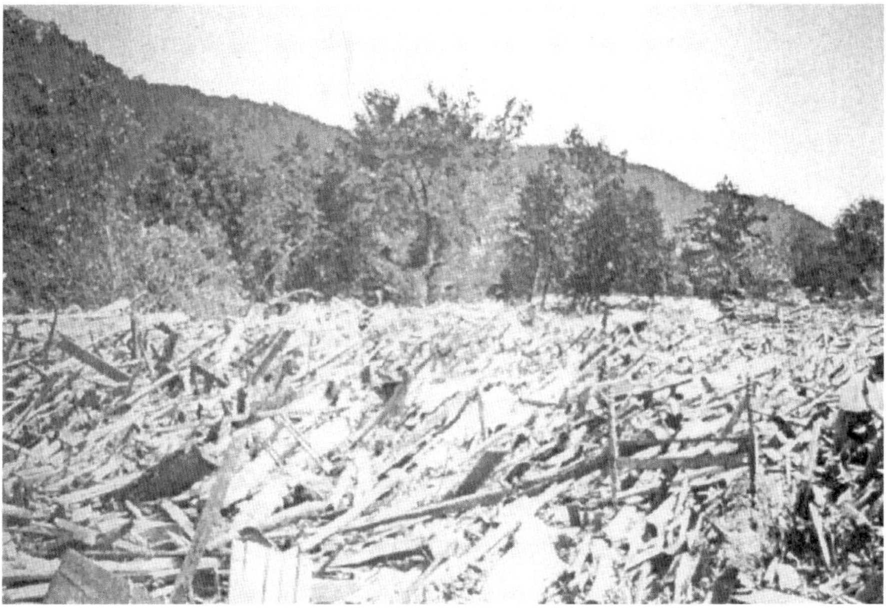

After the May Flood of 1901, debris found along the Nolichucky River in Greene County was discovered to be from the Roan Mountain area.

Rachel, were in Knoxville visiting the sick General Wilder when the waters came. Anxious for news about their children, who had remained at their house in the village of Roan Mountain, the Mahers traveled to Johnson City, then hired a hack to take them home. The hack could make it no farther than two miles above Hampton, at which time the Mahers continued on horseback. They finally completed the journey on foot. Maher described the flood's aftermath for General Wilder soon after arriving home:

> *It began raining again last night and is still raining steadily. The people all along the way and here especially are panic stricken, and the rain frightens them. If you could see the place, or what was the place, you would not wonder. Men, women, and children were overjoyed to see us and they hung around Rachel like a savior. I cannot enumerate the damages in a letter. Of course we are damaged three times more than the rest of the town combined, but the loss of the poor people is complete and absolute and their condition is pitiful…You can believe no one, as no man appears to have been a quarter of a mile from his home, and there are lots of wild rumors, all garnished in the telling.*
>
> *The north side of the town, between the river and the railroad and below the hotel (the Roan Mountain Inn), is a rocky waste, covered with pools—it is all irretrievably gone. The lower meadow, or where the lower meadow was, is in the same condition—a shining, rocky waste…You cannot imagine the desolate look of things. The river covered the valley from mountain to mountain—gorged below and scoured the rocks bare of soil. The house is uninjured—the only one unhurt in the place. One-third of the river now flows through the upper meadow and between the house and the mill. There is not a garden left in this valley.*

To make matters worse, the summer of 1902 produced floodwaters comparable to those of the May Flood. Damages were estimated at more than $10 million, a staggering figure in those days. It was obvious that something had to be done. The Department of Agriculture examined the situation and generated an inch-thick report on conditions in the southern Appalachians, a portion of which was quoted earlier in this chapter. The report documented harmful farming practices, fires, clear-cutting, landslides and erosion problems—all perpetrated in the name of short-term self-interest, whether by landowners or lumbering concerns. The investigators' conclusion was sobering:

> *While the damage from the storm of 1901 exceeds that of any preceding year, it is common knowledge among the mountaineers that annually the*

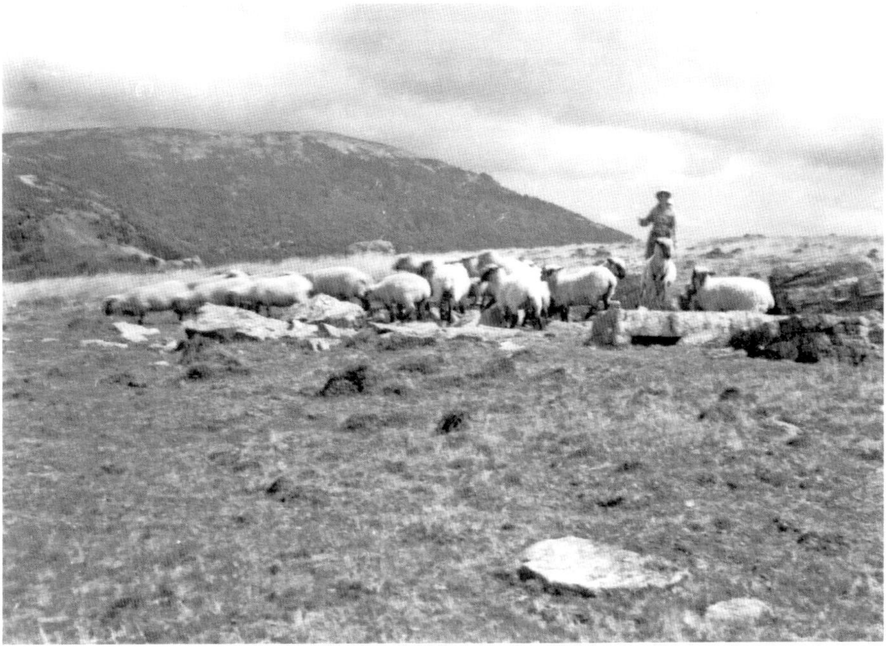

Grazing continued on top of the Roan until the 1940s. Thelma Brown is pictured on Round Bald. 1930s. *D.M. Brown Collection.*

> *floods have risen irregularly but steadily higher, and that their destructive work has been increasing in proportion as the forest clearings and forest burnings have proceeded. We may confidently expect that floods of the future will exceed those of the past.*

The report went on to recommend the establishment of a national park in the southern Appalachians. It was not the first time the idea had been proposed, but the movement started to gather momentum after the floods of 1901 and 1902. Still, it was eight more years before legislation was passed to just begin the purchase of federal parkland in the eastern part of the country. The Weeks Act appropriated $10 million "for the purchase of wild lands in the mountains at the heads of navigable rivers of the Eastern United States." The money was spread among several states. Roan Mountain, along with numerous other sites, was proposed as the location for the park in the southern Appalachians, but the land finally decided upon was a tract due west of Asheville, North Carolina. It boasted one of the last primeval forests east of the Mississippi: the Great Smoky Mountains National Park, now the most visited park in the national system.

The lessons of prudent land management were not fully learned after the floods at the beginning of the century, however. The days of greatest abuse on Roan Mountain and in the surrounding area were yet to come. After General Wilder's death, his property on the Roan was divided among his heirs, who in turn eventually sold their timber. Most of the visitors to the mountain until then had been scientists and vacationers interested in study, sightseeing and relaxation, but they were suddenly replaced by logging companies with an eye only toward financial gain. The massive clear-cutting they undertook was more than any environment could be expected to absorb.

The Champion Coated Paper Company—later called the Champion Fibre Company and the Champion Paper and Fibre Company—was the principal logging company in the vicinity of the Roan, though it was by no means the only one at work in the southern Appalachians. Champion was begun in Hamilton, Ohio, around the turn of the century by Peter G. Thomson. Thomson's process of making paper and coating it on both sides in a single operation brought him a healthy profit, but not healthy enough. Thomson possessed no forests of his own, so he was hampered by having to buy wood from his competitors. In 1905, he purchased ten thousand acres about seventy miles southwest of Roan Mountain near the town of Canton, North Carolina, giving him a supply of spruce for making pulp. Canton had no electricity or central water supply in those days, and it took Thomson $3 million in borrowed money and more than two years to complete his paper and pulp mill. It took another twenty-one years, until 1929, before his operation reached as far north as the Roan.

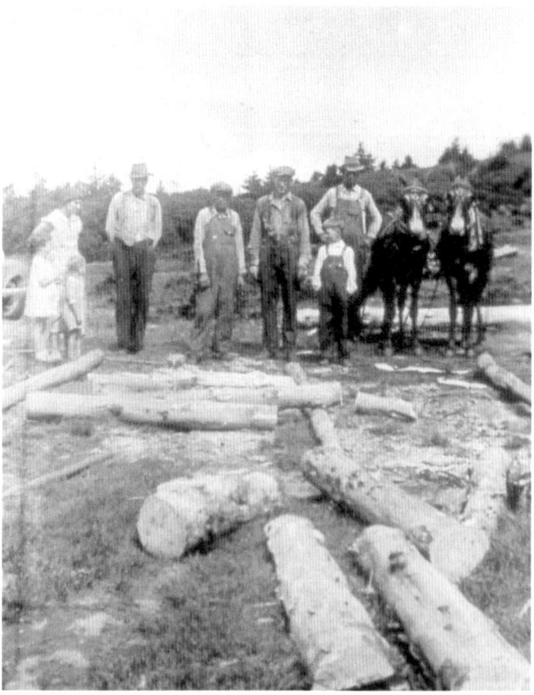

Logging on top of Roan Mountain. Early 1900s. *Courtesy of Thomas O. Maher.*

Logging by clear-cutting severely damages mountain land, but the subsequent

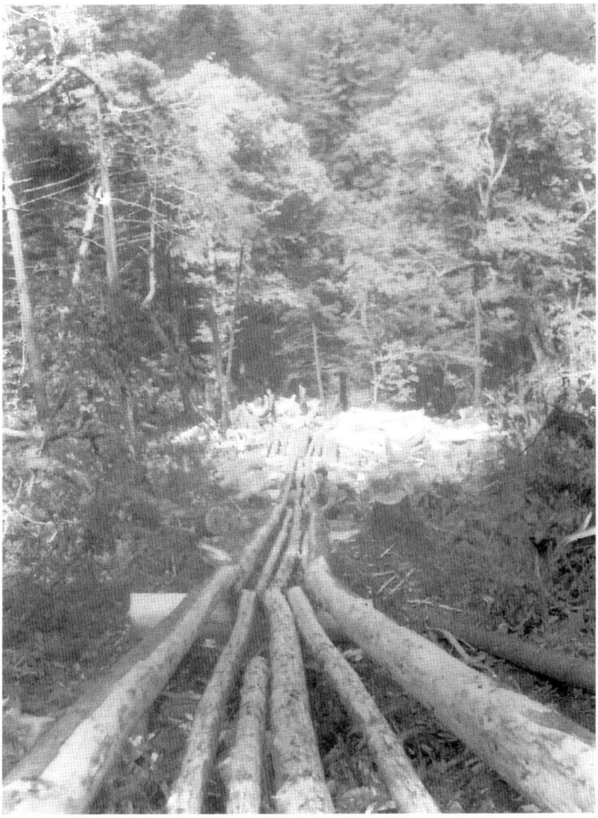

Timber shoot on the Roan. 1934. *D.M. Brown Collection.*

process of transporting cut logs to the mill can greatly damage forests and streams. Michael Frome described the evolution of methods of moving logs in *Strangers in High Places*:

> *The more distant the logger ran his operations from the main line of transportation, the more costly they grew. The mill itself was a relatively small investment. Getting timber out of remote areas was more expensive—therefore, the margin of profit depended upon following the shortest, cheapest way. At first, ox teams were used to drag logs to creeks and streams and on the skid road to the yarding point or deck. They were replaced by horses, which proved faster and easier to handle, besides, a good wood-wise horse often went about his skidding job without reins or words of command. Erosion was caused by clearing lanes for skidders, though nobody cared. And the best way to get lumber down was just to roll it whenever possible. From the high, steep slopes logs were "ball-hooted"—merely started downgrade with peavey, or*

can't hook. A sixteen-foot log, three feet or more in diameter, would gain sufficient momentum to smash even fair-sized trees in its path, and when it passed through a dense young growth it left a track like a miniature tornado.

Then there were splash dams and flumes. In setting up a splash dam, the bed of a creek was freed of protruding rocks and fallen timbers, and cleared of all sharp bends. Hemlock logs, snaked to the stream by cattle, were used to build the dam. As the reservoir grew, animals hauled logs to it over the skid trail. When the rains came, raising the creek level, the water would be released by means of a huge trap door creating a force to splash the logs downstream…The trouble with splash dams was that no logs heavier than water could be moved by splashing and driving, which eliminated oak, ash, and chestnut. The creek shores and bed were torn, wrecked, and ruined, but in the helter-skelter of the day this counted not at all.

Methods of removing cut timber from the forests were more sophisticated by the time Champion came to Roan Mountain. Some logging operations were making use of specialized locomotives, log loaders and skidders, which dragged large loads via overhead cables. But the Roan's unusual geography called for a solution of its own. Champion's approach was to construct a road

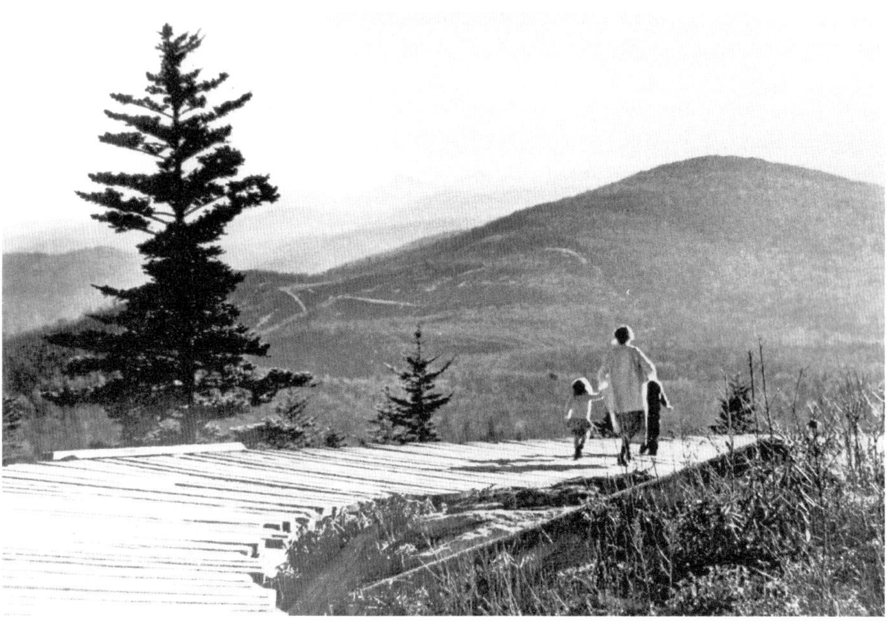

The Board Road was built so trucks could pick up timber in hard-to-reach locations. 1930s.

around both sides of the mountain from Carver's Gap, running right at the elevation where the deciduous and evergreen forests met. It was no ordinary road but rather one constructed entirely of three-inch-thick balsam boards laid across supports that looked much like stilts. Little or no grading was done for the "Board Road," as it came to be called; its only support was the upright poles. These poles were created by cutting the tops off living trees to the height necessary to support the planks, which provided a base for the elevated road. The road snaked around the Roan as if it were floating in the air.

Very few people in the area, particularly on the Tennessee side, remember the Board Road. It must have been a unique engineering feat. I first saw it as a detail in a picture, and later someone gave me a rare close-up photo. I also consider myself fortunate to have actually talked to a man with personal knowledge of the Board Road. He told me that lumber was funneled down long timber chutes to pickup points on the Board Road, where drivers loaded up and headed back toward Carver's Gap. At Carver's Gap, the lumber was transferred to larger trucks and driven into North Carolina by way of the old Calf Pen Road, then into Roan Valley and ultimately to Champion's mill in Canton. He described some of the dangers involved as follows:

> *I remember many a day havin' to drive the big trucks to the spot we had to pick up our load. We had to drive them trucks in* backwards *on that old rickety road so we'd be facing frontways to drive back out. You couldn't go over twenty miles per hour backing in, and then you'd have to go a long ways back to the farthest pickup point. There were plenty of times when the road would* collapse *behind a driver as he was coming out and he'd have to go just as fast as he could to get out. Yet on this whole job, no one was ever killed!*

The Board Road wound for several miles around both sides of the mountain, and it must have been a harrowing midair ride for drivers in their ponderous, log-laden trucks with the road falling like a row of dominoes just behind them. All traces of the Board Road have since disappeared from the forest as completely as it if had never existed at all. As a matter of fact, the logging company removed all of the planks on the road to sell when the road was no longer needed.

Champion's logging operations on Roan Mountain continued until 1937. All trees larger than six inches in diameter were removed. The forests were completely devastated with more than thirty-five thousand cords cut.

Even the rhododendron couldn't seem to hide from the hand of destruction. In the early days of the century, an entire trainload was shipped

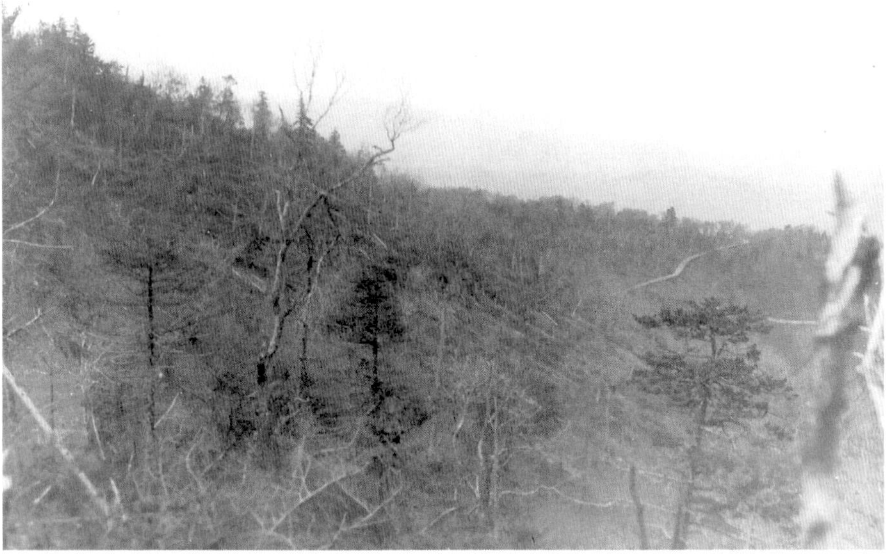

A unique shot of the Board Road snaking around the mountain. 1930s.

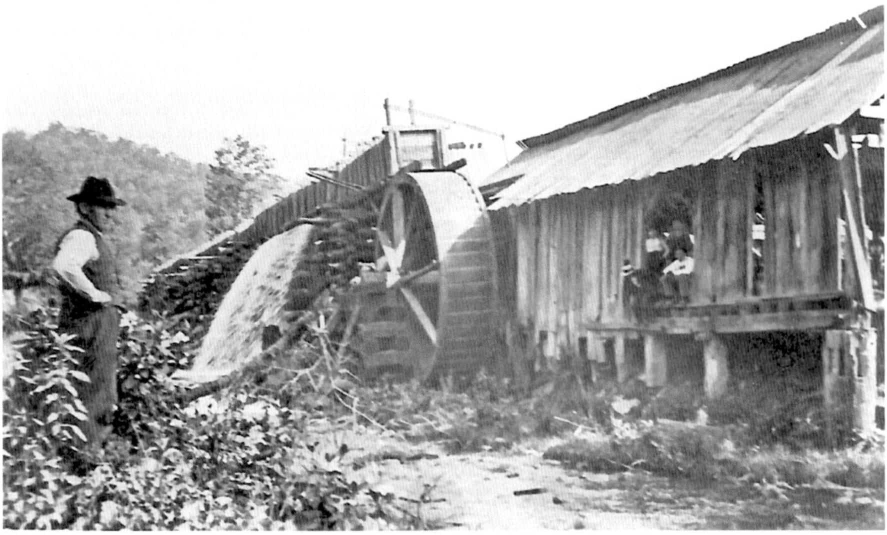

Despite the flood of 1901, forests continued to be cleared into the mid-1900s. Pictured is a water-powered wheel at a local sawmill. *Courtesy of Thomas O. Maher.*

from the Roan to botanical gardens in states to the north, and it was followed between 1927 and 1935 by more than a dozen truckloads destined for landscapers in other parts of the country. Some say that the plateau that supported the largest natural rhododendron field in the United States was all but denuded. It seemed that the Roan had been "loved to death"; that is, had been beaten and abused beyond hope of repair. The subsequent recovery of both the forests and the rhododendron is strong testimony for the need for land management, and it is also a tribute to the resilience of nature itself.

One of the few bright lights during Roan Mountain's darkest years was Dr. D.M. Brown of Tennessee State Teachers College, now East Tennessee State University. During 1934, 1936 and 1937, while the last of the area's virgin timber was rapidly disappearing, Brown came to the Roan to study and record the sizes and locations of the tree species present. He stayed just a small step ahead of the loggers, and the valuable information he collected would have been completely lost if not for his forethought. Brown used a big box camera to record black-and-white images of the mountain at the tail end of its glory years, shortly before the clear-cutting was completed. Like many scientists before him, Brown was puzzled by the Roan's balds, so he planted a group of seedlings on Round Bald, carefully fenced them off and kept track of their progress to see how they would grow. The mystery of the balds remained intact. Brown's trees came to maturity but never did manage to produce viable seeds. They can still be seen standing in a cluster on Round Bald, though they are slowly dying. Brown is credited with completing the

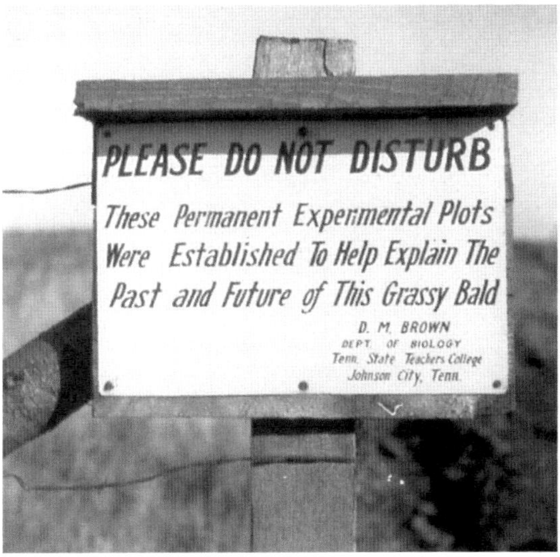

In the mid-1930s, Dr. D.M. Brown planted a small stand of Fraser fir trees to see if they would grow on Round Bald and set seed. 1930s. *D.M. Brown Collection.*

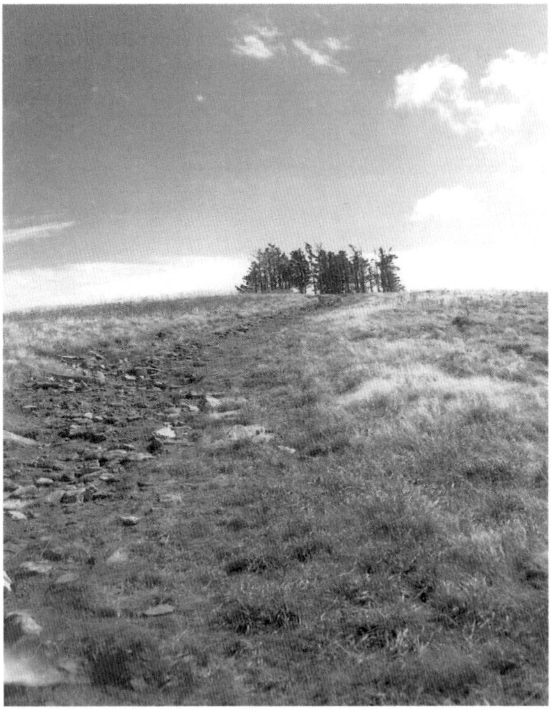

Dr. Brown's trees in the 1980s.

first thorough vegetational study of Roan Mountain. Some look at him as the last of the botanist-explorers who fell in love with the area.

I was fortunate to be able to speak with Lowell Ellis, one of several students who assisted Dr. Brown during his studies on the Roan. Lowell joined Dr. Brown in 1932 and had many fine tales to share. He remembered the extensive logging operations and the infamous Board Road that was constructed around the mountain to gain access to cut timber. Lowell described that road as being a quarter mile from the gap and made from spruce and fir lumber. The road was supported by trees, cut off at the needed height to support planks that were four inches across laid side by side.

The Champion folks even cut the ten- by twelve-foot lumber for Dr. Brown's cabin at Carver's Gap, built thirty feet down from a spring. But in 1937, they took it all back, along with all the planks on the Board Road, hauling it down to Canton, North Carolina.

Squirrels often raided supplies at the cabin, so one evening Lowell decided to cook up "two squirrels with good gravy." Dr. Brown took one bite and pushed his plate away. "It seemed those squirrels tasted like turpentine from eating balsam," Lowell said.

He also described the landscape in great detail, recalling the large numbers of sheep and cattle that covered the mountain. There were no blackberries, except at Roan High Bluff; everything else had been grazed down to nothing but six-inch high bald grass.

Despite their best efforts, people like Dr. D.M. Brown were powerless in stopping the march of the lumber companies. It took governmental

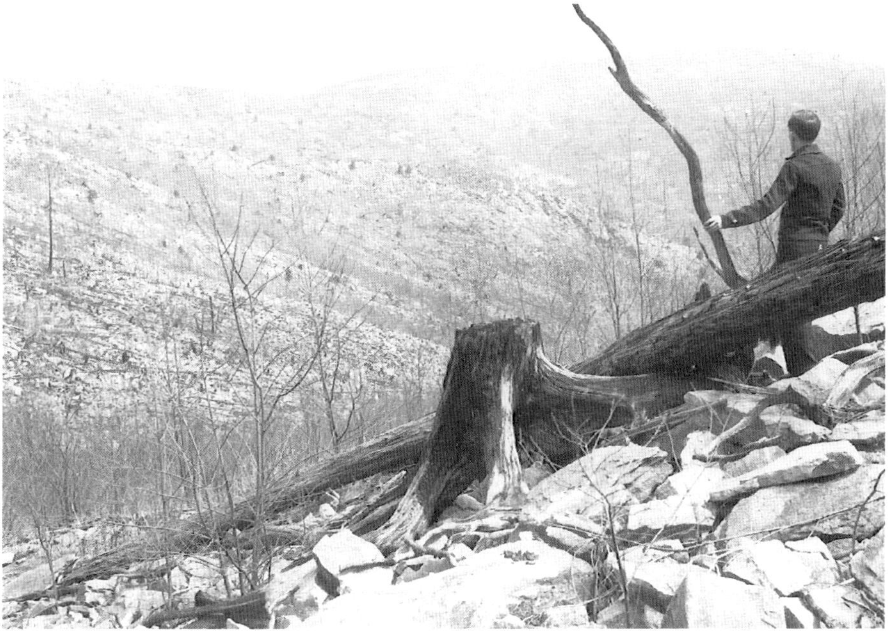

The aftermath of massive clear cutting on Roan Mountain. 1930s. *D.M. Brown Collection.*

intervention in the coming years to restore Roan Mountain—or perhaps more accurately, to allow Roan Mountain the time and the peace it needed to begin to restore itself.

The Iron Mines

The Roan Mountain region was once an area sought after by those who mined magnetic iron ore. Just across the state line, the Cranberry Mines in Cranberry, North Carolina, are well known, once mined extensively, producing large quantities of ore. It became the most famous mine of this region because its non-titaniferous magnetite produced iron that was incredibly low in phosphorus. During its heyday, no other metal from any other source could supply the demand filled by the Cranberry Mines, but it was not the only deposit to be found. The entire region was, and still is, rich with veins of what is considered a very pure ore. Evidence of early mining can be found by traveling through the backcountry of the Roan Mountain area, where prospect holes are often found in remote areas.

There were three primary kinds of ore found here whose values were determined by their purity and amount of added minerals. There were ores whose major component was magnetite, those that were a mixture of magnetite and some titanium and those that were a mixture of magnetite and hematite. At the lower elevations, iron formed in pockets and was easy to refine. In the higher mountains, though, the iron formed in veins that often could be tracked by magnetic surveys and were found to go on for extensive distances. These veins or belts, called boudins (French for sausage), did not stretch during their formation as readily as the surrounding rock. Boudins were distributed through the mountains in continuous lines, the deposits usually in zones parallel to the general structure of the region. In some areas, these parallel lines of ore were close together; in others, they were more widely apart.

Magnetite ore, the principal ore of upper East Tennessee and western North Carolina, had good and bad points. On the good side, it was an ore of very high iron content. This was beneficial as there was very little slag, or waste products, in the raw ore. Since the cost and difficulty of transportation needed to be considered when shipping ore from the remote, mountainous areas, the absence of slag made shipping economically feasible. On the other hand, this pure ore was very hard to refine. The processes involved in melting it down required more heat and more time to get it into a useable form.

Often, iron deposits would be described as their "percentage of iron" compared to some other component—for instance, titanium. Usually these other minerals were included to give an indication of how much, or how little, waste was present in a given vein of ore. Titanium has a high melting point, therefore required more processing, though titanium was present in such small quantities that it gave practically no trouble in the blast furnace. Phosphorus was also considered an impurity, being very hard to remove from the magnetite. If there was hematite present, the ore would tend to be higher in its slag content.

In 1923, W.S. Bayley with the Division of Geology for the State of Tennessee, reported on *The Magnetic Iron Ores of East Tennessee and Western North Carolina*. Mr. Bayley described in great detail every known mine in the Roan Mountain area. His main focus was on the purity of the iron ore and whether or not mining it would be financially feasible versus the cost and processing involved in getting it ready for market. He also quotes H.B.C. Nitze, a geologist for the North Carolina Geological Survey, who reported on the iron ore of North Carolina in 1893.

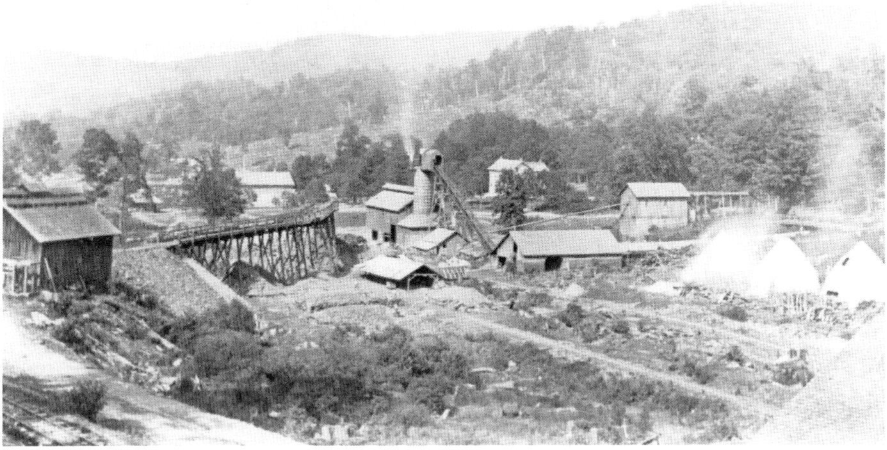

The old Cranberry Iron Furnace. Early 1900s. *Courtesy of the Archives of Appalachia. East Tennessee State University. James T. Dowdy Collection.*

The first openings on the vein northwest of the Cranberry Mines were found three-quarters of a mile south of Elk Park, North Carolina, at the Cooper Place. All that could be seen at this location were several large depressions representing the old open cuts. According to Nitze, these openings were made around 1884 with only a small quantity of ore shipped to Roanoke, Virginia. Also found were a series of pits, or prospect holes, southwest of the Cooper Place, formerly the Crowder Place, on the northeast slope of Hump Mountain, producing ore similar to Cranberry.

Other mines in the Elk Park area included the Ellers and Hardigraves openings, located on opposite sides of Elk Creek. Evidence was found that indicated that the ore belt continued without serious interruption from Cranberry to Elk Park.

Moving into Tennessee, many openings and prospect holes were found in the Shell Creek area below Hump Mountain. The Wilder Mine is located about halfway between Elk Ridge and Shell Creek Stations and about two miles northwest of the Eller's Mine. By today's standards, it can be found just off Highway 19E, east of the Appalachian Trail. The vein is in folds, showing several large open pits, tunnels and underground drifts. It was initially opened before 1880 but was worked on a very small scale. Milt Miller and associates took over the mine in 1896 and shipped five thousand tons of lean ore to the Cranberry Furnace in Johnson City, Tennessee; in July 1918, the last shipment of ten cars of ore was made.

Then, in 1923, the mine was purchased by the Cranberry Furnace Company. A magneto metric survey done by Mr. S.H. Hamilton estimated that 150,000 tons of ore was probable and 600,000 tons possible for this site if it was subjected to fine grinding and concentration. To the west, and higher than the Wilder Mine, were the Greenlee, Ray and Tester properties. These underground cuts and workings showed ore that was similar to the Wilder Mine.

The Red Rock Mine is located about a half mile west of the Wilder Mine, up a steep slope on the west side of Morgan Branch Hollow and a half mile south of the ET/WNC railroad. The property was owned by the Tennessee Coal, Iron and Railway Company and leased to Steven Pittman, who mined some ore and then abandoned it. During this survey in 1923, the place was quite overgrown, and it was difficult to learn much about this site. It was noted that on the mine dump the most prominent rocks found were massive granular aggregates of garnet, hornblende and epidote. In the garnetiferous rock were found nests of almost pure marble. The ore at Red Rock was quite different from other mines in the area. It contained a great deal of calcite, which indicated that the ore-bearing solutions encountered limestone rather than granite in their ascent.

Another abandoned mine was the Patrick Mine on the south side of the road running south along Shell Creek. Other old openings were found between this and Red Rock, indicating that the vein belt is continuous between the two mines. The ore seen here was similar to that found at Cranberry but had not been mined for twenty to thirty years.

Two newer mines were found to the northwest on opposite sides of a little ridge. They were three-quarters of a mile southeast of Shell Creek station on the road up Shell Creek. The mine in Vance hollow is known as the Teegarden, or Shell Creek, Mine, and the one in Ellis Hollow was named the Ellis Mine, or Oakes Entry. About 500 tons of ore were produced here in 1917 while being worked by Ellis and Kirkpatrick. In December 1917, the Cranberry Furnace Company leased the property and operated the Teegarden Mine until the end of May 1919. During the mine's two years of operation, 7,375 tons of ore were shipped from this site. Once the ore's iron content dropped from 43.63 percent to 32.10 percent, it was no longer acceptable at the furnace, and shipment was stopped.

Between Shell Creek and Hampton Creek is an area called the Heupscup Ridge in the spur of Big Yellow Mountain. On the west slope of the ridge near Hampton Creek, a Mr. Young ran a cut into the hillside. The Heupscup Ridge prospects probably yielded some ore based on the size of the opening, but as of 1923, the area was overgrown, and no rock could be seen in its walls.

At the Roan Mountain State Park Visitors' Center, a short trail takes the hiker back to the Peg Leg Iron Mine. The area is a wonderful representation of the enormous amount of disturbance a mined area received in its day. On the quarter of a mile walk are numerous ridges of unnatural appearance, several prospect holes, long ditch lines and much exposed ore. At the top of the trail, an opening can be seen that leads back to underground veins. Behind this, a huge area has been cut out into the bank, all remnants of a past industrial era in the Doe River Valley. An extremely interesting note is that the Peg Leg Mine is probably the oldest iron ore opening in the Roan Mountain area, reportedly being worked since colonial days.

The Doe River Forge was operating on the banks of the Doe River as late as 1885, with ore being taken from the surface to supply this forge. The Crab Orchard Iron Company reopened it again in 1898, shipping about one thousand tons of ore. Again, it was closed and then reopened in 1917, when the Magnetic Iron and Coal Company prospected it.

During his 1923 survey, Mr. Bayley was able to find a large dump of fresh rock about one mile south of Roan Mountain Station on the road

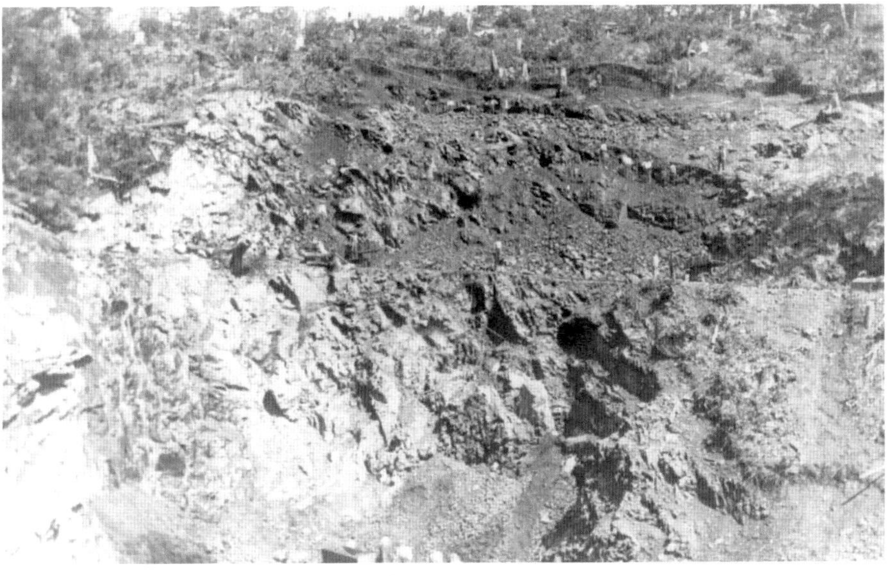

Though much ore was mined beneath the earth, these men were working an open pit mine in Cranberry. 1890s. *Courtesy of the Archives of Appalachia. East Tennessee State University. James. T. Dowdy Collection.*

up the Doe River. Here he described all the varieties of rock that he had seen at Cranberry.

About five hundred feet from the west bank of the Doe River and nearly opposite the Peg Leg Mine are the Old Forge openings. This area was already overgrown in 1923 but was described as having many old pits and float ore, indicating a vein about one hundred feet wide. There appeared to be three streaks of ore, one six and a half feet wide, a second sixteen feet wide and a third with a seven-and-a-half-foot vein. It was then reported that "there need be no fear of the stoppage of the ore, and that the magnitude of the available reserves depends solely upon the cost of mining and concentration."

A few exposures of ore and float ore were found at the Horse Shoe Prospects, which are located about a half mile from the Doe River in the Horse Shoe curve. The Horse Shoe curve can be identified today as the steep curve at the entrance to the Dave Miller Homestead on Highway 143 in the state park. It was assumed by the components of the rock found that this vein was probably different from the Peg Leg veins. Some ore was reported to be of a low grade, while other assayed 31.9 percent iron. It was concluded that

> *the available iron ore resources of the Doe River valley between the Peg Leg and the Horse Shoe mines aggregate from 180,000 to 270,000 tons but that the veins might yield ore indefinitely if it were not necessary to consider the cost of mining.*

After considerable testing, it was concluded that it would require 2.8 tons of crude ore to make 1.0 ton of concentrate, in addition to requiring further processing before charging to the furnace. It was ultimately considered that the Horse Shoe prospect was too costly to mine.

One mile south of the Peg Leg and running in line with the Cranberry vein was a prospect hole found on the west side of "Shorr (Sugar) Hollow Ridge" between Heaton Creek and Sugar Hollow. The area was named the Julian Prospect and is most likely the ridge above today's Sugar Hollow Ridge Road. Very little information was reported on this hole, though it appeared to have low iron content in samples taken.

One half mile west of George's Creek, the Campbell prospect yielded exceptionally rich ore. This holding appeared on the strike of the vein passing through the Peg Leg and Horse Shoe Mines. The initial magnetic survey indicated that there was magnetic attraction present that encompassed a *larger* area than the Cranberry Mines. Work was begun, but before much could be done, some of the backers of the project drowned in the *Titanic* disaster.

Forming the divide between the Doe River and George's Creek is the Chestnut Ridge. On the west side of the ridge and halfway down the slope of Little Rock Knob, a cut and small tunnel were found called the Chestnut Ridge Prospects. In 1890, some ore was shipped from an eastern spur of this ridge, called Strawberry Ridge. A fairly large body of ore was uncovered under the direction of J.R. Engelbert in 1885 and 1890 about a mile west of Little Rock Knob and assumed to be near the Tennessee/North Carolina state line.

At the Engelbert openings, the vein turns sharply south and crosses into North Carolina. The prospects found here are named the Magnetic City Prospect, which is near the present town of Buladean, North Carolina. This ore was located, owned and operated by General John Wilder with the main openings two and a half miles above the mouth of Greasy Creek and one mile south of the Tennessee state line. The forge was located at Magnetic City, North Carolina, and was supplied by the ore of this opening. Three deposits were found in this area and were considered three separate veins, though they were close together.

Deposits continue to be found and reported from Magnetic City on to the Toe River. Outcroppings were found on Bad Creek, Brummetts' Creek, Pigeon Roost, Red Hill and Rock Creek. These occurrences were considered small-scale replicas of the Cranberry vein.

At the culmination of Mr. Bayley's report and explorations, he assumed that there was considerable ore in the Roan Mountain area that could produce great quantities and be mined productively. He went on to estimate the huge amounts of ore that probably existed between Cranberry and Peg Leg but concluded that, without the construction of a railroad to many of these locations, it would not be possible to remove the ore from the mountains and be economically feasible. It was interesting to note that he felt the Peg Leg Mine might be the second largest deposit next to the huge Cranberry holdings when he wrote:

> *At no other localities in Avery County, N.C., or Carter County, Tenn., are there known to be any deposits comparable in size to those in the strip of the Cranberry belt that have been mentioned, except perhaps at the Peg Leg mine, 3 miles south of Roan Mountain Station. Here there has been developed a body of good ore, the size of which, however, has not been determined even approximately.*

Today, the signs of these early days of prospecting are much more subtle. The openings and cuts are still there but often overgrown with trees and vegetation. By noticing an irregular lay of the land, one can sometimes see hints of disturbance. The trail to the Peg Leg Mine in Roan Mountain State Park is an excellent and easily accessible route to get a glimpse of early mining activity. Our knowledge of these actions makes a walk in the woods all the more intriguing. It makes it just as much fun to look down as it does to look up, in hopes of noticing an unusual rock or possibly some hint of human action within what is now a quiet, pristine forest. Our knowledge of the geology of the Roan Mountain area further adds to the mystique and intrigue of this biologically and geologically unique area.

THE NARROW-GAUGE RAILROAD

Prior to the completion of the railroad, travel of any sizeable distance was difficult, dangerous at times and extremely slow. The poor condition of roads in the mountains persisted during and after the Civil War. Single-track dirt roads were noted to be steep, narrow and often cut to pieces from deep axle ruts.

Transporting goods to and from the mountains was a time-consuming and tedious process. The collection and sale of mountain herbs was one such endeavor that was important economically to those struggling to make a living. Roan Mountain was a principal source for many sought-after herbs, especially ginseng, relished for its medicinal properties. In the nineteenth century, ginseng held the distinction of being the most valuable United States export to China.

Herb gatherers would pay drivers of oxen-drawn wagons to haul their plant material to the closest railroad, which was in Johnson City. The trip normally took four to five days because of the road conditions. In the end, those hauling herbs charged quite a hefty price for their services, requiring 50 percent of the money earned through the sale. That was certainly a high price to pay when money was scarce and folks were struggling to survive.

Those who operated local iron ore mines were also hampered by road conditions. During heavy rain or snow, many routes were completely inaccessible—a disastrous situation for the local mining operations when they could not get their ore to Johnson City.

Needless to say, a better means of transportation was imperative to the future of the mountain people. Fortunately, in early 1866, approximately seventy-five Tennessee investors began to examine the possibility of creating a railroad from Johnson City through Elizabethton and the Doe River Gorge and ultimately culminating near Cranberry, North Carolina.

These investors petitioned the State of Tennessee in 1866, requesting the authority to complete the task of building the abovementioned railroad line. On May 24, 1866, by legislative act, the Tennessee General Assembly granted their petition to construct the railroad from the East Tennessee and Virginia Railroad, "commencing at either Carter's or Johnson's Depots on said road, running by way of Elizabethton, Doe River Cove, and Crab Orchard to the North Carolina line, near Cranberry Iron Works."

Thus, the new East Tennessee & Western North Carolina (ET&WNC) was finally chartered, and excitement quickly built hope that transportation to and from the mountains would improve. Shares of capital stock were sold for three months, beginning in October 1866, at twenty-five dollars per share to raise funds to complete the railroad. Once funds were collected, construction could begin with a mandated completion date of two years.

With the project completed just five miles out of Johnson City, the thrill of progress abruptly ended as money ran out. The Tennessee General Assembly granted a two-year extension, but the needed funds were not forthcoming.

After nine years of extensions, a Philadelphia native, Mr. Ario Pardee, bought controlling interest in the Cranberry Iron Works. The ET&WNC Railroad Company was then acquired by the Cranberry Iron and Coal Company in 1875, creating a well-funded venture that led to the completion of the railroad.

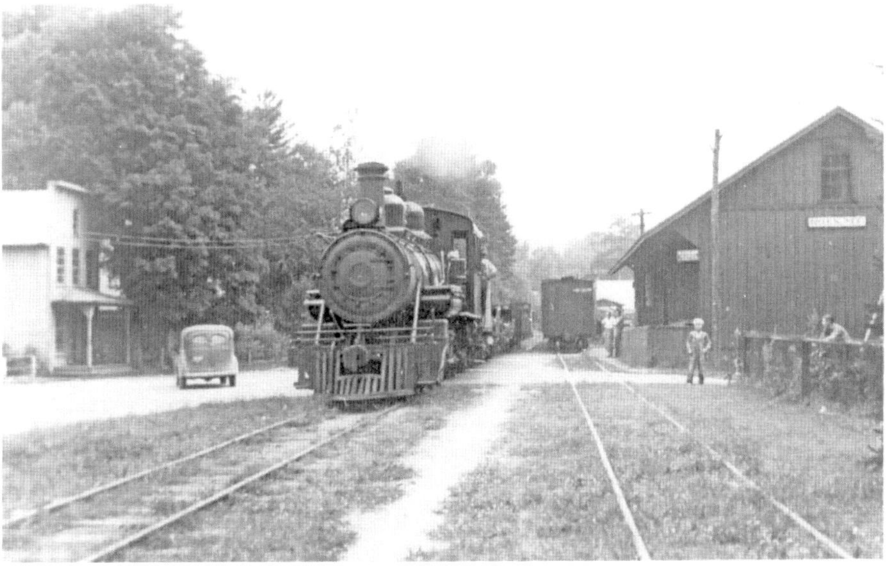

The Roan Mountain Depot along the ET&WNC "Tweetsie" Railroad. *Courtesy of the Archives of Appalachia. East Tennessee State University. James T. Dowdy Collection.*

Now the greatest challenge would be to engineer a route through very difficult terrain. Colonel Thomas E. Matson joined the project as a highly regarded and skilled engineer. His reputation as an excellent road builder through the Pennsylvania mountains provided the needed experience necessary to ensure a safe and stable outcome.

In addition to his work in Pennsylvania, Colonel Matson had designed the historic Covered Bridge in Elizabethton in 1882, was founder and first president of the Johnson City Foundry and Machine Works and served as the Johnson City mayor from 1892 to 1894.

It certainly appeared that the East Tennessee & Western North Carolina Railroad was finally on its way. The eager anticipation by folks along the route was evident, as it was common for older people to walk several miles once or twice a week to check on the progress of the endeavor.

One of Colonel Matson's lauded skills was his method of rapidly cutting a tunnel by working both ends at one time by using small mules and manual digging. The sheer cliffs and solid rock of the Doe River Gorge was worked using block and tackle to lift mules up and over rock faces and then lowering them on the other side to begin work.

Sixteen years after the issuance of the first charter in 1882, the ET&WNC Railroad was completed to its initial destination of Cranberry, North

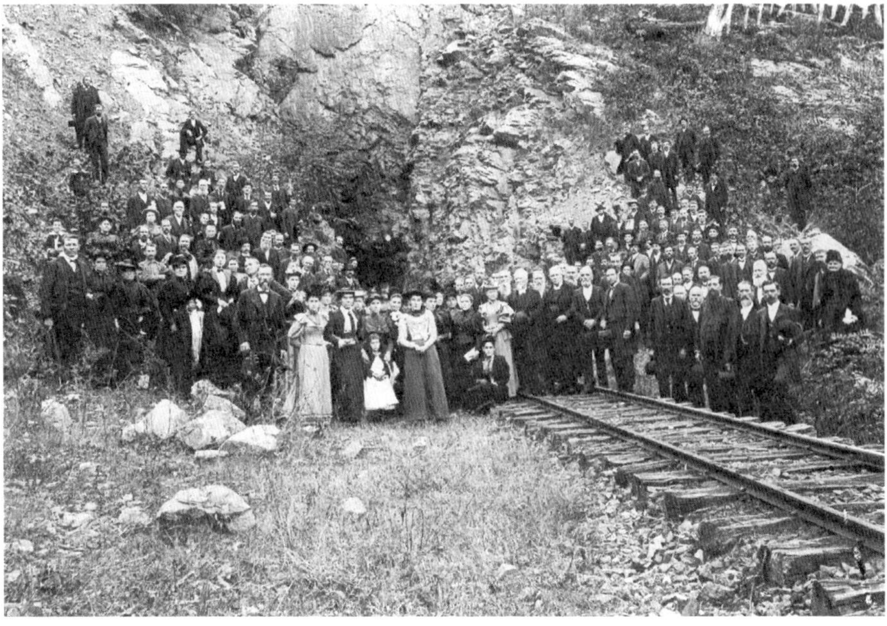

A large group gathers in 1894. *Courtesy of Thomas O. Maher.*

Carolina. Service was extended from Cranberry to Boone, North Carolina, in 1916 via the Linville River Railway. The final product was a narrow-gauge railway, with rails just three feet apart—a fine design for negotiating difficult terrain. In just sixty-five miles, traversing through beautiful mountain land, "Tweetsie," as the railway was dubbed, would cover ground from Johnson City, Tennessee, to Boone, North Carolina.

When the Boone line was dedicated, a local gentleman was noted as saying, "I remember when the only way a person could get to Boone was to be born there"—quite a testament to the isolation people felt prior to the railroad. This connection also became a major boon to those who worked at the Bemberg and Glanzstoff rayon plants in Elizabethton, Tennessee. The train would pick up folks as far away as Boone and deliver them to work early in the morning and home late at night.

The shrill and welcome sound of the train's whistle earned it the nickname "Tweetsie," or occasionally, "Eat Taters and Wear No Clothes." Providing a unique connection to the world outside the mountains, the passenger service continued operation from 1882 until 1950. Tweetsie was not just one train but was a name given to all of the rolling stock of this thriving railroad, including several engines. What began as a business venture soon developed into a railroad line with a personality all its own.

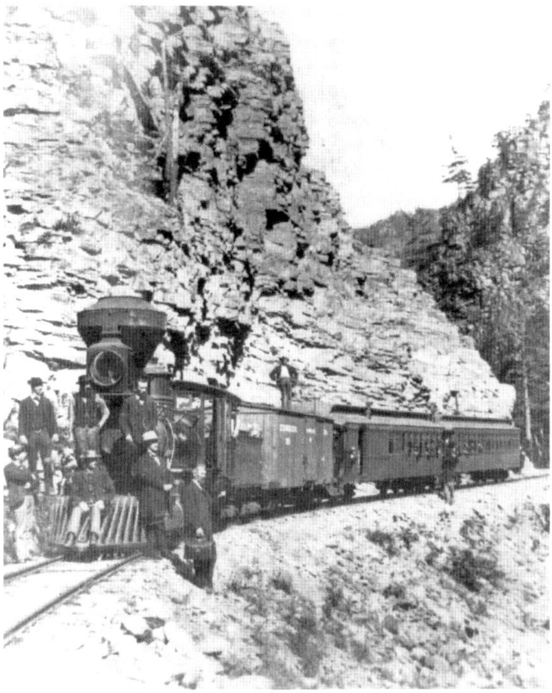

Tweetsie coming through the Doe River Gorge. *Courtesy of the Archives of Appalachia. East Tennessee State University. James T. Dowdy Collection.*

Earning the name the "Railway with a Heart" was not just an accident. Those who worked on the train were people who truly cared about people. It was not uncommon for a mother to bring her children to the train and ask that they be dropped off somewhere else along the line; the conductor and engineer often walked the youngsters safely to their destination. Other days, there might be a shopping list or two handed to the conductor, and during the Great Depression, folks were allowed to ride at no charge if they could not pay. All of these kind tasks were in addition to the "main" work of the railroad, to carry iron ore from Cranberry to the blast furnace in Johnson City. It was not surprising to see the heart-shaped punch on the tickets, designed by conductor Cy Crumley, signifying the spirit and service provided to many generations of Appalachian residents.

This special level of service caught the attention of filmmakers from Universal Studios, who produced the film *Tennessee Tweetsie* in 1938. Always attentive to people's needs along the way, it was not surprising when a woman interrupted the filming, requesting that Cy pick up a spool of thread for her.

Charles Grover "Cy" Crumley was born in 1885 in Elizabethton, Tennessee, and worked for fifty-four years of his life on the ET&WNC Railroad as a brakeman and conductor. Fifteen of those years were spent on Tweetsie on the first train to Boone in 1919 and the last in 1940.

His experiences and recollections paint vivid images of life during the days that Tweetsie was so important to so many living in the hills and hollers. Cy was raised with strong personal ethics to work hard and do good, and that is exactly how he lived his life.

During the flu epidemic of 1918, he would carry doctors from Newland to Linville Gap. From there, they would walk into the mountains to treat their patients. Cy would just stop and wait for them or pick them up on the way back through.

One hot, dry July, Cy noticed thick smoke up ahead while conducting Engine #4. He recalled that there were children in the Ledford home—and it was in the path of the fire. Cy asked the passengers to stay in their seats while they made a quick stop. A well-dressed gentleman shouted, "Stop? You must get me out of here. I don't want to die. I'll give you anything." Of course, Cy and his crew ran to the house, found the family and got them safely on the train.

By this time, the fire had burned around both sides of the train and up to the sides of the engine cab. They just made it out before the Ledford house burned, along with everything else all the way to Montezuma. Those who helped the Ledfords escape were black from the smoke, and worst of all, Tweetsie's paint was "blistered bad." And the man who had panicked? He found Cy after it was all over and told him, "You were right in stopping."

Other excursions offered less frightful events, such as the time a young man asked if his grandma and grandpa could be taken to Hodges Gap. The only method of travel they had enjoyed up until that time was by horse-drawn wagon. At first they were a little skittish and not sure they wanted to ride the train, but once on a roll, Grandma knew she was flying.

Reaching their destination, they decided they did not want to get off. Grandpa was quick to add, "Why, we aim to ride on home with you. Ain't that right, maw? We fancy this here train." But their ride was waiting for them, so they got off the train once they learned that it ran a daily route and they could get back on tomorrow.

Mr. Crumley must have made quite the impression on folks far and wide, for in the summer of 1938, he was invited to appear on a 1939 edition of the New York radio program *We the People*. He and his family gathered up their finest clothes and prepared to go to New York. Being quite a different environment from that to which he was accustomed, Cy was reportedly mystified at many of the habits of big city folks. To Cy, the hotel doorman, who was as still as a statue, appeared near dead. "Do you think he is breathing or not?" he asked. Skyscraping hotels without screens in the windows were also a bit worrisome. "The cars were no bigger than Doe River chiggers," he said.

He asked a maid his most puzzling question: "Why are there not laws requiring screens in the window to keep guests from falling out?" The maid did not appear concerned and indicated that she had worked there for fifteen years and had never heard of a law like that. "Besides, only three have fallen out of this room, anyway," she responded.

When the time came to appear on the radio, Cy was not intimidated by the large audience of five hundred people, not to mention all of those across the country listening. The show's host, Gabrielle Heatter, introduced Mr. Crumley's story as being about a one-of-a-kind railroad in America. From there, he comfortably carried on, "Some years when money is real scarce, we ride passengers for whatever they can pay. Maybe it's eggs or pies, or maybe jars of pickles. Children, we just pick up and drop off where their mammas tells us to."

He even related a frightening tale of coming upon a man who had cut his leg clean off chopping wood. He and engineer Sherman Pippin got the man in the train and tied a string around his leg to stop the bleeding. They ran that train wide open and got the man to the hospital in Banner Elk, saving his life.

After the interview was over, he was greeted by a wonderful round of applause and felt that folks there in New York loved Tweetsie just as much as he did. Though he enjoyed his trip, he told his friend Ken Riddle, "If I lived there, I'd move."

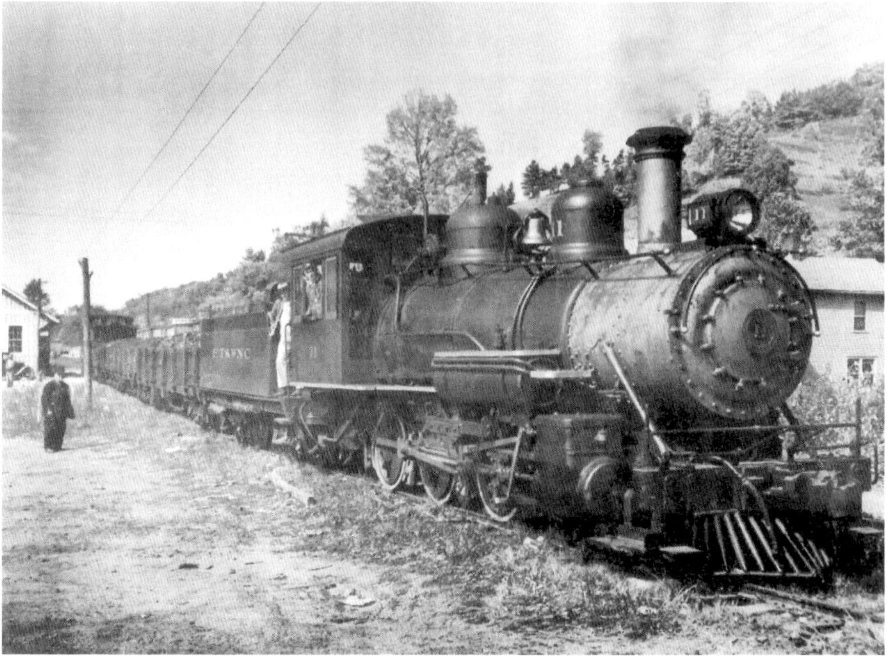

Sherman Pippin in Roan Mountain. 1946. *Courtesy of Thomas O. Maher.*

Sherman Pippin, born in 1883, was a Tweetsie engineer and a resident of Roan Mountain. During the Cloudland Hotel days, he drove a hack (buggy), taking visitors up to the hotel on top of the mountain, but for most of his life, he worked for the railroad.

Pippin lived in a small building at the railroad depot that he hauled around on skids. He preferred to stay in his twelve- by sixteen-foot building, which had a table, icebox, bed and wood stove. When his overnight duty station changed to Johnson City, Cranberry or Boone, Sherman could load the building on a flatcar and take it with him.

Up the road from the Roan Mountain Depot, near Shell Creek, Sherman had a larger home. Thomas Maher, the great-grandson of General John Wilder, recalled Sherman's delightful character: "He was a self promoter and so clever. Behind the barn was an outhouse with white corncobs on the men's side and red corncobs on the woman's side. I couldn't help but ask Sherman, 'Why the color difference?' He didn't hesitate to tell me, 'Shucks, don't you city boys know anything? The red 'uns are softer.'"

By 1954, Sherman had retired as engineer from the railroad, and he had moved his portable living quarters behind his Shell Creek home. On one visit, Tom and his father, Delaney Maher, were to report there promptly at 6:00 a.m. for breakfast. They feasted on a marvelous meal prepared by Julie Wagoner: fried eggs, fried apples, chicken gravy and dumplings, pancakes, homemade butter and coffee cooked in a large tin can. Breakfast had to be over promptly at 6:30 a.m. so Sherman could get to his sawmill across the road from his house.

One thing is for sure, no matter who you spoke with, everyone who remembered Sherman, spoke of him fondly; he was a man who knew the meaning of hard work and undertook it with spirit and energy. Sherman Pippin had the good fortune of living until 1976, many years after his retirement.

Engineer Walter R. Allison quickly learned that running over a woman's pig could not be good. Allison was riding along peacefully when all of a sudden his engine jumped the track in front of a house. The woman of the home came out and talked with Allison while he waited for help to arrive, wondering aloud as to what in the world had caused that train to derail. She abruptly answered his question with a confession; she had greased the track with the lard from a pig that a different Tweetsie engine had run over and killed in that very spot. The railroad had not paid her restitution yet and she was growing weary waiting for her money. So she vowed to grease the track every day until the railroad paid her—which, one might add, was pretty soon after Allison's experience.

In addition to all of the adventures that developed riding the train each day, businesses grew along the depot line, and life became easier as travel from town to town could now be conducted in one day. In and around the Hampton Depot, the town boasted a limestone spring, a good hotel, a watering station (for the locomotive) and a telegraph office.

Continuing along the route, the train passed through the Doe River Gorge, past smaller depots and then arrived at Roan Mountain. From the Watauga River Valley to Roan Mountain, the roadbed climbed fifteen hundred feet.

In the town of Roan Mountain, sitting directly behind the Roan Mountain Depot, General Wilder built the Roan Mountain Inn, which provided a telegraph office and watering station. A perfect stop along the way, folks often spoke of fishing the Doe River off the back deck of the inn. Visitors to the Cloudland Hotel on top of Roan Mountain often spent their first night there in town.

One of the most successful Roan Mountain businesses was owned by the Graybeal Brothers, who operated one of the largest warehouses in eastern America for dried roots and herbs. Opening approximately the same time that the ET&WNC began running through Roan Mountain, it was not

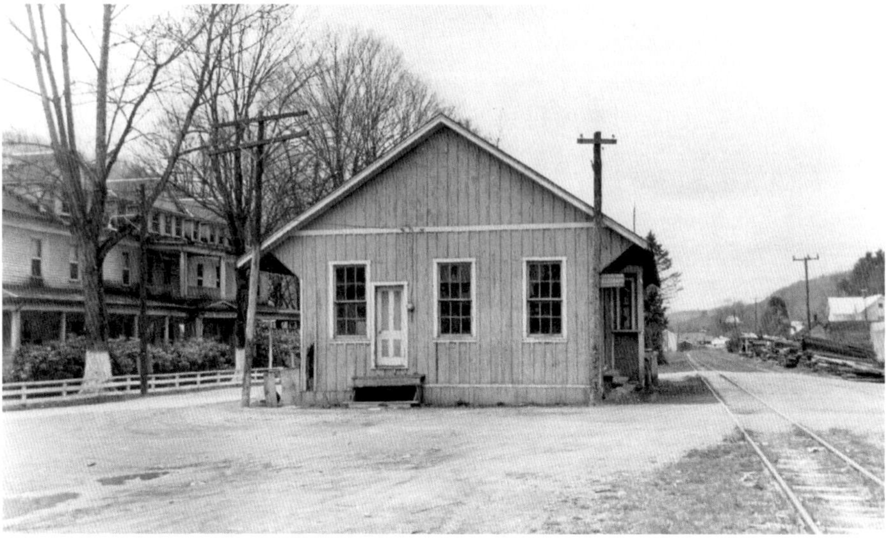

The Roan Mountain Depot with Wilder's "Inn" directly behind it. *Courtesy of the Archives of Appalachia. East Tennessee State University. James T. Dowdy Collection.*

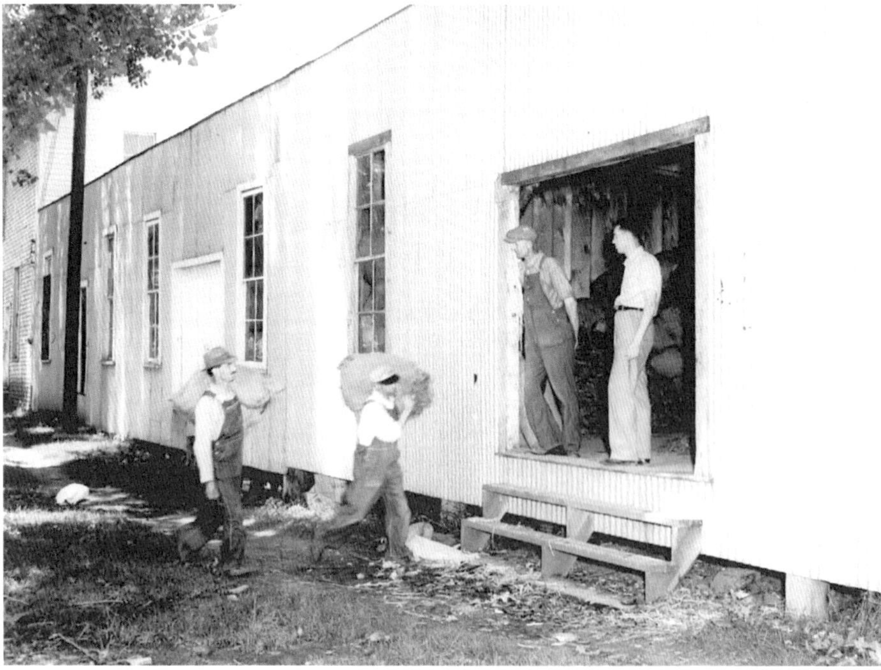

The need for a railroad extended beyond transporting iron ore. Local residents needed a better way to get the herbs they gathered to market in Johnson City. Early 1900s. *Courtesy of the Tennessee State Library and Archives.*

uncommon for folks to walk for miles to sell their gathered herbs for much-needed cash.

In May 1901, the infamous May Flood, sometimes called the May Tide, washed out the track in thirty-nine places and destroyed all but two bridges. More floods in 1940 wrecked havoc on the Linville River Railroad, washing it out beyond repair. Sadly, the North Carolina portion of the line was never rebuilt. And not long after, in 1950, passenger services were discontinued in Tennessee, a sad day for so many.

Though service ended, the train was not forgotten. Tweetsie's coal-fired steam locomotive Engine #12, built for $14,000 in 1917 by Baldwin Locomotive Works, Philadelphia, still survives. Of all the original ET&WNC Railroad narrow-gauge locomotives, Tweetsie Engine #12 is the only one remaining. With an 82.5-ton working weight, which includes coal and water, it is fifty-four feet long, eight feet, four inches wide and twelve feet, six inches tall.

The first new home #12 found was in Harrisonburg, Virginia, as part of the Shenandoah Central Railroad. Hurricane Hazel cut that visit short, destroying the train tracks in 1954. Then it seemed that #12 might be

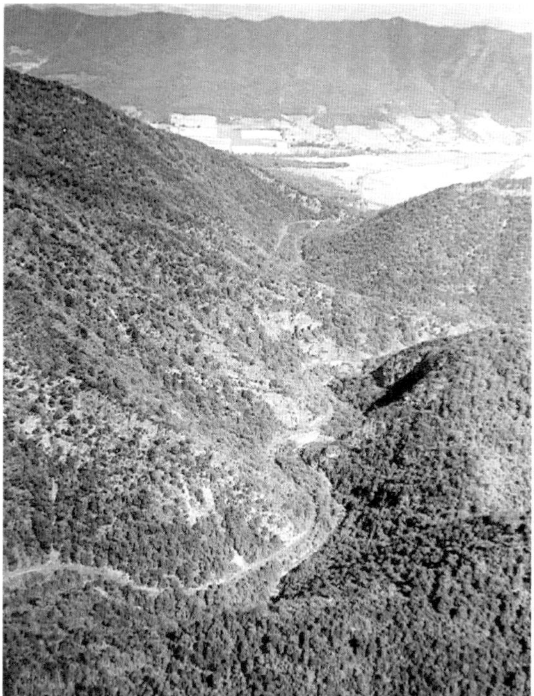

Building a railroad line was not an easy task, as seen by this aerial view of the Doe River Gorge in Hampton. 1947. *Courtesy of the Archives of Appalachia. East Tennessee State University. ET&WNC Collection.*

leaving its home turf for good, when in 1953, Gene Autry signed an option to purchase the engine and move it to California. Deciding the cost to ship the heavy piece of equipment was too high, Autry sold it for one dollar to lumberman Grover C. Robbins Jr. of Blowing Rock, North Carolina. Later, in 1957, Engine #12 made a mile run down a new section of track in the newly opened Tweetsie Railroad Amusement Park.

Doe River's Gorge Ministries have also renovated a small section of the original route in the Doe River Gorge via the Doe River Railway. This railway provides a great opportunity to experience the thrill of riding Tweetsie through the gorge.

The ultimate honor came in 1992, when the United States Department of the Interior listed the Tweetsie Railroad on the National Register of Historic Places. For those who lived much of their lives in isolation, the "Railway with a Heart" was not just an industrial wonder but also an entity that brought hope to the lives of people in mountainous regions in ways that no one could ever have imagined.

III
People and Places

Early Days

The first settlers in the Roan Mountain area were Native Americans, whose legends have long held an important place in their culture. Things not completely understood were often explained through stories and tales. Roan Mountain was a place of mystery to the natives, since its open balds made it distinctly different from the surrounding peaks. They found it to be a fitting subject for legend.

The Catawbas have an important legend about the Roan. It is said that in days long past, when territory was hotly disputed among the native tribes, the Catawbas challenged the Cherokees and all their other foes to a great battle atop the mountain. The prize for the victors was the right to lay claim to the Roan itself. Days passed without an end in sight, and it began to appear hopeless that a winner would ever emerge. Finally, it was the Catawbas who stepped forward and overtook the other tribes. Not wanting such a great battle to go unremembered, the Great Spirit caused the forest to wither from the spots where fighting had taken place. Then the rhododendron, nourished by the blood of the many hundreds who were slain, turned from white to the beautiful crimson seen today. In fact, when the Roan's trademark rhododendron was given a botanical name many years later, it was christened *Rhododendron catawbiense*, or Catawba rhododendron, perhaps to honor the victors of that legendary battle.

No proof of such events exists, of course, but there is evidence of Native American settlement at scattered locations around the base of the Roan. Some of the gaps in the mountain were used for traveling between what is now Tennessee and North Carolina, but the high ridge of the Roan was too cold for year-round habitation, so artifacts are more difficult to come by along the peak.

The first men to explore the southern Appalachians in systematic fashion were the botanists of the eighteenth and nineteenth centuries. Some of them traveled under the sponsorship of European governments. Nurseries were set up in North America to care for the plants they discovered until they could be carefully packaged and shipped across the Atlantic, at which time they became sources of national pride in the gardens of France, Russia and other countries.

Today, it may seem a little difficult to understand the urge that moved men to venture to distant lands and sometimes risk life and limb in their efforts to discover new plant species. John Bartram, a Pennsylvania farmer born in 1699 who became the first man to attempt to catalogue plant life in the southern Appalachians, eloquently captured the spirit of discovery of his time:

> *One day I was very busy in holding my plough…and being weary, I ran under the shade of a tree to repose myself. I cast my eyes on a* daisy; *I plucked it mechanically, and viewed it with more curiosity than common country farmers are wont to do, and observed therein very many distinct parts, some perpendicular-some horizontal.* What a shame, *said my mind, or something that inspired my mind,* that thee shouldst have employed so many years in tilling the earth, and destroying so many flowers and plants, without being acquainted with their structures and their uses! *This seeming inspiration suddenly awakened my curiosity* [sic], *for these were not thoughts to which I had been accustomed. I returned to my team, but this new desire did not quiet my mind; I mentioned it to my wife, who greatly discouraged me from prosecuting my new scheme, as she called it; I was not opulent enough, she said, to dedicate much of my time to studies and labors which might rob me of that portion of it which is the only wealth of the American farmer. However, her prudent caution did not discourage me; I thought about it continually—at supper, in bed, and wherever I went. At last, I could not resist the impulse.*

Bartram's botanical excursions took him through Maryland, Virginia, the Carolinas and as far as Florida. After a time, he could justifiably boast that "by a steady application of several years, I have acquired a pretty general knowledge of every plant and tree to be found in our Continent." The difficulty of traveling by horse and foot through new territories in those days cannot be underestimated. It must have taken a special kind of resolve to tackle high mountains like the Roan. Bartram's letters describe the rigors of surviving in the backwoods of the southern Appalachians in vivid detail. Insects were a problem, as were wild animals. "The panthers have not seized any of our people, that I have heard," Bartram wrote in 1738. "But many have been sadly frightened with them. They have pursued several men, both on horseback and foot. Many have shot them down, and others have escaped by running away."

The spirit of exploration must have gotten into the Bartram blood. John Bartram's son, William, followed in his father's footsteps. In 1773, William began a four-year botanical excursion in the Southeast under the sponsorship of a prominent London physician, Dr. John Fothergill. His journeys found him in the mountains primarily during the fall of the year, when he would collect ripe seeds for return to his father's botanical garden in Philadelphia. His legacy survives in the William Bartram Trail, which passes through the Appalachians well south of the Roan, skirting portions of North and South Carolina.

The Bartrams were instrumental in preparing the way for André Michaux, the true giant among the botanist-explorers in the southern Appalachians. Michaux was born near Versailles, France, in 1746. His wife died in childbirth in 1770, and after that he seemed to focus his attention on botany in an effort to overcome his grief. In 1785, the French government was looking to acquire plants and trees from eastern North America for its parks, and Michaux was commissioned for an expedition. His mission, in the words of his government, was "to make an intensive study of the trees and shrubs and to conduct such experiments as might be necessary to determine their fitness for transport to France."

He sailed to New York and the following year made it as far south as Charleston, South Carolina, where he organized his principal nursery. Michaux remained in North America until 1796. Among his important discoveries in the mountains of western North Carolina was the rare, beautiful plant *Shortia galacifolia*, commonly known as Oconee bells. He also taught local settlers the value of ginseng and showed them how to prepare it for the market in China. From the point of view of a conservationist, it is a wonder that all of Michaux's collecting did not damage the integrity of mountain vegetation; in the fall of a single year, for example, he carried away more than twenty-five hundred trees, shrubs and plant specimens from Burke and Yancey Counties in North Carolina alone. In 1794, he explored the Roan and other area peaks, discovering several alpine species that had previously been observed only in Canada.

Toward the end of his time in North America, financial support from France started to wane, and Michaux began to feel like a forgotten man. He set sail for home from Charleston in 1796, his ship carrying a full array of his finest specimens. Michaux's first stroke of bad luck fell when the vessel wrecked off the coast of Holland. He fastened himself to a piece of plank and later washed ashore unconscious; his precious plants were saved, though they were saturated with salt water. Further disappointment awaited him when he arrived in Paris, as he discovered that only a small number of the six thousand specimens he had sent to France during his decade in North America were still surviving. The gardens of Paris, it seemed, had been among the victims of the French Revolution. Michaux recovered enough from the blow to return abroad in 1800, but he died of fever on the island of Madagascar two years later.

André Michaux left his mark on the world in his classic botanical guide, *Flora-Boreali Americana*. Within its pages are descriptions of the thousands of plant species he discovered, examined and collected during his years of travel.

John Fraser, a Scotsman, was a noted botanist who explored the Roan in 1787, 1789 and 1799 under the patronage of the Russian government. Asa Gray, a botanist of a later generation, described the moment of one of Fraser's greatest discoveries on Roan Mountain: "On a spot which commands a view of five States, namely, Kentucky, Virginia, Tennessee, North Carolina, and South Carolina, the eye ranging to a distance of seventy or eighty miles when the air is clear, it was Mr. Fraser's good fortune to discover and collect living specimens of the new and splendid *Rhododendron catawbiense*." Fraser is also credited with discovering the fir that now bears his name and stands as a remembrance of a man who considered the Roan one of his favorite botanizing locations. *Abies fraseri*, the Fraser fir, occurs naturally in areas of high rainfall about forty-five hundred feet in elevation, though it has lately been cultivated on plantations as low as fifteen hundred feet. The tree's beautiful shape, its dark green foliage, its strong branches, its pleasant aroma and its excellent needle retention make it ideally suited for service as a Christmas tree. The Fraser fir's popularity has spawned an entire industry in the mountains.

There is a story that Fraser traveled for a time in the mountains with rival André Michaux. Michaux, it is said, feared that Fraser was dogging his footsteps so as to be certain not to miss out on any of the specimens Michaux intended to send to France. When he'd had his fill of Fraser's

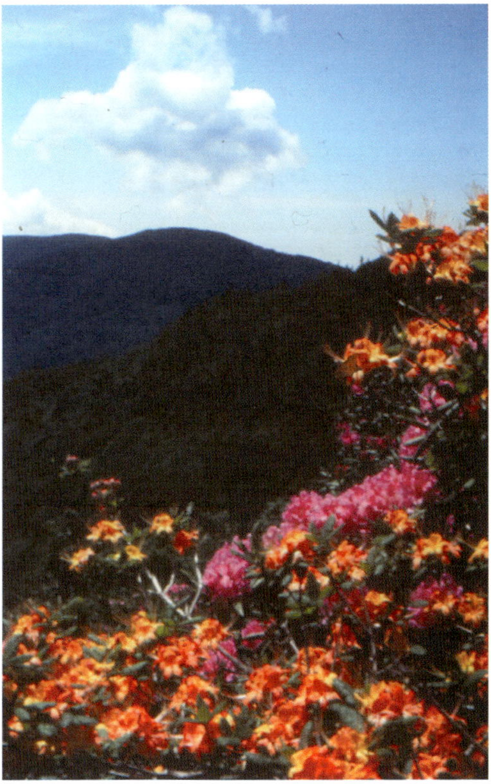

Right: Flame azalea and rhododendron bloom on the balds.

Below: The vibrant Gray's lily, named for botanist Asa Gray.

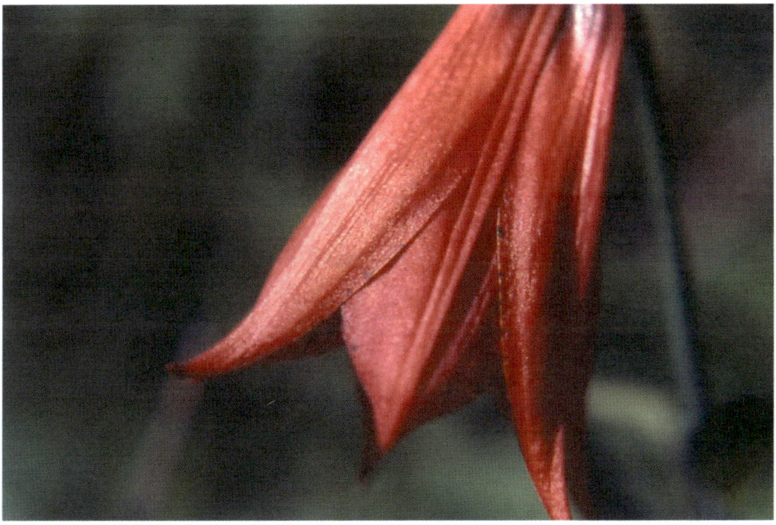

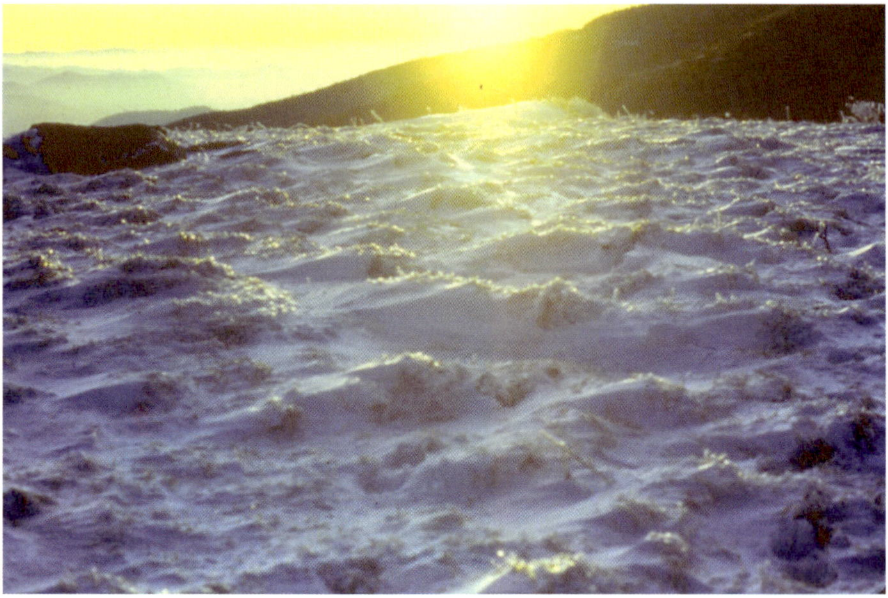

Sunset on Round Bald.

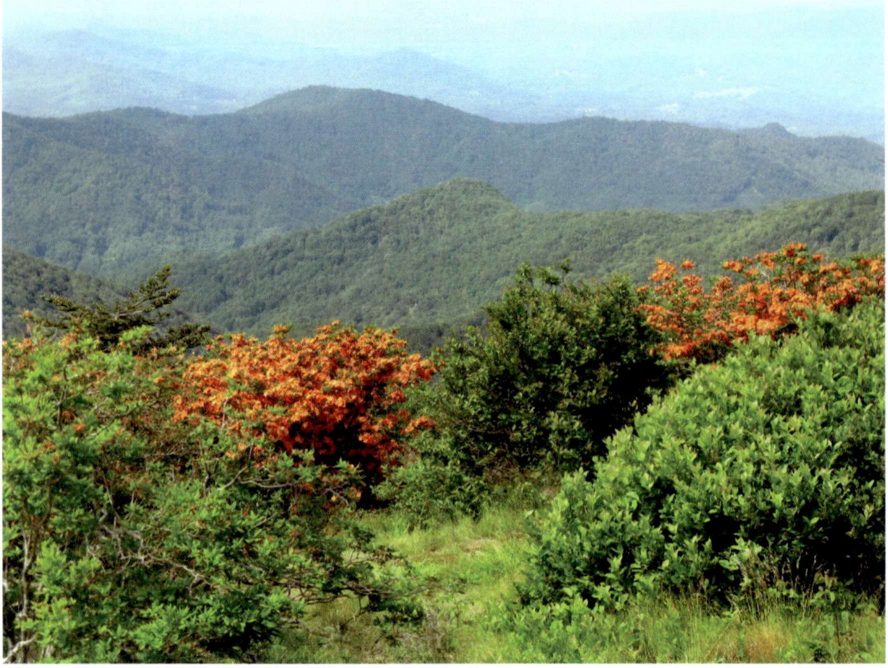

Flame azalea near Engine Gap looking into North Carolina.

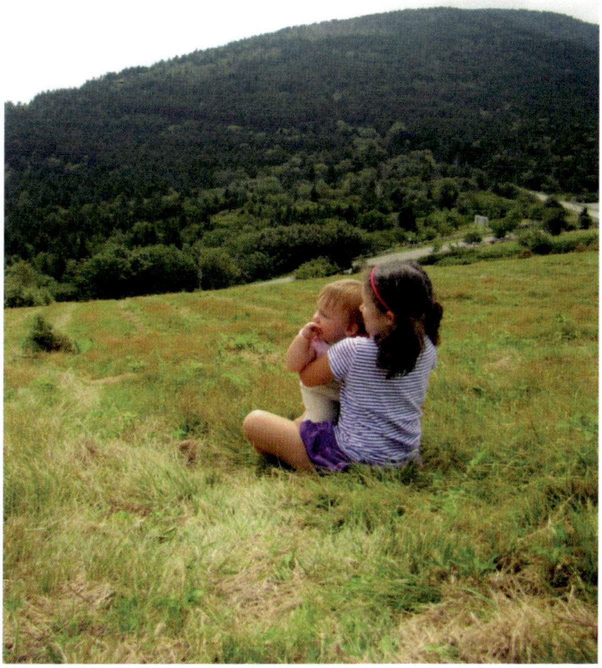

Right: Two young ladies enjoy an afternoon on Round Bald with Carver's Gap and Roan High Knob behind. *Courtesy of Carrie Maye Sullins.*

Below: No matter what the age, Roan Mountain brings out that thrill of discovery. *Courtesy of Carrie Maye Sullins.*

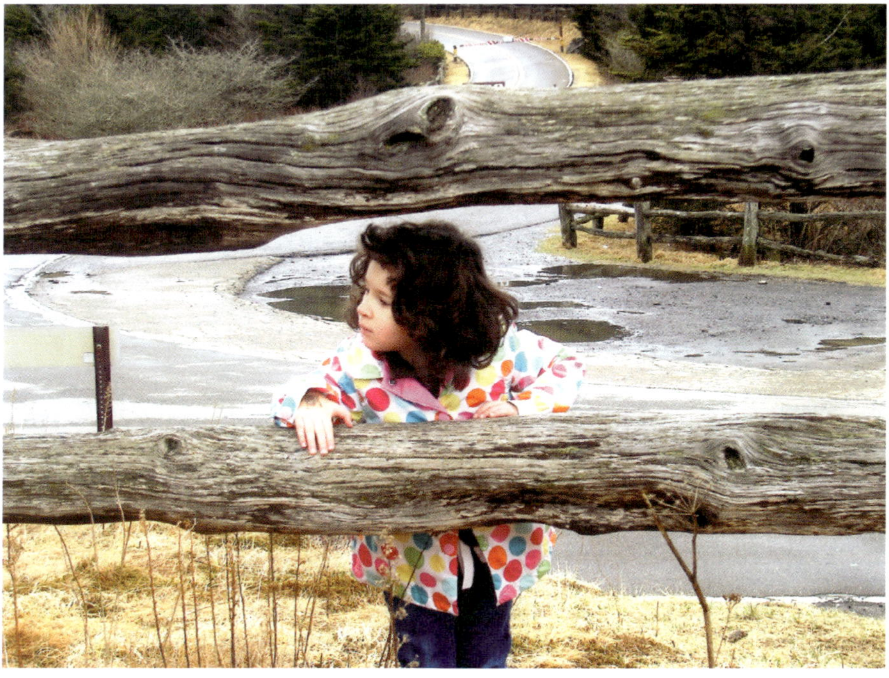

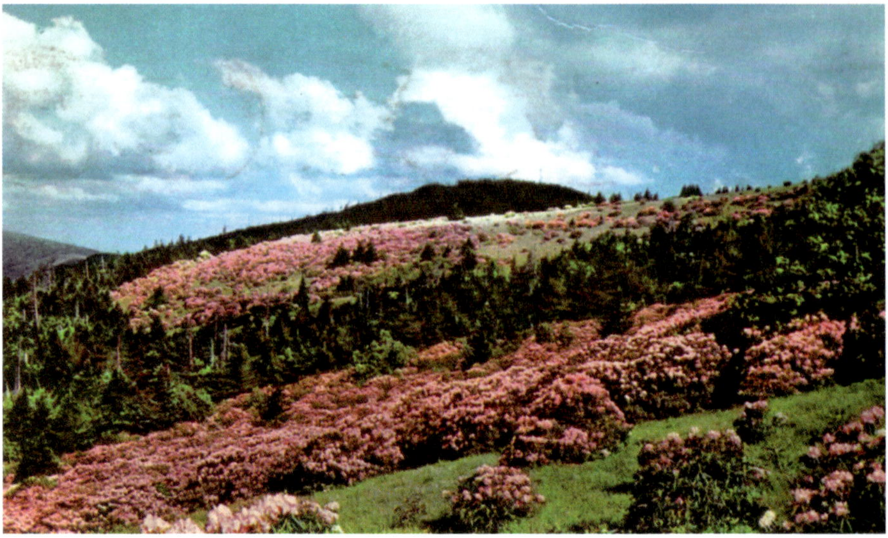

An early postcard boasts the beauty of the Rhododendron Gardens in full bloom. *Courtesy of Pete Barr.*

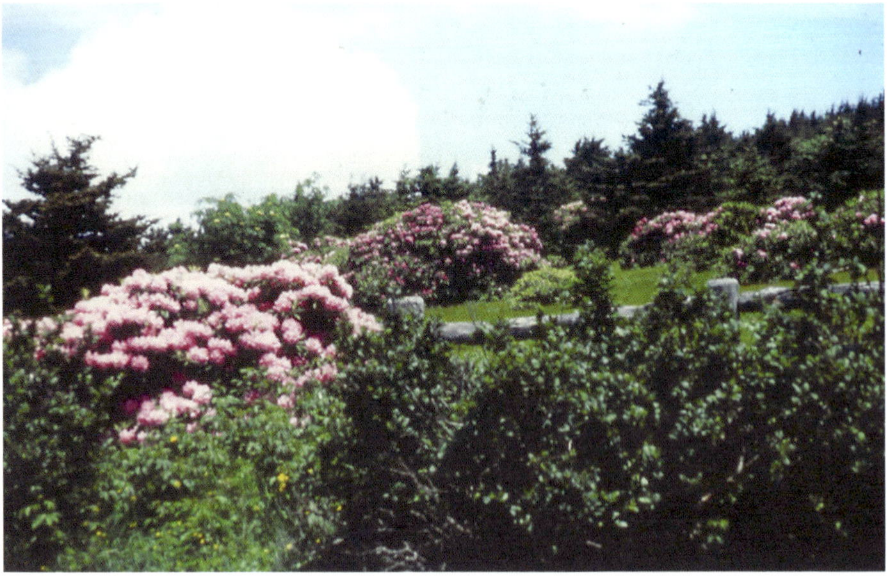

One of the earlier color photographs of the rhododendron blooming on the balds. 1940s.

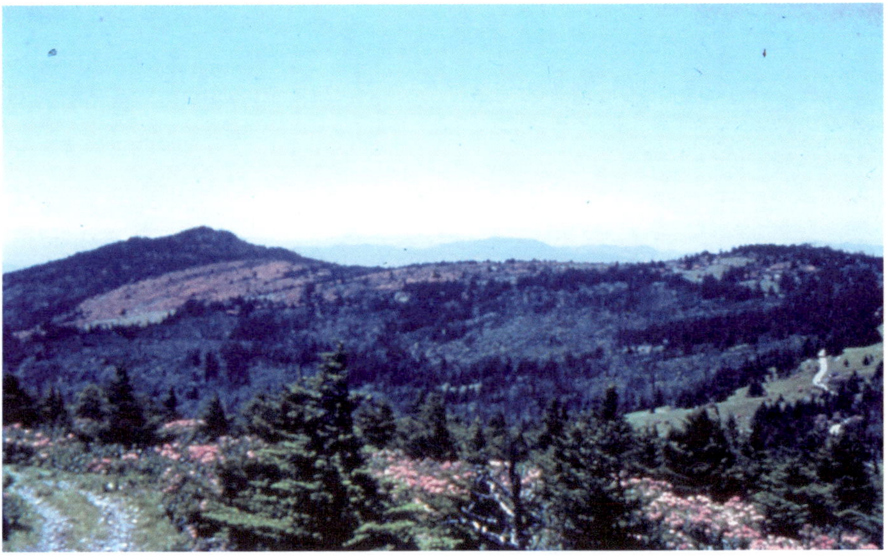

This panorama was probably even more sparsely vegetated when Elisha Mitchell boasted of galloping his horse along the crest of the Roan. 1940s.

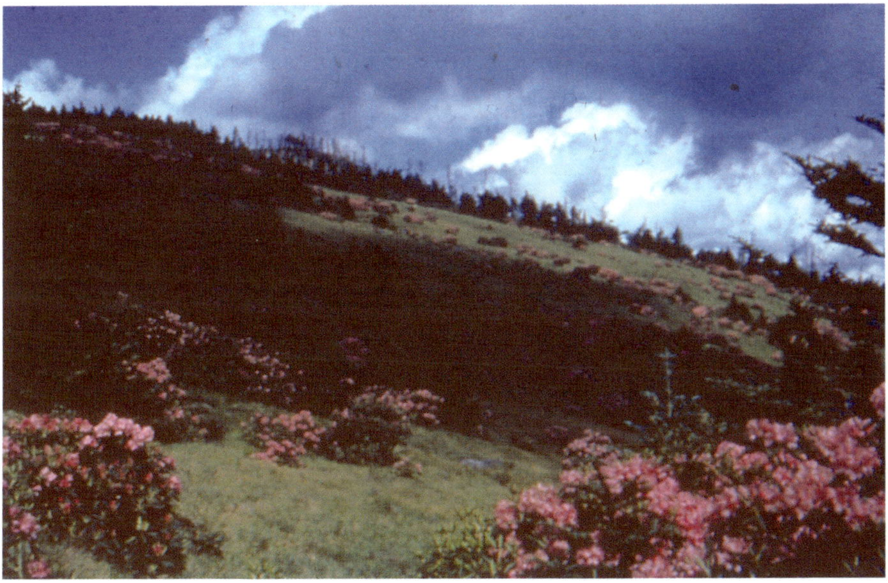

The Catawba Indians believed that the blood lost from a great battle gave color to the rhododendron. 1940s.

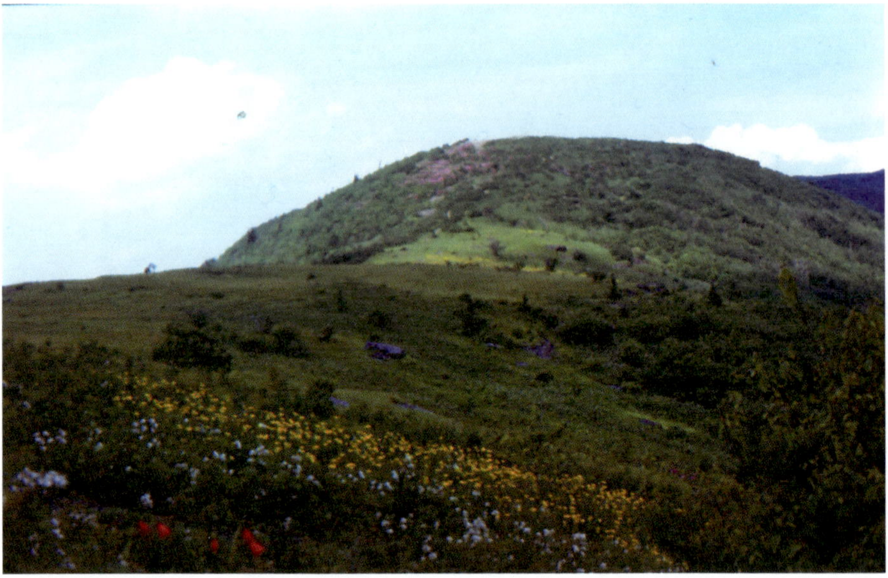

By late June, the grass and shrubs balds take on a rainbow of color.

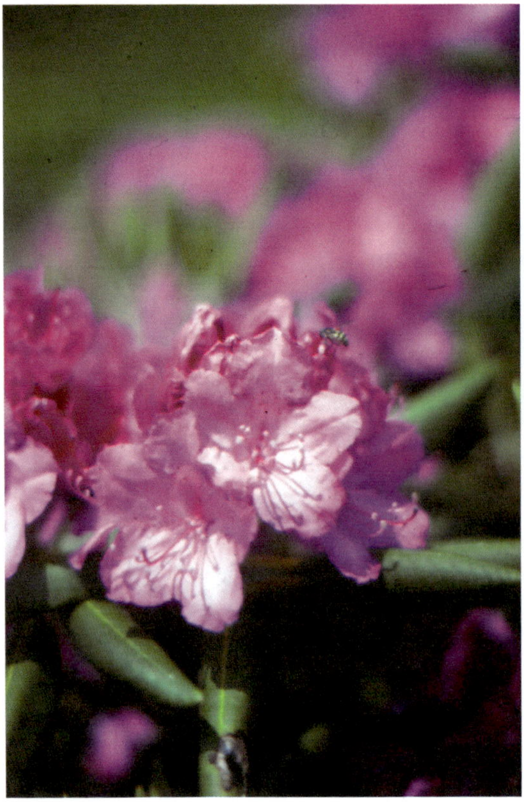

Looking into the center of a rhododendron bloom, intricate patterns and colors are evident, giving the plant an excellent opportunity to attract pollinators.

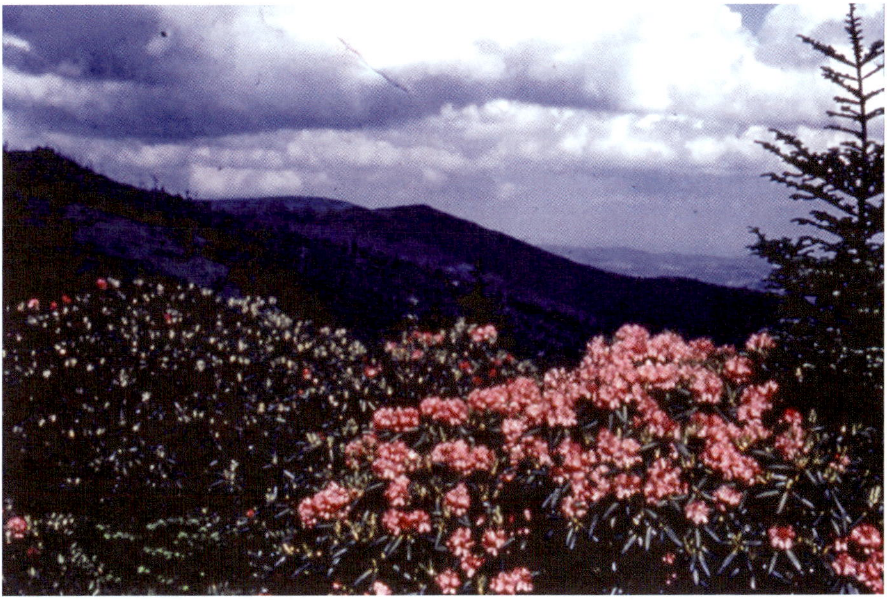

Looking into the North Carolina mountains in the 1940s.

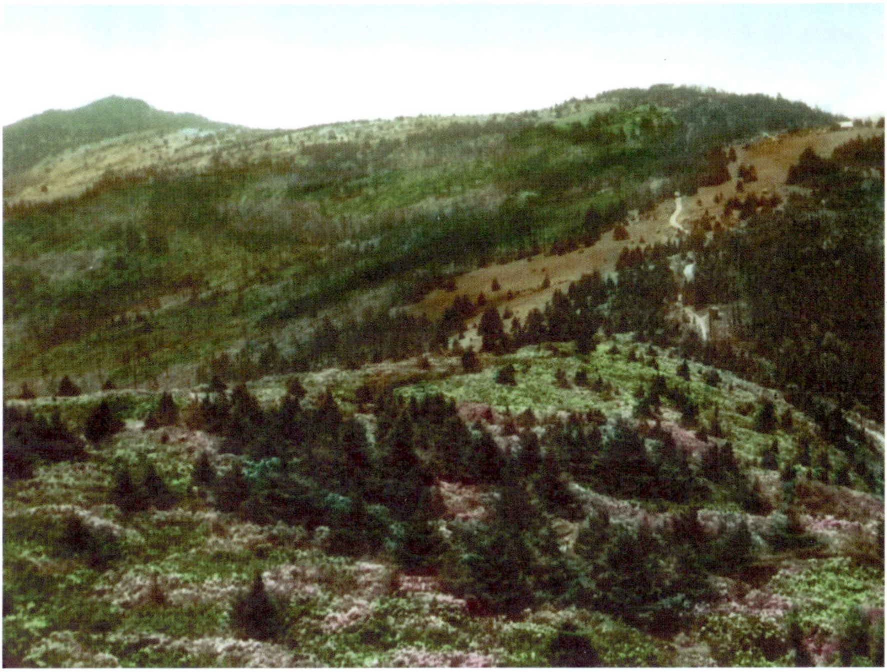

A unique image captured on a glass lantern slide in the 1930s shows the openness of the landscape. *D.M. Brown Collection.*

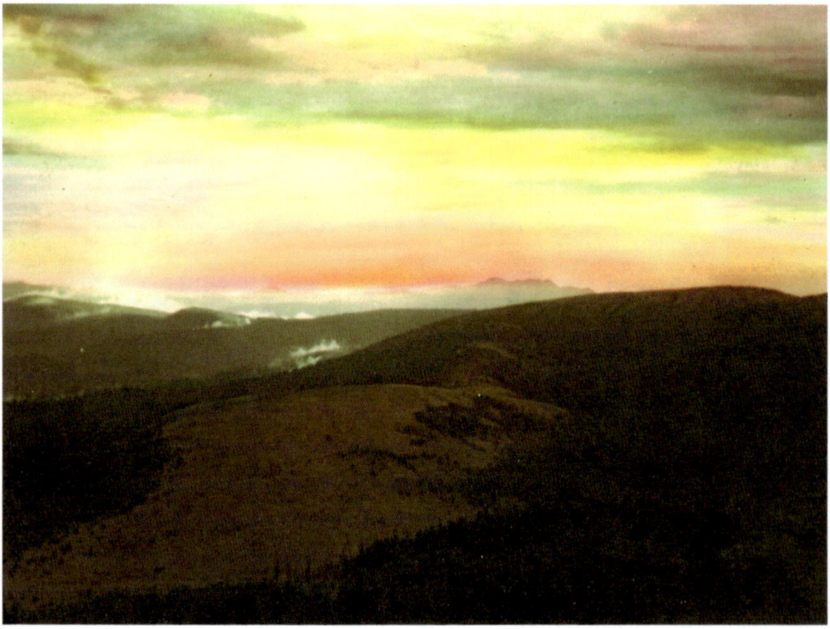

An ocean of painted color on a glass slide as the sun rises over the balds. 1930s. *D.M. Brown Collection.*

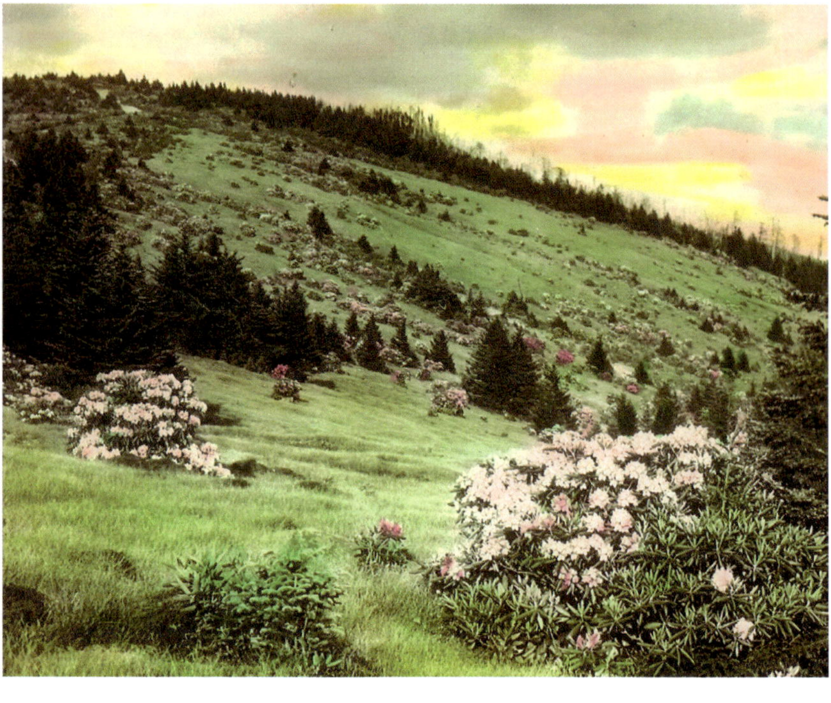

Traces of the old ridgeline road can be seen in this 1930s glass slide. *D.M. Brown Collection.*

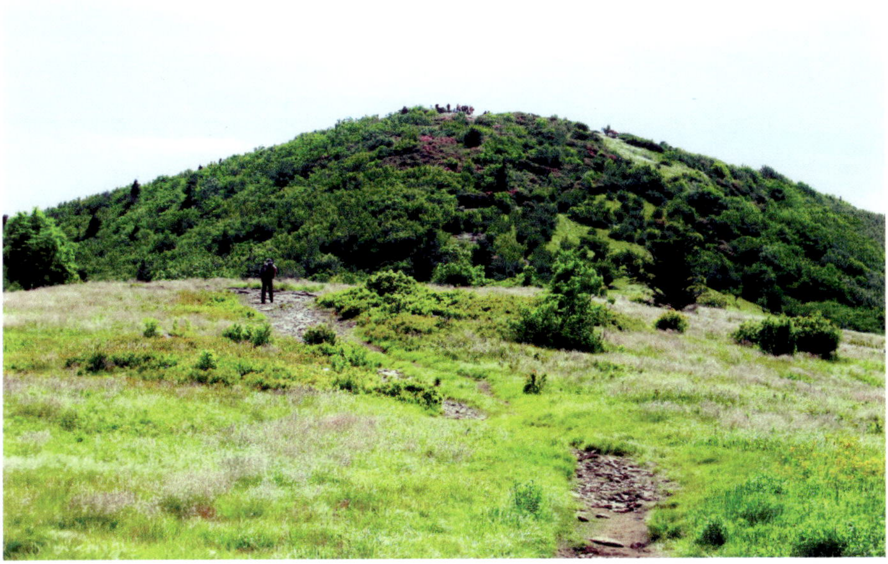

Jane Bald, named after Jane Cook, who cared devotedly for her sister, Harriett, as she fell ill on the bald that now bears her name.

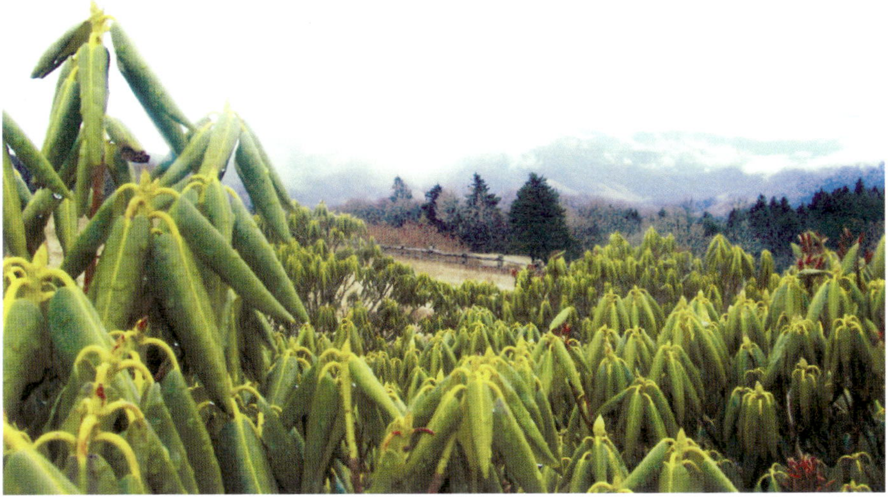

The first travelers who negotiated the mountain wilderness negotiated rugged terrain, across elevations reaching more than six thousand feet above sea level. *Courtesy of Carrie Maye Sullins.*

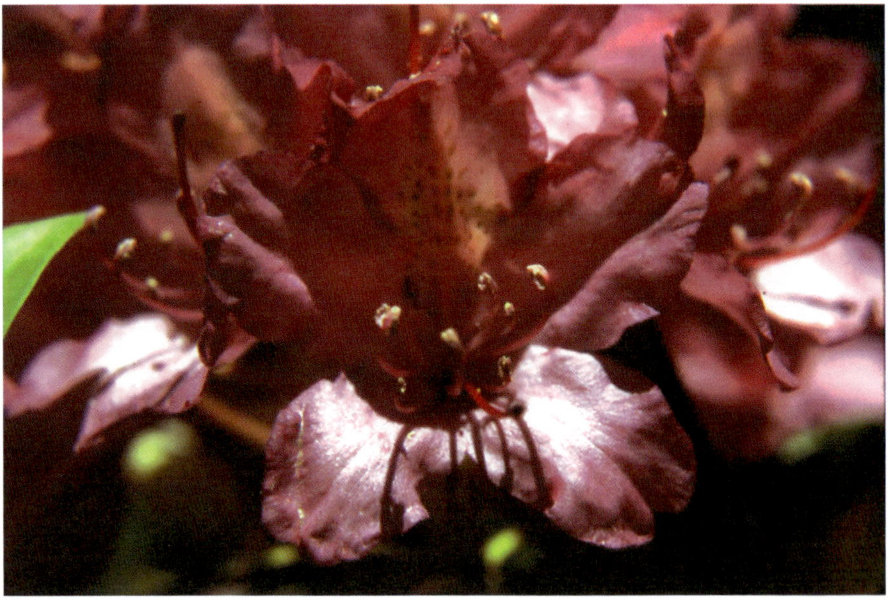

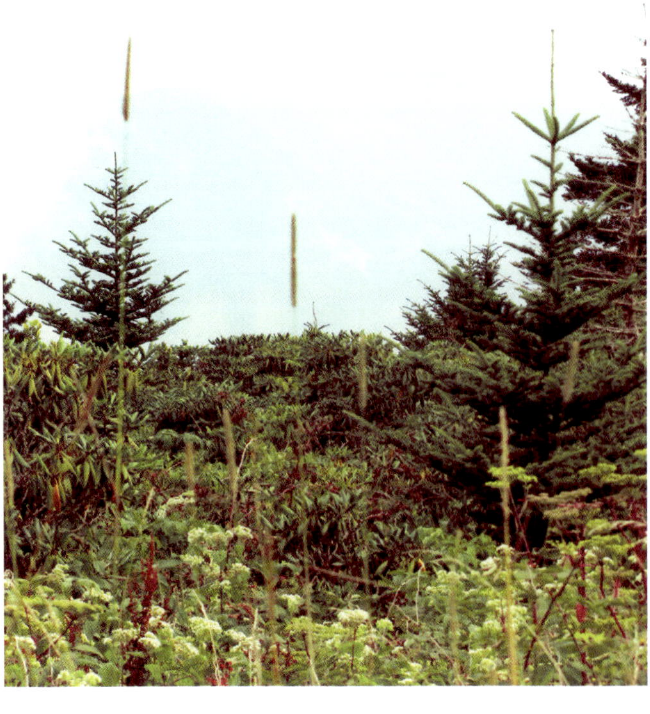

Above: *Rhododendron catawbiense.*

Left: The towering heights of the North Carolina mountains as seen from the top of the Roan. *Courtesy of Carrie Maye Sullins.*

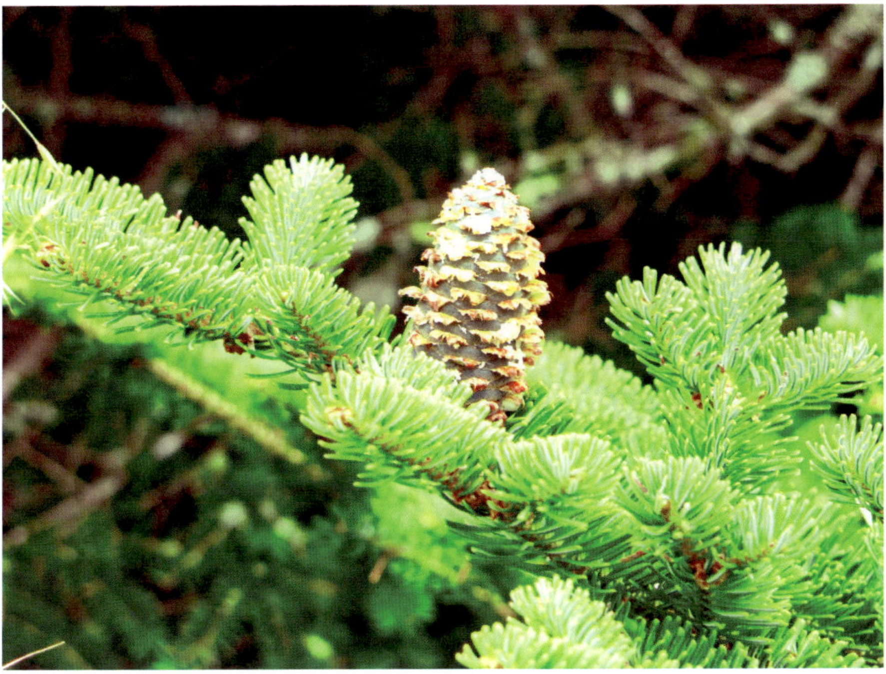

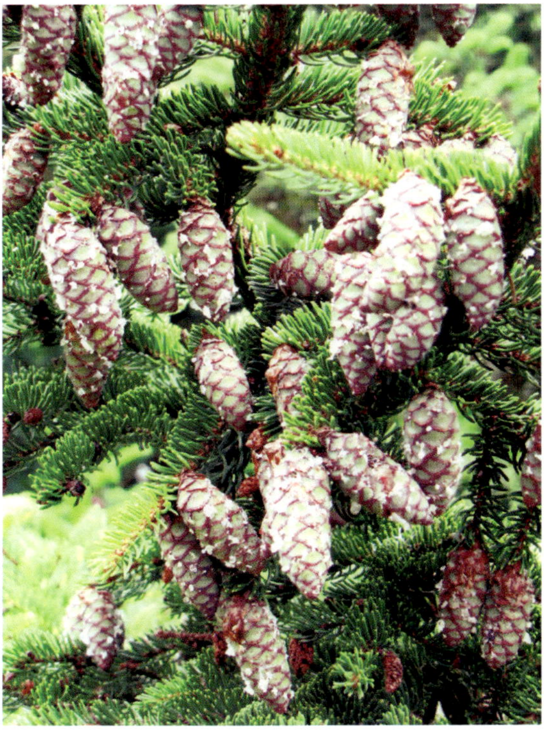

Above: Fraser fir, named for John Fraser, producing its crop of cones for the season. *Courtesy of Carrie Maye Sullins.*

Right:: A prolific crop of female seed cones on the red spruce tree, a critical habitat for the northern flying squirrel. *Courtesy of Carrie Maye Sullins.*

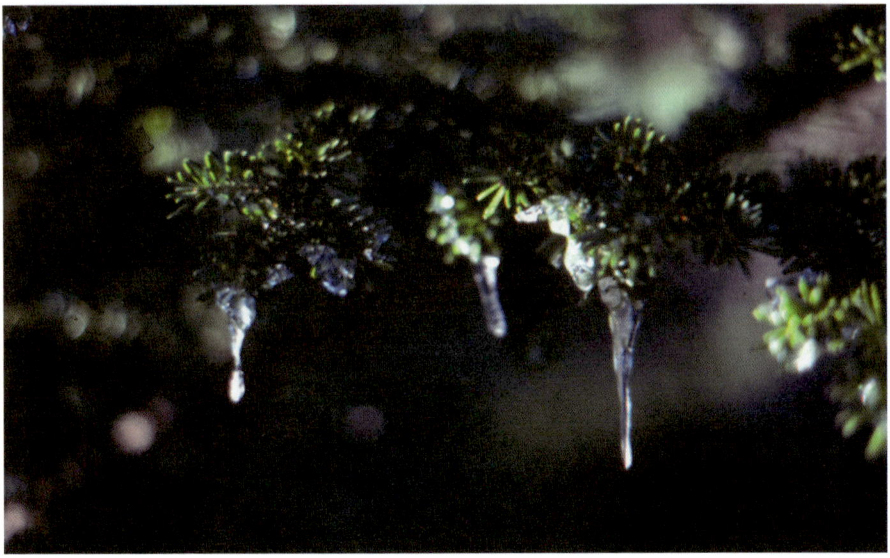

Fraser fir, a Canadian zone species, is adapted to survival in a cold, snowy environment.

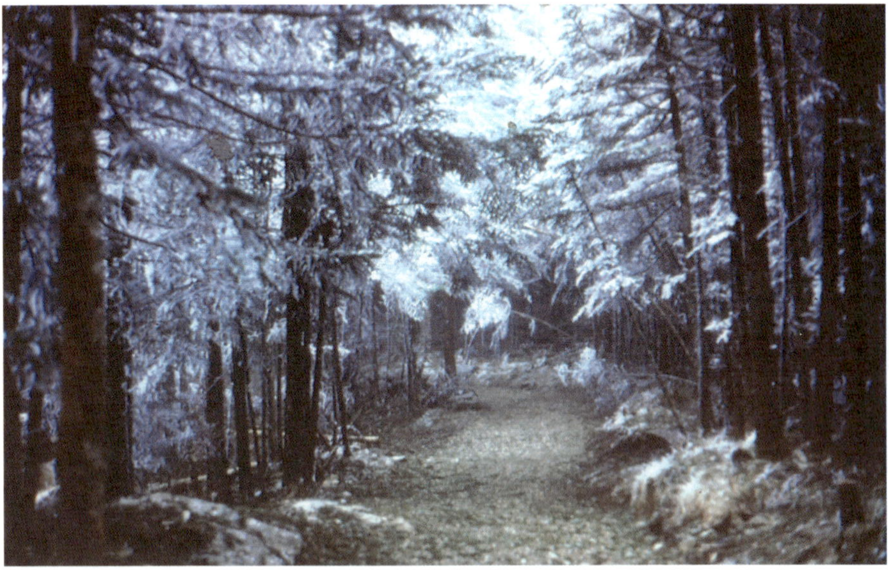

The quiet beauty of the spruce-fir forest.

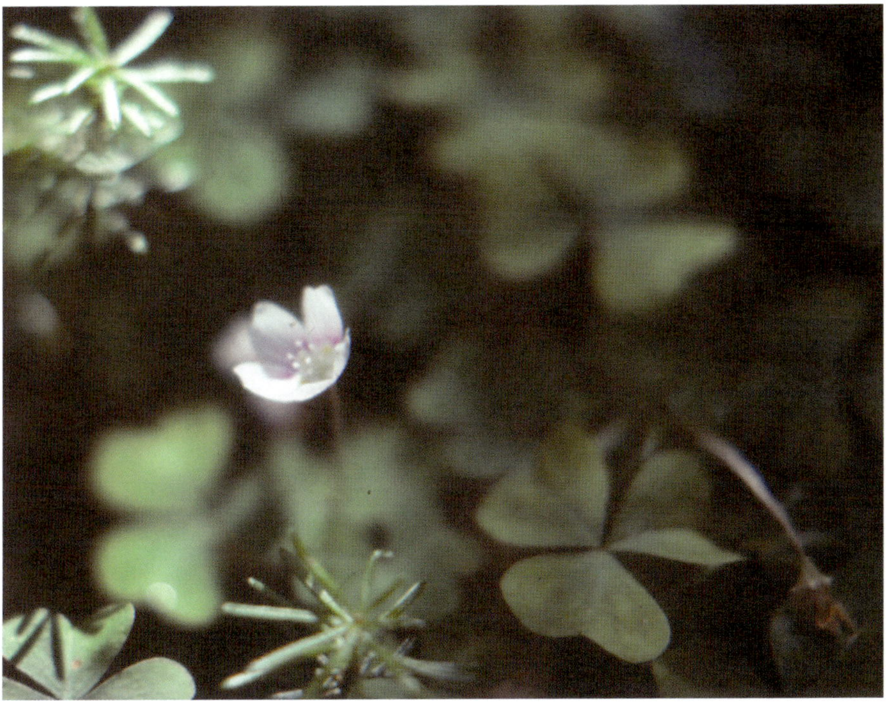

Wood sorrel, *Oxalis Montana*, survives under the cool shade of a spruce-fir forest.

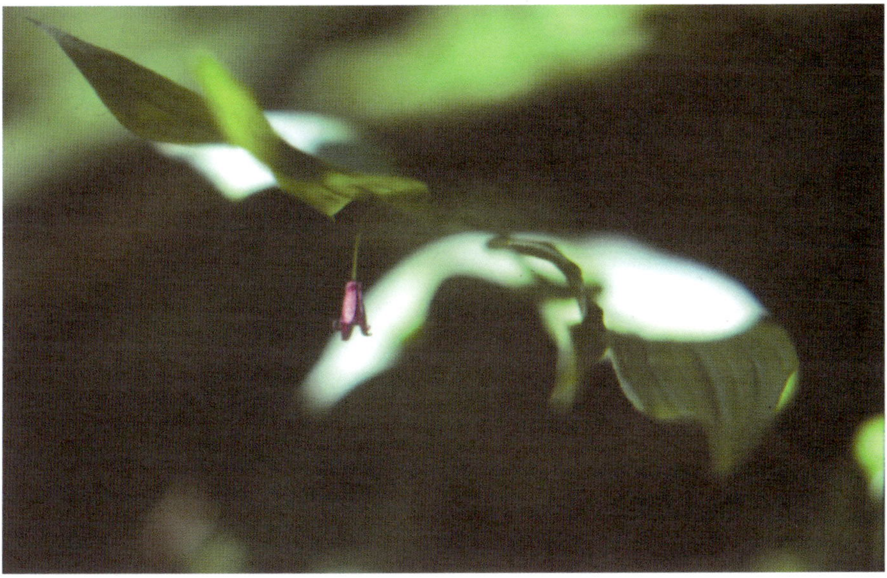

Rose twisted stalk, *Streptopus roseus*, is sparingly found in rocky, wet areas.

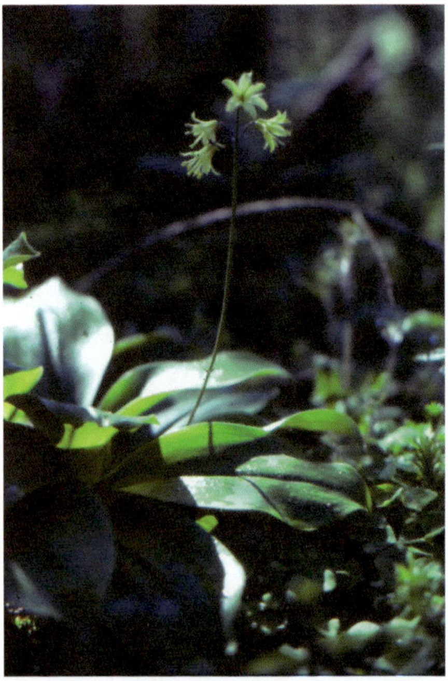

Clintonia borealis, Clinton's lily, a plant endangered through most of its range.

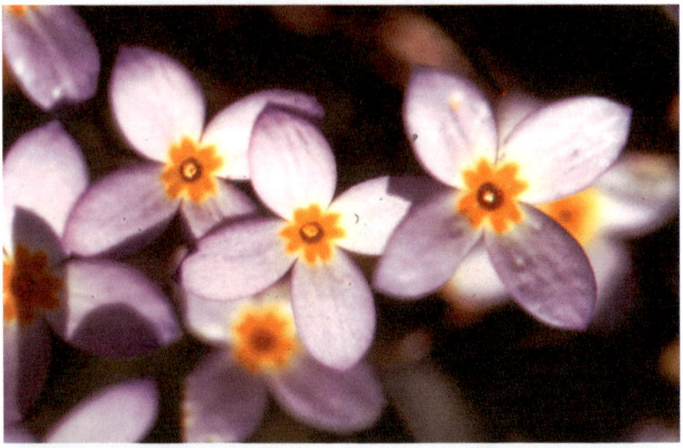

The Thymeleaf bluet, *Houstonia serpyllifolia*, is commonly seen along the Appalachian Trail on the balds.

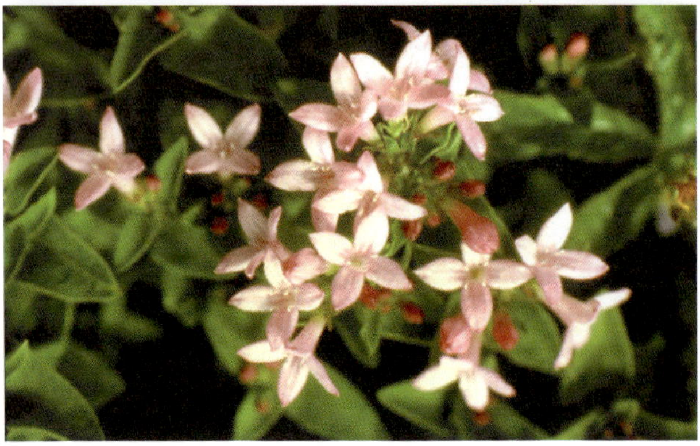

The endangered Roan Mountain bluet, *Houstonia purpurea var. Montana.*

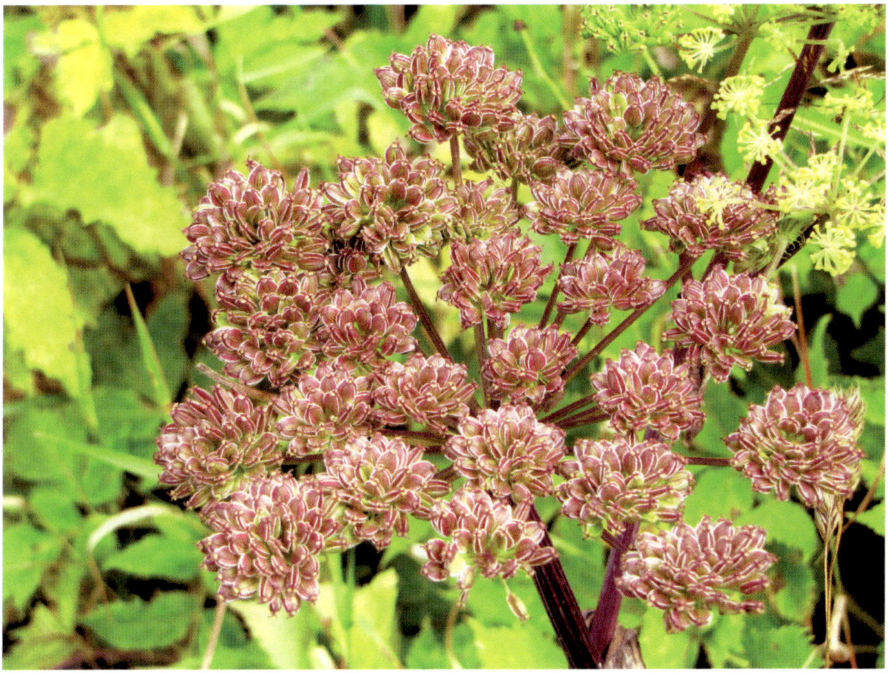

In the fall of the year, filmy angelica, *Angelica triquinata*, produces a distinctive head of seeds. Bees that find nectar on the flowers often appear intoxicated! *Courtesy of Carrie Maye Sullins.*

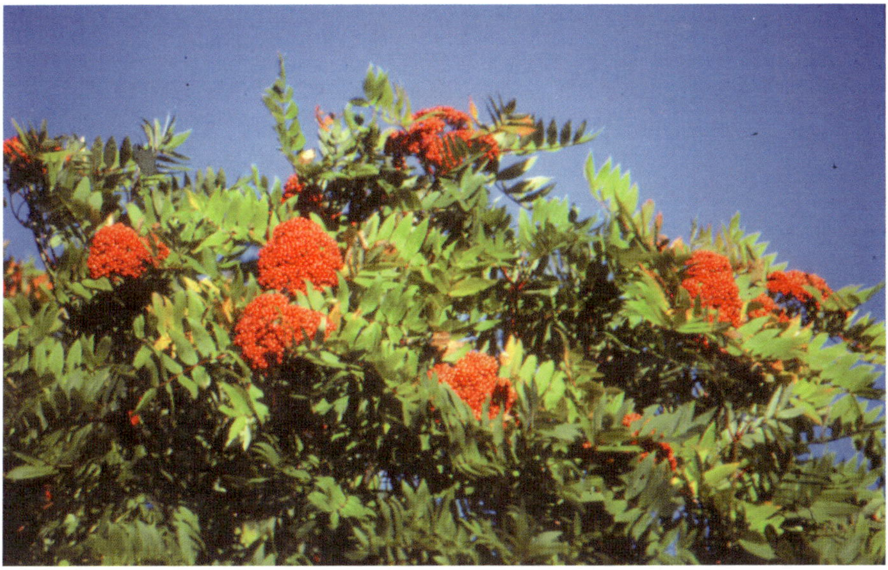

The vibrant red berries of the mountain ash, or Rowan tree, are the source of one of the legends that attempt to uncover the mystery of how Roan Mountain got its name.

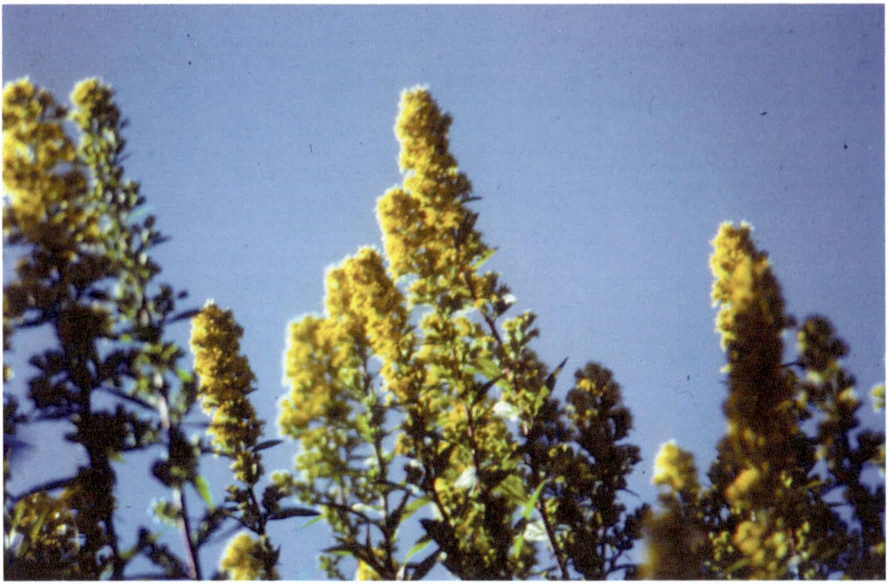

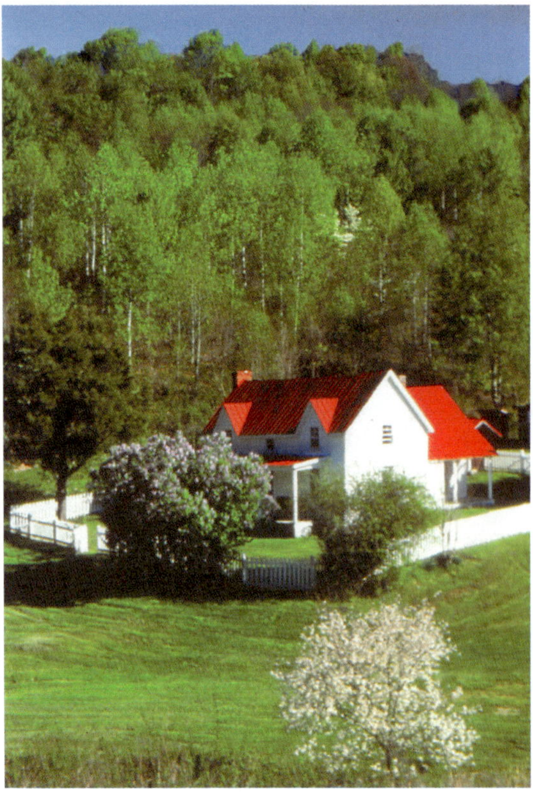

Above: Roan Mountain goldenrod against a bright blue sky in late summer.

Left: The Miller Homeplace in Roan Mountain State Park.

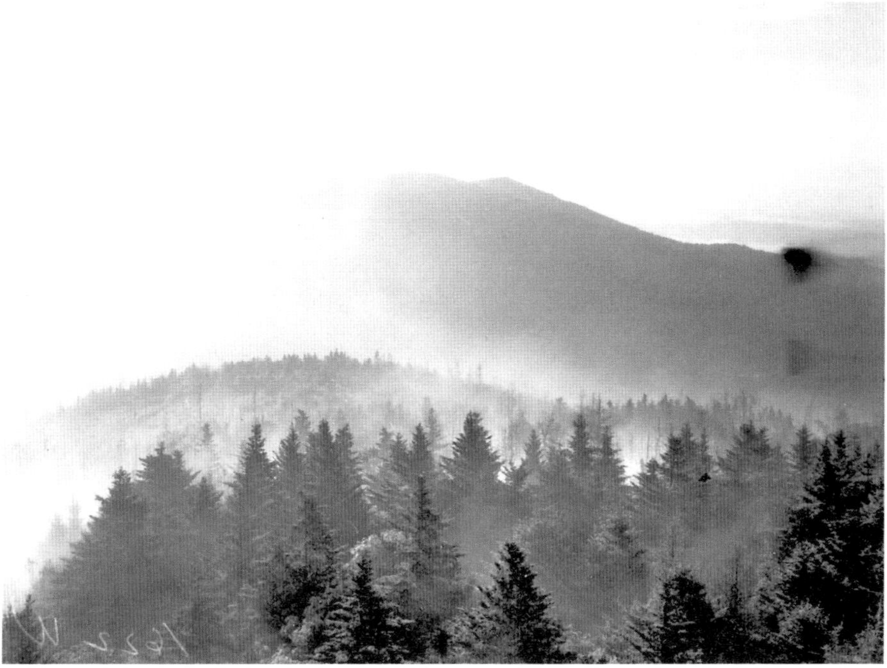

Botanists from around the world have explored the Roan for several centuries. The Fraser fir, seen here, was named after botanist John Fraser. *D.M. Brown Collection.*

company, Michaux left him under the pretext of having to track down some horses that had strayed, and the two went their separate ways from that point onward. Such was the competitive spirit among botanists at that time. Fraser had his son return to North America in 1807, and his son spent many years on the continent sending seeds and plants back to Great Britain after Fraser's death in 1811.

John Strother and the rest of the team that surveyed the Tennessee/North Carolina state line in 1799 were not botanists by trade, but they were certainly important figures in the early exploration of the Roan. Strother wrote of the hardships of travel in the mountains: "This day's march [up the Roan] was very severe, water scarce and that a considerable distance from the line. Had but an indifferent night's rest. The ground being very steep where we encamped was the cause of our resting but little. Add to this the severity of gnats." Strother was impressed with both the stiff wind and the view atop the Roan. "There is no shrubbage grows on the tops of this mountain for several miles, say, five," he wrote. "The wind has such a power on the top of this mountain that the ground is blowed in deep holes all over the northwest sides. The prospects from the Roan Mountain is more conspicuous than from any other part of the Appelatchin mtns."

Elisha Mitchell was a professor at the University of North Carolina in the days when that school boasted only three faculty members and ninety-odd students. Mitchell is most noted for his uncannily accurate measurements of the Black Mountains of North Carolina. He died in 1857 in a fall on the mountain, later named in his honor. At 6,684 feet, Mount Mitchell is the highest peak east of the Black Hills of South Dakota. Professor Mitchell considered the Roan "the easiest of access and the most beautiful of all the high mountains" of the region. Of Roan Mountain's unique geography, he wrote:

> *With the exception of a body of* [granite] *rocks, looking like the ruins of an old castle, near its southwestern extremity, the top of the Roan may be described as a vast meadow, (about nine miles in length, with some interruptions, and with a maximum elevation of six thousand and thirty eight feet), without a tree to obstruct the prospect; where a person may gallop his horse for a mile or two, with Carolina at his feet on one side, and Tennessee on the other, and a green ocean of mountains raised into*

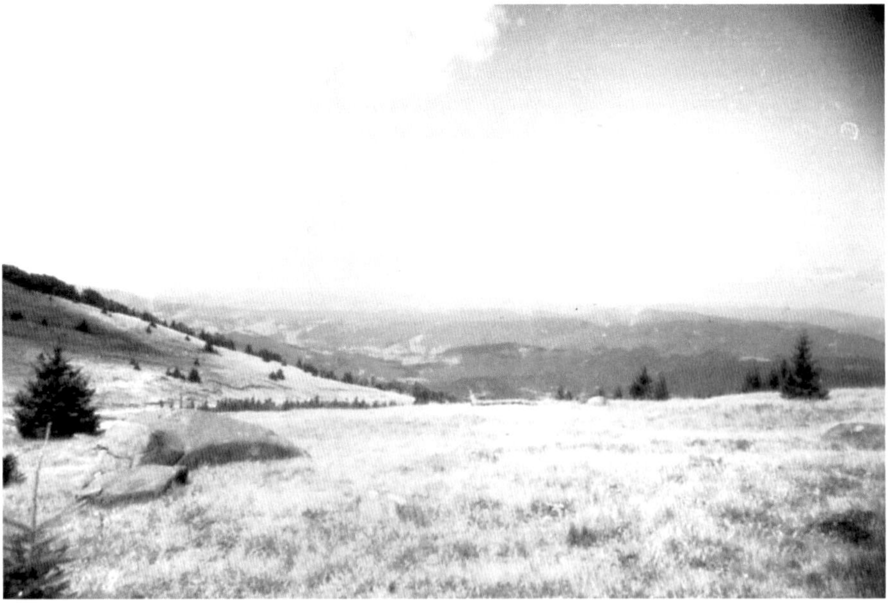

Elisha Mitchell spoke fondly of Roan: "The top of the Roan may be described as a vast meadow...without a tree to obstruct the prospect; where a person may gallop his horse for a mile or two, with Carolina at his feet on one side, and Tennessee on the other." *D.M. Brown Collection.*

> *tremendous billows immediately about him. It is the pasture ground for the young horses of the whole country about it during the summer. We found strawberry here in the greatest abundance and of the finest quality, in regard to both size and flavor, on the 30th of July.*

The name of Harvard botanist Asa Gray is another familiar one throughout the area. Gray explored the Roan in 1840 and called it "without doubt, the most beautiful mountain east of the Rockies." Gray was born in Paris, New York, in 1810. He earned a medical degree but never used it, as his love of "the vegetable kingdom" pushed him instead toward a career in botany. His most famous article, "Notes on a Botanical Excursion into the Mountains of North Carolina," published in 1842, contained an impressive list of the plant species he discovered during his research. It was on the Roan where Gray found the lily he called *Lilium canadense*. With its deep red color and its throat speckled with black spots, it differed considerably from any lily previously known. Not long afterward, Dr. Sereno Watson set it aside as a distinct species and renamed it *Lilium Grayi*, or Gray's lily, in honor of the man who discovered it. Gray's lily still blooms in the Rhododendron Gardens atop the Roan.

The mountain continued to attract scientists from all parts of the map through the latter stages of the nineteenth century. Describing the atmosphere of the discovery on the Roan during the summer of 1880, J.W. Chickering noted that "an almost continuous scientific convention has been informally assembled on the summit." Early explorers in the area constituted a who's who of the botanical community, and the list of their findings is long and impressive.

If unusual plant species were responsible for bringing the first systematic explorations of Roan Mountain and the southern Appalachians, then timber and minerals were responsible for bringing industry to the region. Industry's interest in the mountains' timber actually predated interest in exploiting mineral resources, but major loggers were slow in pushing their way as far south and west as Roan Mountain, and it was after 1900 before the mills were operating in full swing.

North Carolina has been called "the Specimen State" in mining circles. The title is a bit disparaging, since it implies that while the Tar Heel State is home to a great many kinds of minerals, few are present in great enough quantity to make exploiting them worthwhile. In the state's defense, it should be noted that iron, copper, mica, talc, kaolin, barite, corundum and lime have all been discovered in paying quantities in North Carolina territory.

There are legends about ancient mining operations in the southern Appalachians. A tradition among the Native Americans of the region tells of white men on mules coming from the south during the summertime and carrying off a white metal with them. The legend probably contains a good measure of truth.

Thomas Lanier Clingman was an explorer, a congressman and a key figure in the development of the North Carolina mountains throughout much of the nineteenth century. In 1867, Clingman discovered a small quantity of silver ore at the Sink Hole Mine, located just seven miles southwest of Bakersville, the closest community to Roan Mountain on the North Carolina side. Initial estimates suggested that the mine would yield about three hundred dollars' worth of silver per ton—a gross overestimate, as it turned out, but nonetheless the kind of promise that sets miners to digging with vigor. Clingman ordered a shaft to be sunk and two tunnels to be constructed but was disappointed to find nothing but mica.

Clingman and his men knew they were digging at an old mining site, but they were surprised when it came to light just how old the Sink Hole Mine really was. The Sink Hole site is a series of excavations sixty to eighty feet in diameter extending for about a third of a mile along a ridge. Old stone digging tools were found in some of the holes, and there was evidence of the use of metallic tools as well. More importantly, there were trees greater than three feet in diameter growing from some of the mounds of dirt removed in previous excavations. Clingman estimated that the timber rooted in the excavated earth was three hundred years of age, and in fact local resident Charles D. Stewart removed one such tree in 1872 and discovered that it contained three hundred rings in its trunk.

The revelations at the Sink Hole Mine lent credence to the theories that Spaniards in search of gold and silver explored the area way back in the sixteenth century. Hernando de Soto conducted an expedition in 1540, but he never made it as far north as the Roan Mountain area. Juan Pardo, who arrived in 1567, and the Spanish explorers of his generation are more likely candidates. Thus, there may have been significant interest in the area's mineral resources more than four centuries ago. But if there ever were notable deposits of silver around the Roan, then the Spaniards and their mules must have carted it all away.

It is interesting to note that Clingman and his men considered the mica they removed from the Sink Hole Mine to be worthless, simply discarding it as waste. A man named Heap stumbled upon Clingman's operation, took a block of mica with him over the mountains to Knoxville, Tennessee, and discovered that there was a market for it. He later returned with a partner, and the two of them successfully mined mica at the site for several years. In those days, mica was either pressed into sheets or ground, and it was used in such things as stoves, lamps, electrical machinery, insulation material and wallpaper. Bits of the shiny, reflective material can still be found on the Sink Hole property.

The most important mine in the vicinity of the Roan is undoubtedly the Cranberry Mines, located in North Carolina just three miles off the Tennessee border on Cranberry Creek, named for the abundant berries on its banks. Experts have called it one of the most remarkable iron deposits in the United States. The Cranberry vein actually stretches some twenty-two miles in a southwesterly direction, crossing the state line at Hump Mountain, at the northern end of the highlands of the Roan. In its day, it was a vein of remarkable purity, with high percentages of magnetic oxide of iron and metallic iron, but completely free of sulphur, the bane of the iron industry. The steep slopes at the Cranberry Mines were once covered with blocks of ore, many weighing hundreds of pounds. At times during the mining process, massive vertical walls of ore ten to fifteen feet thick were exposed. The main outcrop was fifteen hundred feet in length, ranging from two hundred to eight hundred feet in width.

The iron ore of Cranberry was first discovered in 1780, but it was not until 1920 that a Catalan forge was erected at Cranberry Gap. Also called a bloomery, it was the earliest form of smelter used to produce a porous mass

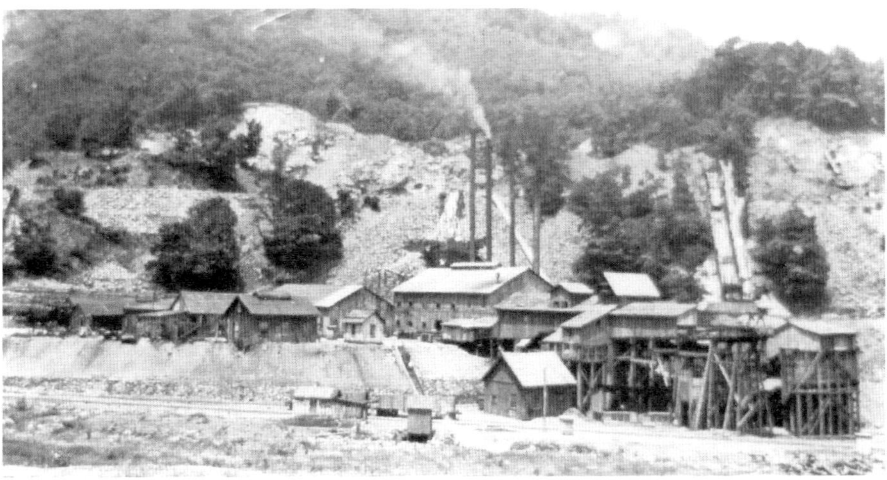

The Cranberry Mines. 1890s. D.W. Mackie Collection. *Courtesy of Sam S. Mackie.*

of iron and slag (the compounds that are removed). In the early twentieth century, this slag was ground into a powder. The antique glass termed "slag glass" was made from this powder. Later, the bloomery was replaced by the blast furnace, which produced a brittle, high carbon pig iron. Pig iron required further processing to produce commercial steel and iron.

There is an interesting story surrounding the later re-discovery of the Cranberry vein. Three brothers from Crab Orchard, Tennessee—Joshua, Ben and Jake Perkins—attended a log rolling near their home in 1826. They became involved in a scuffle with a man named Wright Moreland and attempted to rob him of his clothes. After the incident, the incensed Moreland obtained warrants for their arrest. To avoid prosecution, the Perkins boys fled over the mountain to North Carolina, where they sought to support themselves by digging ginseng along the banks of Cranberry Creek. It was Joshua Perkins who found iron ore instead. The brothers were smart enough to take advantage of a North Carolina statute allowing anyone discovering ore on vacant land to construct a tilt-hammer forge; according to the statute, once the operators produced five thousand pounds of iron at their forge, the state would grant them three thousand acres at the site in an effort to encourage development. The Perkins boys were on their way.

During the Civil War, the Confederacy took over the output of many local iron mines from 1862 until the end of the war. Iron ore was hauled using oxen- and mule-drawn wagons to small forges. Some went to Morganton and some to a handmade forge on the Doe River in Elizabethton, operated by William C. Brownlow. Brownlow used his ore to make tools for farmers. Of interesting note, *Governor* Brownlow served the state of Tennessee from 1865 to 1869.

Other miners staked their claims to portions of the deposit, and the Cranberry vein passed through a variety of owners—including General John T. Wilder, probably the most influential man in the development of Roan Mountain—during the remainder of the nineteenth century. It quickly became obvious that a modern transportation system was needed to ship the ore out of the mountains. Railroad companies were chartered for area service by the Tennessee General Assembly as early as 1866, but it was 1882 before the main line from Johnson City was opened. Production then skyrocketed. Between 1884 and 1893, about two hundred thousand tons of ore were mined at Cranberry. The ore was processed at a large black furnace constructed in Johnson City, and the finished iron was then shipped to steel mills in Ohio and Pennsylvania to be used in the manufacture of high-quality steel. The railroad system built to exploit Cranberry's resources

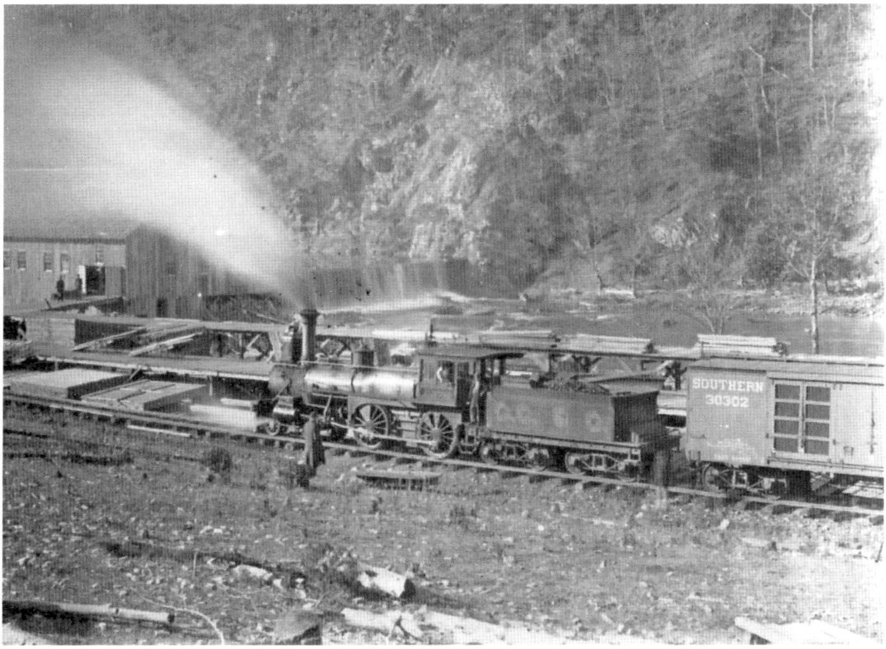

General John T. Wilder was instrumental in the development of the railroad throughout our region. He is pictured here standing by the tracks along the Nolichucky River at Chestoa. 1900. *Courtesy of Thomas O. Maher.*

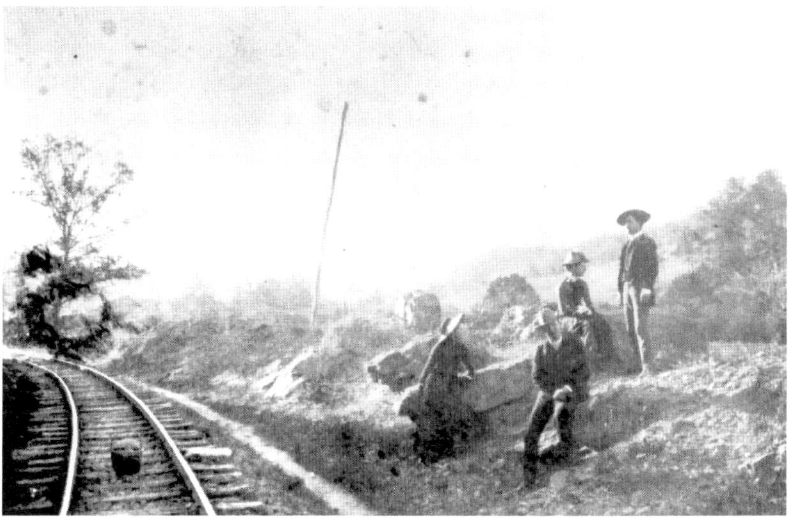

Cloudland Hotel advertisements claimed that the railroad trip to Roan Mountain was "beautiful beyond description, and far finer than anything else in the whole history of railroad engineering." 1880s. *Courtesy of Thomas O. Maher.*

also opened the area for tourists, heralding Roan Mountain's heyday as a popular resort.

Operations at Cranberry were expanded during World War I, with annual production reaching sixty thousand tons. The facilities were closed during bad economic times in 1921, then opened again in 1923 and closed again in 1929. Some people say that the Great Depression didn't really come to the southern Appalachians; it was already there. By the time the stock market crashed, the ore deposits at Cranberry had been largely depleted, the hillsides had been stripped of timber and flooding had become a dire problem.

The discoveries, challenges and contributions of the earliest explorers set the stage for what would ultimately grow into a prosperous community. From 1880 into the early 1900s, Roan Mountain experienced changes that would never have been imagined by those who first explored this mountain wilderness.

GENERAL JOHN T. WILDER

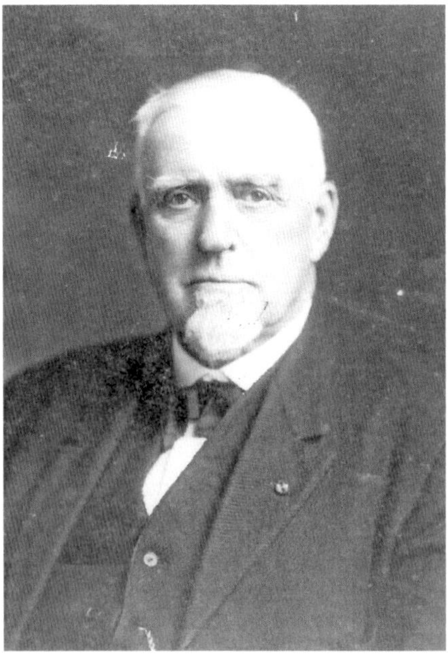

General Wilder, born in 1830, pictured here in 1890. *Courtesy of Thomas O. Maher.*

John Thomas Wilder was an industrialist, an inventor, a Civil War hero and an influential figure in the development of East Tennessee. He also stands as the single most important personage in the history of Roan Mountain. The Roan's glory days were Wilder's glory days.

Wilder was born in Hunter's Village in the Catskill Mountains of New York State on January 31, 1830. From his boyhood days, and without any formal training, he exhibited an avid interest in geology, collecting and arranging specimens in a small cabinet in his home. A restless soul, Wilder decided to head westward to try to make his fortune at the age of nineteen. He arrived in Columbus, Ohio, nearly penniless. An excerpt

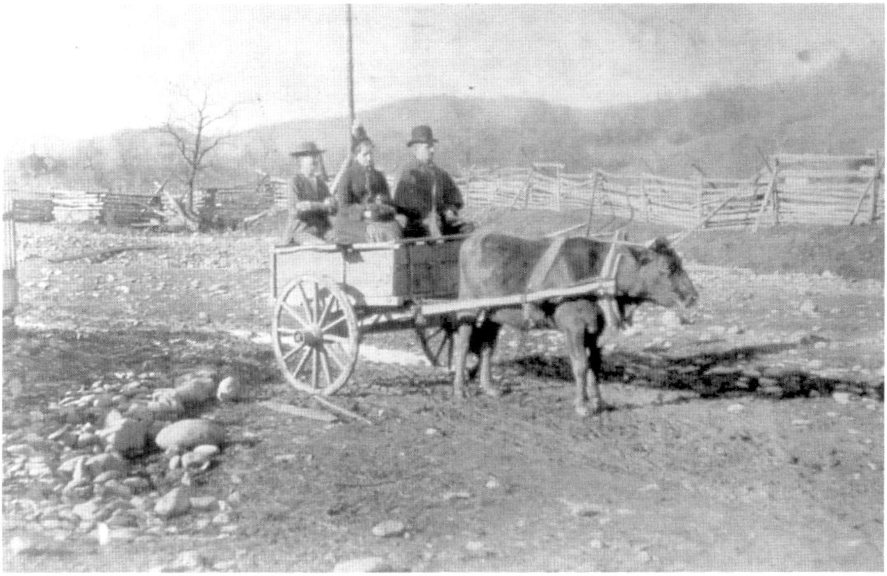

An oxen-drawn wagon provides an opportunity to "court," with supervision of course. 1880s. *Courtesy of Thomas O. Maher.*

from the November 3, 1927 edition of the *Columbus Journal* bears testimony to the hardships of those early days but also to the determined character that helped carry Wilder through:

> *One day while walking along Broad Street he espied a coin on the ground, which he seized and hastened to High Street to get a bun; but, when he reached the restaurant, he concluded that he would wait until he got hungrier before spending the coin, so he walked away with it in his pocket; and he kept that coin in his pocket through all of his eventful days.*

Wilder did not go hungry for long. He landed employment at Ridgeway's Foundry, where he worked as an apprentice draftsman and pattern maker and was introduced to millwrighting. The owner of the foundry was so impressed with Wilder's talent and initiative that he offered to make him co-owner with his son upon his retirement if the two would operate the business together. Never lacking in confidence, Wilder declined the generous offer. He had bigger plans.

In 1857, he moved to Greensburg, Indiana, and opened his own modest foundry and millwrighting establishment. He married Martha Stewart, daughter of one of the town founders, shortly thereafter. In the years that followed, Wilder sold equipment and built mills and hydraulic works in the states of Indiana, Illinois, Wisconsin, Virginia, Kentucky and Tennessee. He patented a turbine wheel and gained wide recognition as an expert in hydraulics. By the outbreak of the Civil War, his plant in Greensburg employed about one hundred men.

Wilder supported the Union cause, and he was determined to be part of the war effort. He closed his foundry, melted his metal down into bullets, raised a company of local men and organized them into a light artillery company, the first three-year regiment recruited in Indiana. When it was determined that Wilder's artillery company did not fit into Union plans, the company was mustered into service with the Seventeenth Indiana Infantry, part of the Army of the Cumberland.

Within a month, Wilder was promoted from captain to the rank of lieutenant colonel without ever having been a major. His troops were eventually mounted on horseback and armed with Spencer Repeating Rifles. The news of their speed and toughness spread quickly, and they came to be known as Wilder's Lightning Brigade. Confederate cavalry leaders like Nathan Bedford Forrest, John Mosby and Jeb Stuart held the advantage over their Federal counterparts early on, but as the war progressed and resources were exhausted, Union cavalrymen like Phil Sheridan and Wilder more than held their own. Wilder and the Lightning Brigade earned respect from Union and Confederate forces alike, particularly distinguishing themselves in action at Chickamauga, Georgia, where they helped hold off victorious Confederate troops while the Union army retreated to Chattanooga. Wilder had been made a brigadier general by the end of the war.

When the hostilities were over, Wilder resolved to move to Tennessee. There were a couple of reasons for the change. His health had suffered greatly during the war, and he hoped that a milder climate might do him good. And during his wartime forays into the Volunteer State, his entrepreneurial eye had been struck by the abundant natural resources waiting to be developed.

There is an amusing story surrounding Wilder's first ventures in the Chattanooga area shortly after his arrival in 1866. He was visiting the farm of a man he had fought alongside; Colonel Robert K. Byrdand Byrd was trying to convince him that his farmland was highly suitable for development as a town site. "Colonel, what about the Emory River? Won't it flood these bottoms?" the skeptical Wilder purportedly asked. Byrd replied in the negative, but it was only a short time later that Wilder spied a small log lodged in a tree several feet off the ground. "Bob, what devilish boys put that log up that tree?" he promptly asked his companion. Wilder then

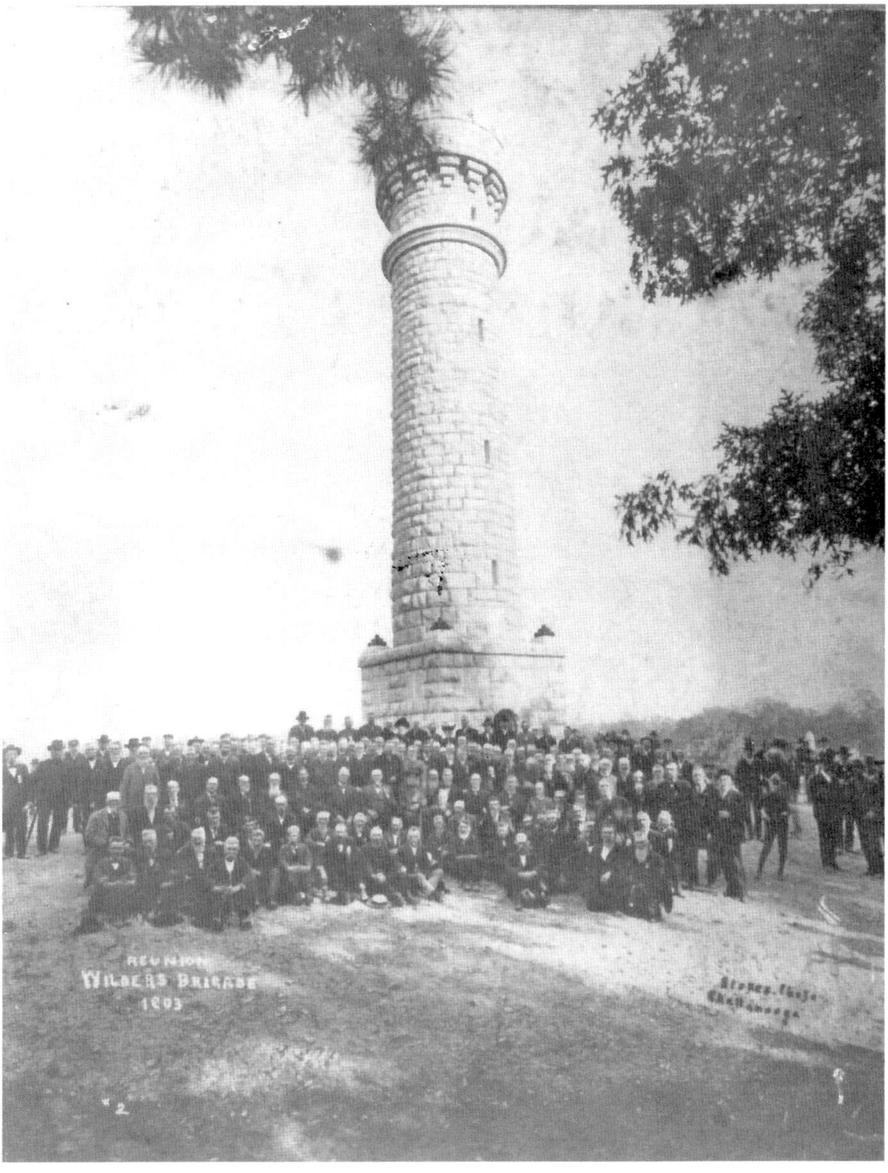

The 1903 reunion of Wilder's Lightning Brigade in Chattanooga. *Courtesy of Thomas O. Maher.*

proceeded to select another site near the Tennessee River, ninety-two miles above Chattanooga. There, he discovered a four-foot-thick vein of iron ore, along with deposits of coal and iron that would be needed in the operation of a foundry. John Thomas Wilder was back in business.

In 1867, Wilder and two associates organized the Roane Iron Company, laid out and christened the town of Rockwood and erected a blast furnace, the first using coke to operate in the South. A second furnace was built nearby soon afterward, and Wilder's reputation as an industrialist began to spread anew. He next concentrated his energies on Chattanooga and established the Roane Rolling Mills and Wilder's Machine Works, the former for the manufacture of railroad rails and the latter for the production of his patented turbine wheel. Sometime around 1870, he purchased seven thousand acres along the top and sides of Roan Mountain at a cost of $25.15 per acres. He also organized the Southern Car and Foundry Company, the Dayton Coal and Oil Company and the Durham Coal Company, which operated on deposits found near the battlefield at Chickamauga, where he had once waged war.

Around the late 1870s, Wilder acquired a portion of the famous Cranberry Mine in North Carolina. The duke of Marlborough once visited Wilder in Johnson City and was treated to a tour of Cranberry. "General, how far downward does this vein of ore extend?" the duke inquired. "Your

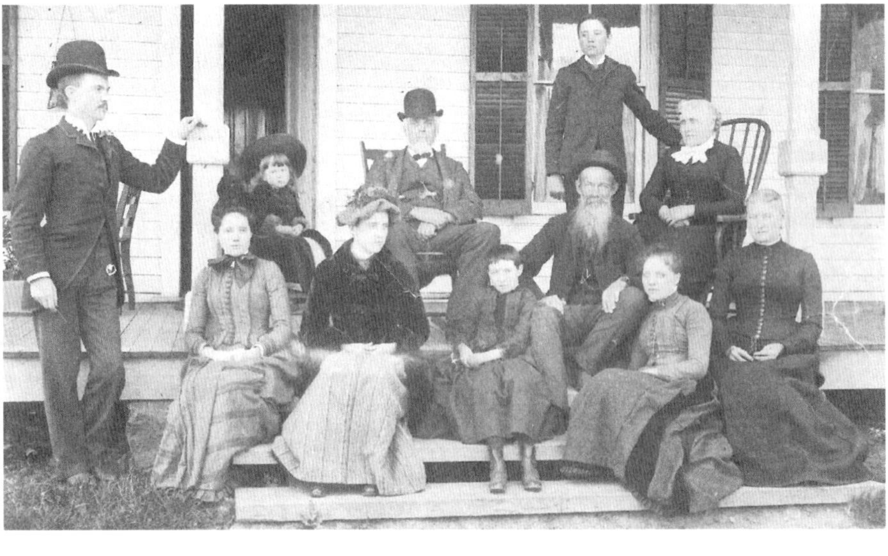

Wilder (center) and family are pictured on the front porch of their home in the village of Roan Mountain. 1886. *Courtesy of Thomas O. Maher.*

Grace," Wilder purportedly answered, "it is my opinion that the devil is now making iron from the bottom of it." Industrial ventures toward the end of the general's career included the Carnegie Land Company in Johnson City and the Fentress Coal Company, located at the site of the present-day mining town that bears the name Wilder, appropriately enough.

It is important to draw a distinction between Wilder and the carpetbaggers of his generation, whose purpose was to exploit whatever had value in the South in postwar turmoil. By contrast, Wilder gave more than he took. His first Tennessee furnaces were built at a time when the market was unstable, financial resources were limited, high interest rates were rampant and technical knowledge was scant. His ventures were bold and risky but not opportunistic. Wilder deserves a good share of credit for helping establish Chattanooga as an industrial center of the middle South.

His interests outside mining bore witness to his farsightedness and energy. While living in Johnson City, he served as vice-president of the Charleston, Cincinnati & Chicago Railroad, which later grew into the Carolina, Clinchfield & Ohio, one of the South's great coal carriers.

Wilder also envisioned the development of Tennessee's water resources. He anticipated the Tennessee Valley Authority by more than twenty years when he helped organize a power company and acquired water rights along the Little Tennessee River; again, his role was that of pioneer, as others, not Wilder himself, profited from his vision in the years that followed.

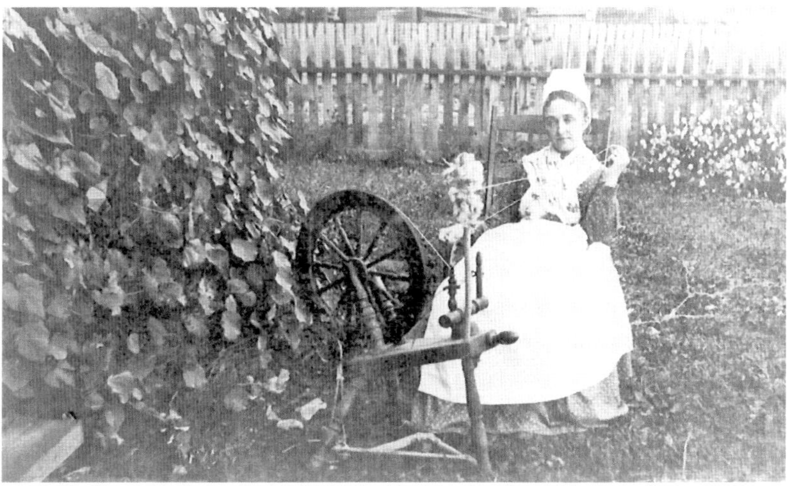

Josie Pippin, a relative of Sherman Pippin, at her flax wheel in the village of Roan Mountain. 1880s. *Courtesy of Thomas O. Maher.*

He was less a success as a politician. Some said his forthrightness worked against him in that sphere. He was elected mayor of Chattanooga in 1871, only to resign eight months into his term. He was the Republican candidate for Congress from the Chattanooga district in 1876. He made up a large margin in the polls but ultimately lost. His judgment also failed him in his friendship with Alexander Graham Bell, as he declined the opportunity to invest in Bell's "toy" because he believed it would never amount to much.

Of great importance to Roan Mountain, Wilder built the Cloudland Hotel and opened the area to tourists from all points on the compass. He also constructed a home and a hotel in the village of Roan Mountain. Built in the 1880s, the Roan Mountain Inn often served as a one-night stopover for people en route to the Cloudland Hotel, located on top of the mountain. The Roan Mountain Inn sat right on the Doe River, behind the Roan Mountain railroad depot, with advertisements boasting that guests could catch fish off the back porch.

Samuel C. Williams, a former justice of the Tennessee Supreme Court, effectively captured Wilder's appearance and personality in a historical monograph published by Indiana University Press in 1936:

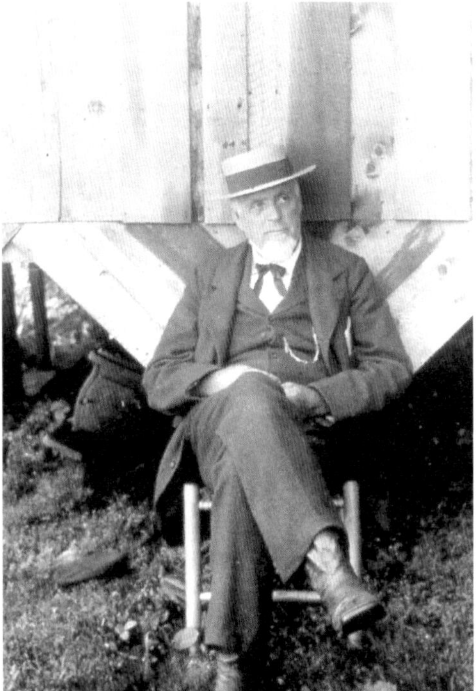

Wilder, relaxing atop the Roan. 1880s. *Courtesy of Thomas O. Maher.*

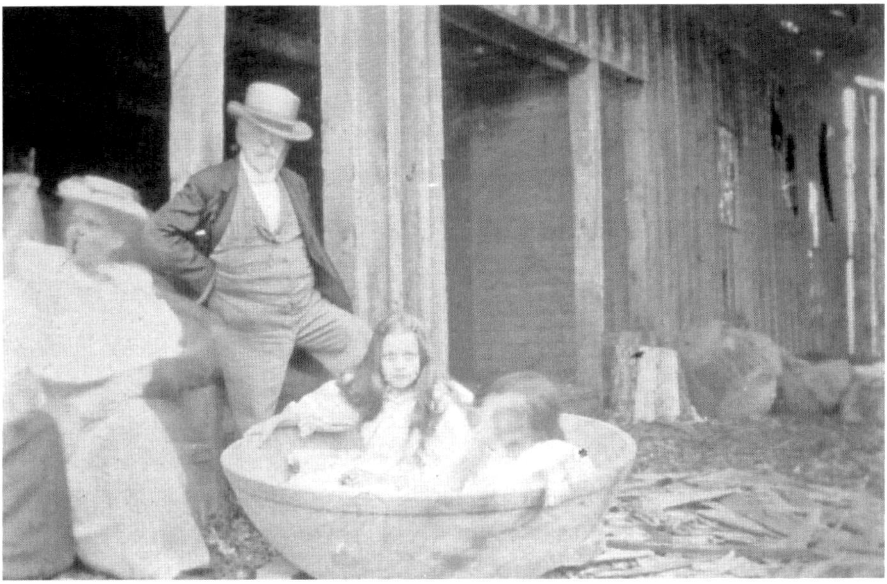

Wilder looks on as two young relatives sit in a bowl carved from a single knot from one of Roan's giant trees. 1880's. *Courtesy of Thomas O. Maher.*

> *As to personal appearance: General Wilder was six feet two inches in height, but well proportioned. As age advanced he took on flesh but until after eighty years he moved with ease and a degree of grace. His eyes were particularly penetrating and bright; they were readily kindled by merriment. He had unusual conversational powers; his speech was spicy and at times emphasis was attempted to be lent by strong and explosive words, after the manner of many military men. His information was wide and in some directions ample, such as in the field of the history and traditions of the regions in which he resided, and in reminiscences of the great and near-great with whom he had come in contact. He was a total abstainer from intoxicants and made no use of tobacco; but at the board he was no mean trencherman, especially when confronting a juicy beefsteak.*

Wilder's life was not a bed of roses. He lost a great deal of money in the panic of 1893, and his finances never fully recovered. In fact, his losses cut so deeply that his daughter Edith was forced to drop out of college. Edith Wilder recovered better than did her father, as she went on to marry Arthur Hoyt Scott, who played a part in the development of paper towels and tissues and who helped bring the fledgling Scott Paper Company into the international marketplace.

Despite his financial woes, General Wilder's popularity remained high. One of the most remarkable features about his life was his surprising status among ex-Confederates and Southerners in general. He became chairman of the Chickamauga National Park Commission, with responsibilities that included overseeing a site dedicated to the soldiers on both sides who met in one of the Civil War's great battles. He intervened to prevent the arrest and prosecution of former Confederate general Nathan Bedford Forrest on charges of parole violation, and he was later rewarded when the Nathan Bedford Forrest Post of the United Confederate Veterans made him an honorary member. During the Spanish-American War, Wilder traveled to Washington at his own expense to promote Knoxville as the site of a proposed training camp. That camp was christened Camp Wilder in his honor, and it became the home of the Sixth Tennessee Regiment. And in 1903, when a monument to Wilder's Lightning Brigade was to be dedicated, his old friends at the Nathan Bedford Forrest Post turned out as a body. As one of the post's members, Colonel Tomlinson Fort, said at the ceremony, "His name is a household word in the South; particularly in all East Tennessee, where he has lived continuously since the close of the

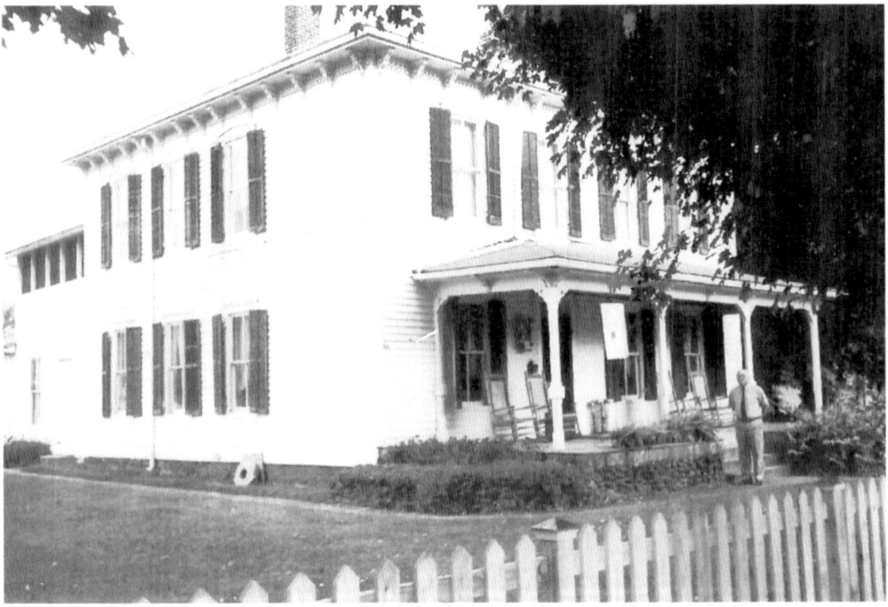

Shown in the 1980s, the Wilder House in Roan Mountain is now on the National Register of Historic Places. Standing in front of the home is Thomas O. Maher, the great-grandson of the general. *Courtesy of Thomas O. Maher.*

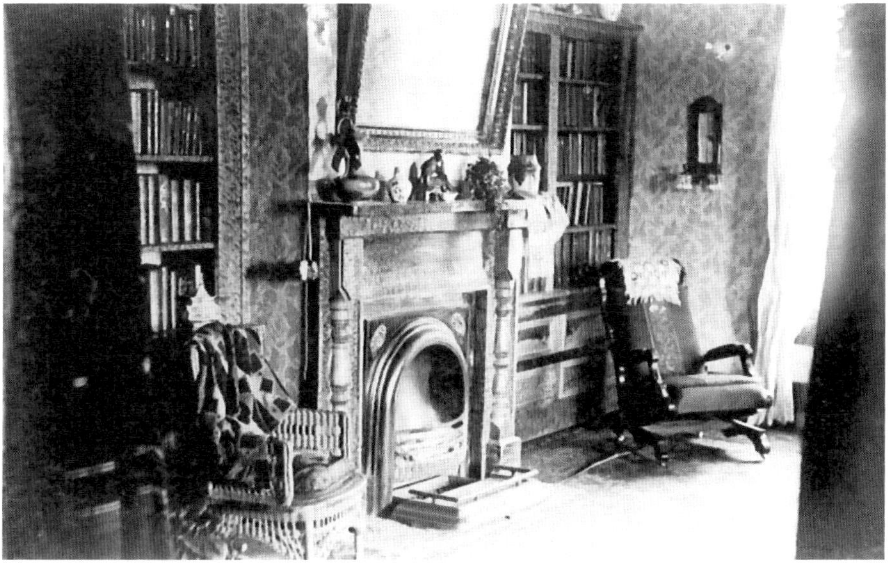

An interior view of the sitting room of Wilder's home, fondly named Nasturtium Cottage. 1890s. *Courtesy of Thomas O. Maher.*

war; and no man has done more than General Wilder in bringing order out of chaos."

The willingness to serve his country was something Wilder had in his blood. He was fifty-eight years of age at the outbreak of the Spanish-American War. When he learned that President McKinley was offering brigadier commissions to ex-Confederate generals Fitzhugh Lee of Virginia and Joseph Wheeler of Alabama, he immediately sought service himself. Wilder subsequently learned that such appointments were being offered only to former Confederate generals, in acknowledgment that the South was sending tens of thousands of volunteers for the current war effort. He then tactfully backed off from his request.

Wilder died on October 20, 1917, in Jacksonville, Florida, where he had gone to avoid the rigorous fall and winter seasons native to his home of Monterey, Tennessee. An ex-Confederate delivered his funeral sermon. He was buried in Forest Hill Cemetery in Chattanooga. His legacy in Roan Mountain carries on in the spirit of his home in the village, which is still standing and on the National Register of Historic Places.

CLOUDLAND

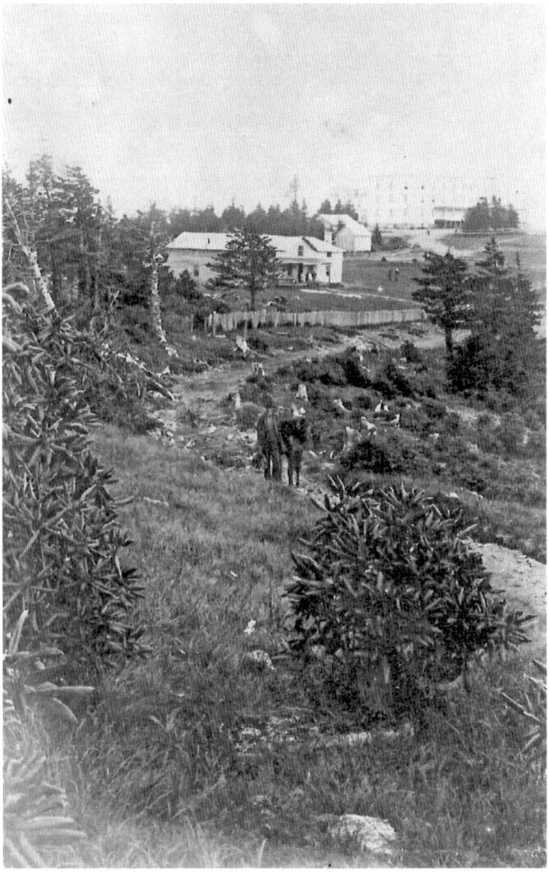

The new Cloudland Hotel in 1884. It was suggested that the original hotel was torn down to make room for the grand one, but this rare view documents that they stood at the same time. A log cabin is located between the two. *Courtesy of Thomas O. Maher.*

It is not known exactly what motivated General John T. Wilder to build a resort hotel on a portion of the seven thousand acres he owned on top of Roan Mountain. Wilder himself had moved to Tennessee after the Civil War in an effort to improve his failing health, so perhaps he was hoping that other people with illnesses would come to partake of his cure. His resort eventually did become a haven for hay fever sufferers.

The area atop the Roan was affectionately known as "Cloudland" to early visitors due to the thick fogs and clouds that appeared out of nowhere to interrupt the view into the valleys below; the top of the mountain is actually shrouded about 75 percent of the time. The summit of Roan Mountain is also one of the few places in the world where a person can see his or her shadow in the clouds. To the people of Wilder's day, the name Cloudland bespoke excitement, surprise, a spirit of exploration and a place where miracles happened. He adopted the name for his resort.

In 1877, under Wilder's direction, L.B. Searle constructed a twenty-room spruce log structure on top of the Roan, assisted by John Gouge of Glen Ayre. It proved to be quite a summer haven for those who were tired of city

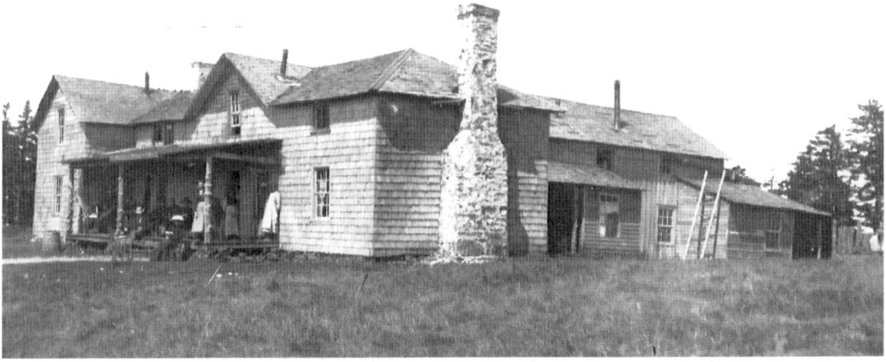

Mary Wilder photographed the first hotel on top of the Roan, built years before the three-story Cloudland Hotel. *Courtesy of Thomas O. Maher.*

life or just enjoyed the clean air of high elevations. A few years prior, Mr. Searle had also built a small cabin for Wilder near the same site.

That first hotel was only a prelude, however. The larger Cloudland Hotel was reported by local residents to be completed and opened in 1885. A three-story frame structure at over sixty-two hundred feet in elevation, it was quite possibly the highest human habitation east of the Rockies. Local accounts of the number of rooms it contained varied from a little over 100 to just fewer than 300; most estimates made the room count either 166 or 266. Everyone agreed on the number of bathrooms on the premises, though—there was only one! Mary Fanslow reported in her thesis that Frank Shell, serving as clerk for five years, from 1900 to 1905, recalled four bathrooms. She suggested that renovations in 1892 might have accounted for differences in local memory.

Wilder himself was reported to announce in early 1884 that his Roan Mountain Depot Hotel (now referred to as the Roan Mountain Inn) and the Cloudland Hotel would be ready for guests on June 20 of that year. At that time, he also indicated that the Cloudland Hotel was 414 feet long, 42 feet wide and three stories tall—the largest summer hotel in the South. According to Wilder, his resort would provide 218 bedrooms and would be managed by Frank Stratton.

The construction project must have been a monumental one, though the reported cost of $40,000 seems a pittance by today's standards. The lack of public access to the site was one of the primary problems. Wilder and

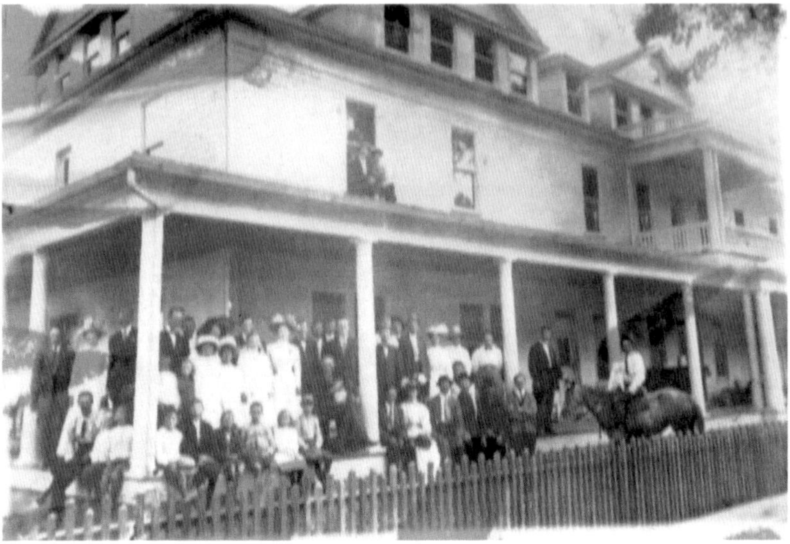

The Roan Mountain Inn was opened by Wilder in conjunction with Cloudland on top of the Roan. This rare image was discovered after a fire, many years ago. *Courtesy of Jeanne Pippin Grizzard.*

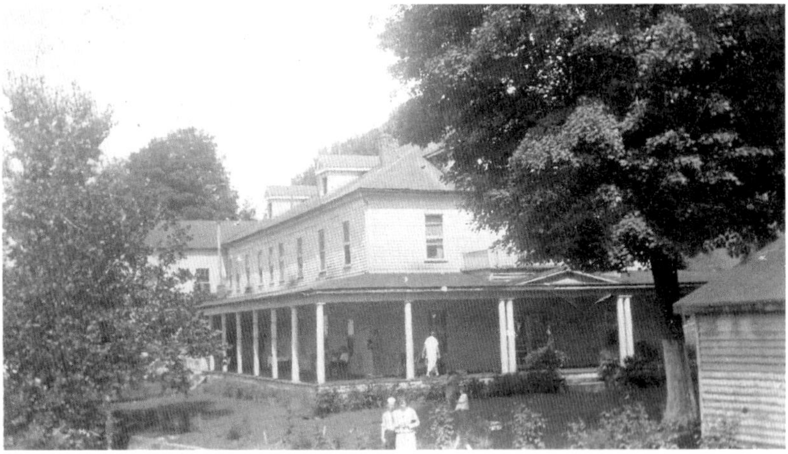

The back porch of the Roan Mountain Inn sat directly above the Doe River. The front porch looked toward the Roan Mountain Railroad Depot. *Courtesy of Jeanne Pippin Grizzard.*

the others involved in the effort applied for and were granted permission to construct the first Carver's Gap Road, from Wilder's Forge on Big Rock Creek across the Roan to Carver's Gap and down the valley of Little Rock

Creek to a ford near the home of John G. Burleson. In Tennessee, Rube Mosley helped to build the first six miles of "hack line" that began in Burbank on the Tennessee side of the mountain.

To hasten the building of the hotel, a steam sawmill was erected on the site so lumber could be sawed and planed locally. The majority of the structure was built of the balsam that grows on top of the mountain. Cherry was used for a good deal of the furniture, while hard maple cut to one-inch widths was shipped in to make a dance floor. The hotel was steam heated—rather innovative for its day. Huge fireplaces were kept blazing most of the time, with the steam turned on when the temperature dropped at night. Water was supplied by a spring on the south side of the mountain some eight hundred feet below the top; hydraulic units lifted the water and deposited it in two storage tanks located at the rear of the hotel. The individual guest rooms boasted spring beds, copper bathtubs and rugs.

There were facilities on the grounds for bowling, fishing, croquet and golf. Pauline Stone, the daughter of N.L. Murrell, one of the hotel's operators, remembered the opening of the golf course this way: "My father took a club and ball and teed off for the first time, and the ball made it from tee to green. The upshot of that was that they got special balls because the air at that altitude was such that any duffer could be a pro."

Within a year of the completion of the big hotel, the first hotel and its surrounding buildings were burned to clear the area. A paved parking lot overlooking Tennessee now stands on the former site of the first hotel.

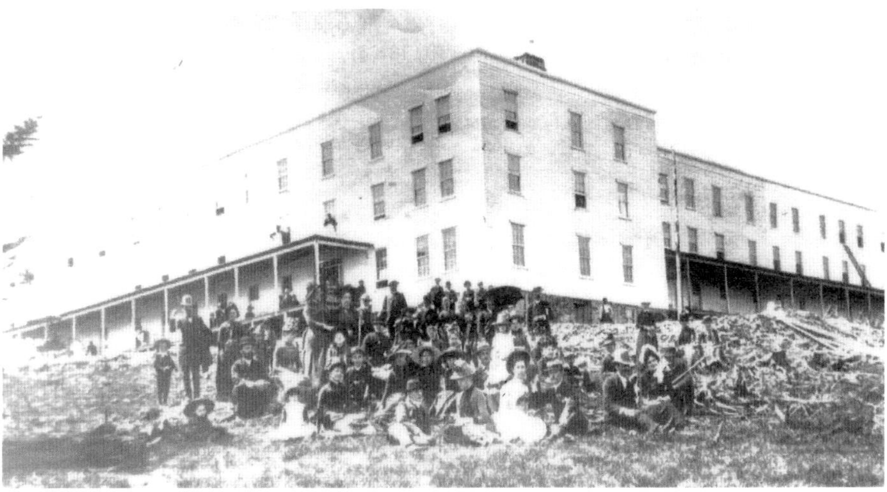

The grand opening of the Cloudland Hotel in 1884. *Courtesy of Thomas O. Maher.*

Once the Cloudland Hotel was in full operation, the main task was attracting enough guests to fill its many rooms. Cloudland's advertisements, like the one included here, were models of mild overstatement. The emphasis, particularly with the testimonials that accompanied the descriptive copy, was on the health benefits of the Roan Mountain area, but the advertisements also touched on such minor matters as the welcome absence of insects, reptiles and thunderbolts. Wilder understood that the local population could not provide the principal support for his hotel, so his first ad campaigns were directed at major American population centers and even at the European market:

CLOUDLAND HOTEL
Top of Roan Mountain
6,394 FEET ABOVE THE SEA,
WESTERN NORTH CAROLINA,
ROAN MOUNTAIN HOTEL COMPANY,
PROPRIETORS.

***

Address: ROAN MOUNTAIN HOTEL CO., Cloudland,
Mitchell Co., N.C. or, ROAN MOUNTAIN HOTEL CO.,
Roan Mountain, Carter Co., Tenn.—Daily Mails

***

PERFECT EXEMPTION FROM HAY FEVER

***

COME UP OUT OF THE SULTRY PLAINS TO THE "LAND OF THE SKY"—MAGNIFICENT VIEWS ABOVE THE CLOUDS WHERE THE RIVERS ARE BORN—A MOST EXPENDED PROSPECT OF 50,000 SQUARE MILES IN SEVEN DIFFERENT STATES—ONE HUNDRED MOUNTAIN TOPS OVER 4,000 FEET HIGH IN SIGHT.

Description

Cloudland Hotel is situated on Roan Mountain, Mitchell County, Western North Carolina, twelve miles from Roan Mountain Station, on the E.T. & W.N.C. R.R., which runs from Johnson City on the East Tennessee Railroad, to Cranberry Mines in North Carolina.

Roan Mountain is an uplife in the heart of the Western North Carolina Mountain system, overlooking the Unakas on the North and Blue Ridge on the South. "It is," says Prof. Asa Gray, of Harvard College, "the most beautiful mountain east of the Rockies."

The mountain top is a beautiful grassy prairie of 3,000 acres, dotted over the red Rhododendrons, Azalias, and Mountain Heather, on clumps from a yard to ten acres in area, set in the beautiful green sward, fringed with rich Balsams and Spruces, growing from beds of most luxuriant mosses. Here are deep woods, tangled thickets, wild glens and great cliffs of naked granite, hundreds of feet high, with deep, dense gorges beneath them whose stillness a human footfall has rarely broken. Thunder storms often fill the valleys while sunshine bathes the mountain top; and no grander view is ever seen than that presented on such an occasion. A hundred mountain peaks rise out of the storm clouds like islands in the sea, while lurid lightnings cleave the cloud lakes lying in the valleys below. The top of Roan Mountain being above dangerous lightning storm clouds, is free from thunder bolts. No insects or reptiles found at this altitude.

Clear Cold Water, only thirteen degrees above freezing; beautiful brooks teeming with mountain trout, summer temperature from 48 to 73 degrees (usually 60 degrees); the most even temperature known—balmy, bracing air, its like can not be found by going North; a clean, healthful, pleasant, beautiful summer resort. Try it.

The hotel is the highest human habitation east of the Rocky Mountains, free from sudden changes.

The atmosphere is perfectly pure, and as a Health Resort, there can be no location more desirable. Consumption is unknown and malaria finds no refuge among these mountains.

Particulars

House open for the reception of guests, June 20th. Rhododendrons, Azalias, Heathers and Houstonias bloom in June. Most magnificent cloud views in September and October.

The hotel property and mountain are surrounded by a fence ten miles long entered by three gates.

CAMPING ON THE MOUNTAIN IS NOT ALLOWED.

Board, $2.00 per day, $10.00 per week, $30.00 per month for four weeks.

Fires in private rooms, $5.00 per month for each room. Children under ten years, and servants, at half rates. Children occupying seats at first table to the exclusion of other guests at full rates. We have no other family rates. Hack rates on extra baggage (all over 80 lbs.), $1.00 per hundred pounds.

Rooms neatly and comfortably furnished, floors carpeted, spring mattresses on all beds.

ROAN MOUNTAIN STATION HOTEL

Is new and well furnished. Rooms carpeted; good spring beds, thoroughly comfortable and is 950 feet higher than any hotel on Lookout Mountain and 2,650 feet above sea level; a cool, restful resort, Cold water, cool nights. All at the same rates as at Cloudland Hotel. It is on the railroad, with daily trains and W.U. Telegraph line. Good boating and fishing. Post office, Roan Mountain, Carter Co., Tenn.

***

HOW TO GET THERE

Go by the East Tennessee system to Johnson City, and there take the Cranberry (Stem Winder) Narrow Gauge Railroad to Roan Mountain Station, twenty-six miles from Johnson City, passing through Doe River Gorge, one of the wildest rides in the world. The Doe River Canyon is four miles long and 1,500 feet deep. Up this the railroad winds its way through four tunnels and over five bridges, in rocky clefts about 100 feet above the river, through one of the most romantic spots on the continent. The country along this line is beautiful beyond description, and far finer than anything else in the whole history of railroad engineering, alone fully repaying one for the time and expense of the entire trip. At Roan Mountain Station is a new, clean, and well-furnished hotel, owned by the company; also, a livery stable from which a hack line runs to the top of Roan Mountain to the Cloudland Hotel, a ride of twelve miles up a new and beautiful road, winding up the sides of the mountain, passing the most magnificent scenery at every turn, brings us to Cloudland Hotel on top of the mountain, 6,394 feet above sea level.

A very interesting horseback or wagon ride can be taken across the country from Marion, Round Knob Hotel, Asheville, or Warm Springs, N.C., to Roan Mountain, passing through the heart of the Alleghenies, the finest mountain trip in any country.

SPECIAL EXCURSION RATES and coupon tickets, good for the season, from all principal railroad points. Covered hacks run from the railroad to the mountain top; only reasonable fares charged. Eighty pounds of baggage free.

TELEGRAPH AND EXPRESS OFFICES at Roan Mountain Station.

***

TESTIMONIALS

EXEMPTION FROM HAY FEVER.

Dr. D.B. Goodwin, of Pine Grove, Clark County, Ky., takes pleasure in stating for the Benefit of Hay Cold Patients, that he has escaped his annual on Roan Mountain, N.C.

***

Mrs. Robt. Hereford Hare, of 2,031 DeLancey Place, Philadelphia, Penn., takes pleasure in stating for the benefit of Hay Cold Patients, that during the ten years that she has suffered with Hay Fever, she has sought and found relief by the seaside, at Caesar's Head, at Mountain lake and at the White Mountains, but nowhere in the United States has she found perfect exemption from the disease, until now at Cloudland Hotel on the top of Roan Mountain.

***

816 F Street, Washington, D.C., February 7, 1892.
Our party, without exception, were very greatly benefited by our summer on the Roan. I know of no summer vacation that has been of so great and permanent value to all of us as the one which we spent with you, and we certainly agree that none have been pleasanter.

My experience of two summers has created a most hearty desire for another visit in the near future, a wish shared by all our party.

William B. King

***

Renewed Bouyancy and Vitality,
House of Representatives, Washington, D.C.
Feb., 8, 1882.
I often recall with pleasure my sojourn at Cloudland last summer. The place needs only to be extensively known to be more liberally patronized. The mountain scenery is unsurpassed; I do not suppose there is a grander view east of the Rocky Mountains than that which is presented to the eye from Roan Bluff. The deliciously cool and invigorating mountain air seems to impart renewed buoyancy and vitality.

N.C. Blanchard. from Shreveport, La.

***

Climate Can Not Be Equaled
Washington, D.C., January 30, 1882.
I often think of the pleasant time I spent on Roan Mountain last summer. For beauty of scenery, cool and healthful climate, and freedom from summer's heat. I think it can not be equaled.

G.W. Gray.

***

Roan Mountain Cured Her.
Eaton, Tenn., May 17, 1880.
My daughter was attacked in February, 1879, with pleura-pneumonia, very badly, which resulted in complete hepatization of one lung, with an extensive effusion of serum and pus, which rendered it in this latitude, a hopeless case. But I am happy to say that she is entirely relieved, and was never in better health than now. I know that the trip to Roan Mountain cured her.

Respectfully, J. W. Robinson, M.D.

***

Lung and Throat Troubles.
Dayton, Ohio, February 3, 1882.
Could I express my opinion of the Roan it would be a glowing description of, to me, the most beautiful spot on earth. No one could find a more healthful place, or more grand and beautiful scenery. Every minute on the Roan was full of pleasure and my health was much and permanently improved. Before going there I was greatly troubled with pain in my lungs, also with chronic sore throat; both of which almost entirely left me, and had I stayed until the close of the season, I believe I should have been perfectly restored. I feel that I was benefited more than words can tell.

Mrs. William Shepler.

***

Asthma—Saved Her Life.
Port Gibson, February 21, 1882.
My daughter, Nettie, sixteen years of age, suffered one year with a severe attack of asthma, sleeping often in a chair. I tried many remedies and all to no avail. My physician finally recommended a change of climate. I accidentally saw in a railway guide that Roan Mountain was of high elevation; without a second thought I proceeded thither, and she had but one attack while on the

Mountain, and that in the valley, at Bakersville. Since then she has attended to her studies and has been free from this dreadful and troublesome disease.

I am of the opinion that her stay on the Mountain, roaming everywhere daily, wet or dry, in your invigorating climate, saved her life.

L.T. Newman.

***

Charleston, S.C., February 9, 1882.

I would so relish a draught of your glorious Mountain air. The dear old Roan and pleasant summer with you I remember with the very greatest pleasure, and am already planning to get up in June instead of July. One small objection to the Roan is the inability to return to the lower world with comfort, however gradually we make the descent. Don continues the hearty boy you did so much for last summer.

Mrs. Edwin P. Frost.

***

Must Be Financially Interested.

12 Dauphine Street. New Orleans, February 2, 1882

I speak so constantly of Roan, its bracing air, splendid climate, etc., that my friends think I must be financially interested in Cloudland, and I am seriously thinking of asking you to certify that such is not the case.

C. Edmund Kells, Jr., D.D.S.

***

Wonderful Floral Display.

Petersburg, N.J., March 10, 1882.

I often think of my visit to Roan Mountain last June and of the wonderful floral display I thee beheld in your beautiful Rhododendron park. Truly the pure air, the delightful temperature, the clear, cold spring water, and the perfume-laden woodlands, make your "Land of the Sky" a veritable Arcadia.

C. W. Reynolds.

***

Magnificent Roan Mountain.

New York City., N.Y., January 31, 1882.

It was my good pleasure to visit the magnificent Roan Mountain last June and behold the beauties of nature as viewed from this place 6,394 feet above the level of the sea. To anyone in search of rest and quiet it is the spot. We arrived wearied with our long journey, and were thinking how old and tired we would be in the morning, but to our surprise, after a night of the sweetest sleep, we were feeling finely. I have traveled extensively but never found such pure and bracing air, and where one would recuperate so fast. I have seen the much admired prairie flowers but never saw anything equal to the beautiful wild flowers of Roan Mountain.

Henry R. Hartshorn.

***

The Half Had Not Been Told

Wilmington, Delaware, February 3, 1882.

My recollections of Roan Mountain are of the most delightful kind. I would come and stay all summer with you if I could. Since my first visit in 1866 I have been three times on "The Roan." Before each of these visits I have feared that my recollections of its own beauty and of the grandeur of the views from it, might have caused me to be too enthusiastic in describing it to parties about to visit it for the first time, and that the result would be disappointment to them and to me. This has never occurred; all have confessed that the half had not been told them of this, the most beautiful of our mountains.

Wm. M. Canby.

***

> *Dr. Dan. C. Holliday, of New Orleans, in the* New Orleans Democrat *says, writing under date of August 6, 1881: "Here we are at Cloudland, enjoying a temperature of morning 48 degrees, noon 65 degrees, night 43 to 52 degrees, and this only 48 hours from New Orleans! It appears really like* fairy land."

The hotel's guest register is lost, so the list of luminaries who came to Roan Mountain will probably never be known. It *is* known that the governor of Louisiana, some European royalty and Grafton Greene, a chief justice of the Tennessee Supreme Court and the man who would later write the court's opinion in the Scopes Monkey Trial, were among the guests. Often referred to as the father of American psychology, William James also visited the mountain, as evidenced by his letter to his sister from Roan Mountain on August 23, 1891.

The register also served as a kind of journal for the recording of the numerous plant species discovered on the mountain, so it would be of immense value to our knowledge of the early botany of the Roan. F. Lamson Scribner gave a hint of what the register might contain in an article published in the *Botanical Gazette* in 1889: "In the old register of the hotel are recorded the finds of the several botanists or botanical parties who have visited the locality. The first of these was made in 1878 by Dr. George Vasey, who, under the head of 'Grasses of Roan Mountain,' enumerates the four

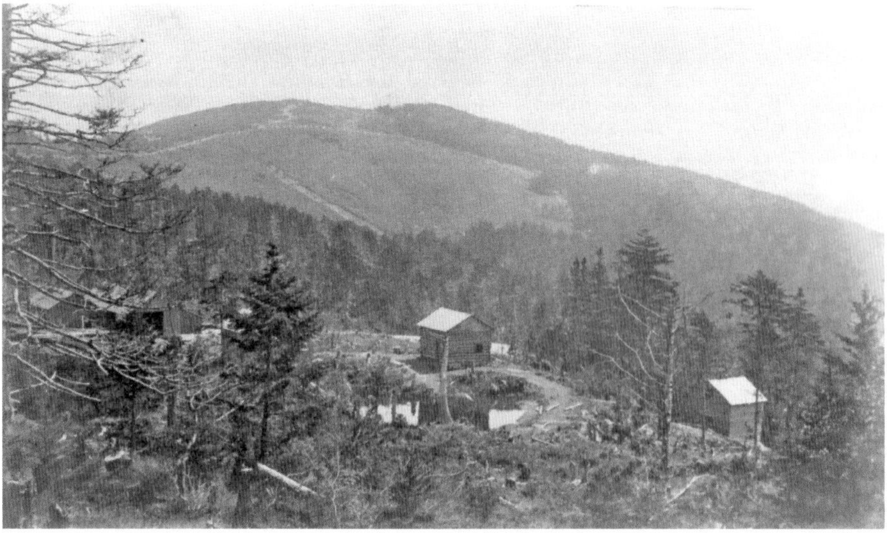

The water source for the Cloudland Hotel with Roan High Knob and a portion of the ten-mile fence in the background. *Courtesy of Thomas O. Maher.*

or five species observed by him." Indeed, the register is considered such a treasure that, for the better part of a century after Cloudland closed, history buffs still entertained hopes that it would one day be recovered from some forgotten, dusty attic.

The majority of visitors came not to list their botanical finds in the guest register but rather for health reasons, as General Wilder might have envisioned. There is a remarkable tale of one young girl who had been flat on her back with severe asthma for most of her life. Her family heard tell of the Roan's remarkable curative powers and brought her there as a last resort. The girl lay on blankets and pillows in the back of an old buckboard as her driver started the slow climb up the winding road to Cloudland, but miraculously enough, she was up and sitting beside him by the time they reached the hotel. Such were the powers of the high mountain air. So many migrated to the Roan seeking relief from their allergies that they became known as the "Hay Fever Brigade." It is interesting to note that the hotel did not even open for the summer season until June 20. By today's standards, the rhododendron bloom might have peaked at this time or may have come and gone.

The ride up the mountain to Cloudland did not usually inspire such cures. In fact, it was by many accounts the most trying part of a vacation on the Roan. Sherman Pippin, one of the men who drove their hacks from the railroad depot up to Cloudland, was meticulous enough to launder his blankets every day. Thus, his hack became particularly popular among female visitors to the mountain. He was transporting a load of ladies up the road one terribly hot summer day when the conditions were so miserable that they all thought they would die of thirst. It just so happened that Pippin was also carrying a cask of whiskey destined for the hotel bar, so he took a penknife, bored a hole in the barrel, distributed good cheer to all present and cut a plug to fit the hole. His patrons arrived at Cloudland well satisfied, and the barkeeper was never the wiser.

Sherman was quite the storyteller, entertaining his riders all the way from bottom to top. Tales of wolves, panthers, horrid blizzards and crashing trees all kept his guests on the edge of their seats. In the 1970s, Tommy Swindell interviewed Sherman and had the opportunity to hear, firsthand, of his many adventures. Sherman bragged of avoiding head-on collisions by watching his horse's ears: "They'll hear a hack a' comin', they'll put their ears up, then when you'd come to a place where you could pass, you'd stop and wait." On one particular trip, Sherman missed his trusty horse's cue and was a little miffed when the horse pulled over for no apparent reason. Moments later, a hack came flying by, its brakes squealing; it surely would have wiped

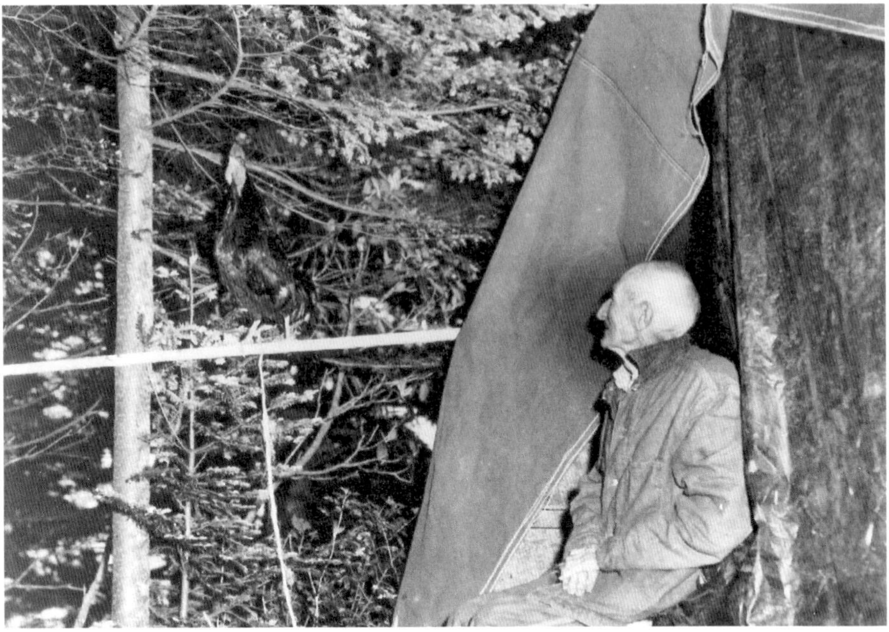

Sherman Pippin, hack drive and Tweetsie engineer, pictured with his rooster, which traveled with him everywhere. *Courtesy of Thomas O. Maher.*

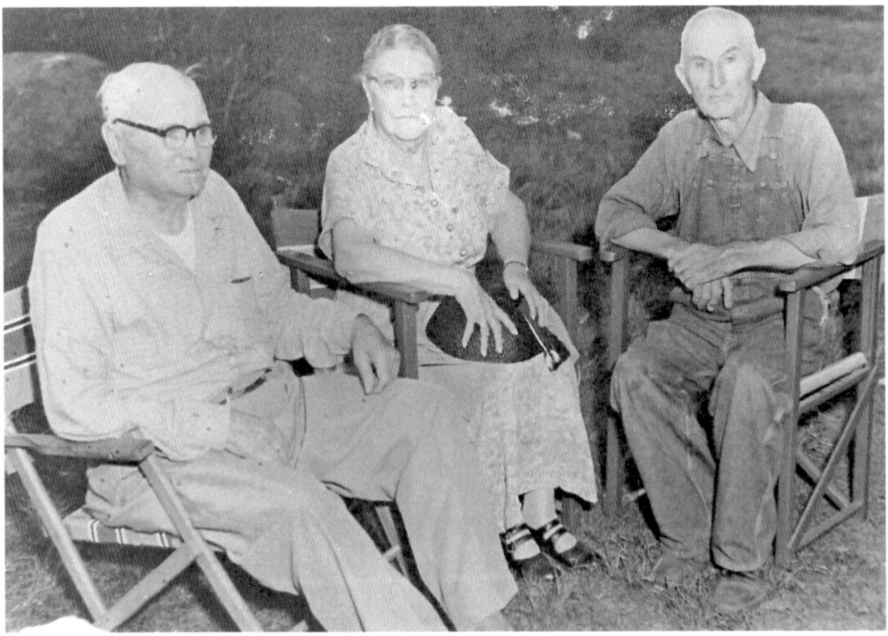

Sherman Pippin, pictured with Frank and Oley Shell. *Courtesy of the Archives of Appalachia. East Tennessee State University. Murrell Family Collection.*

out Sherman and his passengers had his horse not stopped. Oddly, without request, the horse moved on once danger had passed.

After Wilder's hotel operation and the hack line closed, Sherman would make weekly trips to the mountain, with his rooster along to wake him up. It so happened that a fellow from up North came upon his campsite one trip. Sherman recalled, "He was an awful nice fellow, but he didn't know a lot about Scripture. He said, 'What kind of rooster is that there,' 'Why,' I said, 'that's a descendent of the rooster that betrayed Peter.' And that satisfied that person."

Once they reached the top of the mountain, most Cloudland guests commented favorably on the mild weather, the variety of plant life present and the quality of the air. In *The Heart of the Alleghenies*, Wilbur G. Zeigler and Ben S. Grosscup wrote eloquently of the view from Roan Mountain:

> *While I was at the hotel a terrific thunder storm visited—not the summit of the Roan but the valleys below it. It came after dark, and from the porch we looked out and down upon the world in which it raged. Every flash of lightning was a revelation of glory, disclosing a sea of clouds of immaculate whiteness—a boundless archipelago whose islands were the black peaks of the mountains. Not a valley could be seen; nothing but the snowy bosom of this cloud ocean, and the stately summits which had lifted themselves above its vapors. In the height of the storm, the lightning blazed in one incessant sheet, and the thunder came rolling up through the black awful edge of the balsams, producing somewhat similar sensations to those which fill the breast of a superstitious savage at the recurrence of an every-day storm above him.*

Noted mountain traveler Charles Dudley Warner visited Cloudland in 1885. "The hotel," he remembered, "provided two comfortable rooms for office and a sitting room with partitioned off sleeping places in the loft. It set a good table, but rocked like a ship at sea when the wind blew."

The fees charged at Cloudland come as something of a shock. Guests could rent a room for two dollars per day, ten dollars per week or thirty dollars for four weeks. If they wanted a room with a fireplace, they had to pay five dollars per month extra. Cloudland's prices seemed so low that the *Johnson City Press-Chronicle* was moved to publish a wistful article titled "What This Country Needs Is a Good $2 Hotel" back in the spring of 1970. The article told the story of how an Illinois man, Julian P. How, had unearthed one of Cloudland's old advertising brochures among his father's papers. How's imagination was captured by both the flowery wording of the advertisement and the wonderful place it described, so he put the brochure in an envelope, addressed to "The

Proprietor, The Roan Mountain Hotel, Carter County, Roan Mountain," and jokingly inquired as to whether a room could still be had at the quoted price. Just as he anticipated, the answer came back that the rates were no longer in effect and that the Cloudland Hotel had in fact passed from existence.

Two dollars bought a lot before the turn of the century. Cloudland kept a doctor, a butcher, a baker and a barber in residence. The property was surrounded by a fence ten miles long, entered by three separate gates. A post office was eventually set up in the hotel, with mail addressed to Cloudland, North Carolina. It was possible to have mail delivered in winter, though it sometimes took an industrious person to make it to the top of the mountain.

Waitresses at the Cloudland Hotel were assigned eight tables each. Their pay was twelve dollars a month plus tips. Room service meals to elderly patrons sometimes brought five-dollar tips.

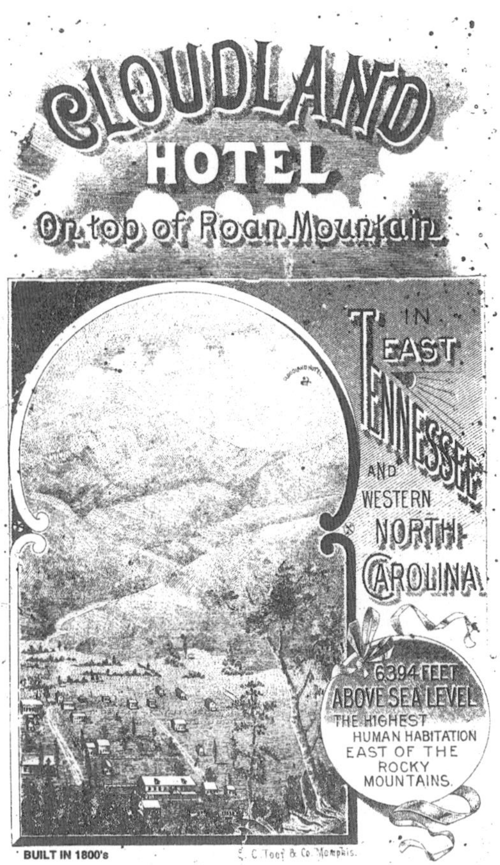

Under Murrell's management, new advertising was designed for the Cloudland Hotel. *Courtesy of the Archives of Appalachia. East Tennessee State University. Murrell Family Collection.*

The guests did not go hungry. Flour, sugar and other bulk staples were hauled up the mountain by wagon, while items like vegetables, eggs and fresh fruit were often carried on horseback. Food that was prone to spoiling was kept in a house above a spring whose water was, as Cloudland's advertisements liked to boast, "only thirteen degrees above freezing." Breakfast always consisted of bacon, liver, steak, fried apples, fried potatoes, flannel cakes, biscuits, coffee and eggs. The main meal was served at midday, with a choice of two soups, two meat entrees—perhaps one of them the juicy beefsteak so favored by General Wilder—six vegetables and a selection of four desserts. Supper was a bit lighter, with cereal, meats, eggs, flannel cakes and portions left over from the midday menu. Musical entertainment accompanied the evening meal as an aid to digestion.

One of the most notable facts about the Cloudland was that, like the ridgeline of Roan Mountain itself, the hotel straddled the Tennessee/North Carolina boundary. Guests could sleep in one state and dine in the other. The hotel drew the maximum effect from its geography, even going so far as to paint a white line through the dining room and down the length of the long banquet table, with the names of North Carolina and Tennessee painted on their appropriate sides. The demarcation was done mainly in jest, but it had its practical side, too: drinking alcoholic beverages was legal in Tennessee but illegal in North Carolina, so guests needed to be certain where they stood when they imbibed. It was said that the local sheriff from North Carolina spent many an idle hour at the Cloudland waiting for someone to slip up and become a new customer for his jail.

Cloudland Hotel

6394 FEET ABOVE SEA LEVEL.
ON TOP OF ROAN MOUNTAIN.

Perfect Exemption from Hay Fever.
Highest Habitation East of the Rocky Mountains.

ADDRESS **N. L. MURRELL**, PROPRIETOR,
DAILY MAIL, TELEGRAPH AND HACK LINE. CLOUDLAND, N. C.

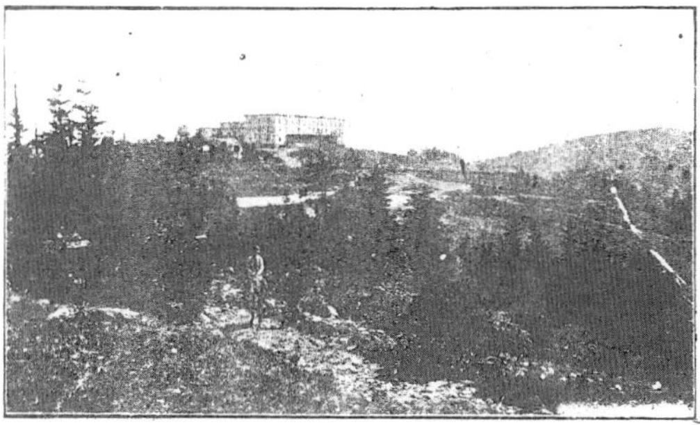

HOW TO GET THERE.

Go via Southern Railway to Johnson City, Tennessee. There take the East Tennessee and Western North Carolina Narrow-Gauge Railroad, through the wildest gorge of the Alleghanies --four miles long and over 1000 feet deep, through which Doe River flashes and tumbles--26 miles to Roan Mountain Station, where there is a nice, clean and well-kept hotel, under entirely new management. Thence in surreys, an entrancing and exhilarating ride of 12 1/2 miles up Roan Mountain to Cloudland Hotel, squarely on top of the mountain, where you have thousands of square miles of territory in sight below, within a radius of 150 miles, over valleys and mountains, in seven different States--West Virginia, Kentucky, Virginia, North Carolina, Georgia, South Carolina and Tennessee--the finest mountain view on the continent.

PARTICULARS.

Hotel opens for the reception of guests July 1st.

Rhododendrons, azaleas, heather and houstonias bloom in great profusion. Most magnificent cloud views in September.

BOARD.

Per day, $2.00 to $2.50; per week, $10.00 to $14.00.

Children under ten years of age in children's ordinary, half rates. Children at first table to the exclusion of other guests, full rates.

White servants, three-quarter rates. Colored servants in colored servant's quarters, half rates.

Table waiters are well-trained young ladies.

Rooms all heated with steam.

Hack rates, $3.00 round trip; hand baggage, free; trunks, $1.00 each way.

CLOUDLAND.

Is a well-built, well-furnished hotel, with ample parlors and verandas; now under entirely new and competent management. It stands on top of a high summit of Roan Mountain, on the State line between North Carolina and Tennessee, in the counties of Mitchell, N. C., and Carter, Tenn. The State line runs through the hotel, and by a peculiar geographical feat, North Carolina is West of Tennessee. The hotel has accommodations for more than three hundred guests. The rooms "all outside," and from all are magnificent views. There are 110 mountain tops in sight below that are more than 4000 feet high. The view reaches into seven different States.

Cloudland Hotel is 6394 feet above sea level; over 4000 feet above hotel on Lookout Mountain; 4644 feet above Asheville, N.C.; 5050 feet above Johnson City, Tenn.; 5194 feet above Warm Springs, N. C.; 200 feet above Mt. Washington, N. H.; 1200 feet above Denver, Colorado; 4600 feet above Mont Eagle, Tenn.; 5400 feet above Knoxville, Tenn.; 5700 feet above Chattanooga, Tenn.; 5144 feet above Tate Springs, Tenn.; 4400 feet above Catskill Mt. House, N. Y.

Cloudland Hotel advertising after 1897. *Courtesy of the Archives of Appalachia, East Tennessee State University, Murrell Family Collection.*

Henry T. Finck, a New York music critic, first visited the Cloudland Hotel on August 8, 1898, and seemed quite impressed with the upstairs rooms, where one could sleep in two states at once—your head in one and feet in the other. One might guess that sleeping on an upper level might have alarmed him somewhat, realizing the unexpected effects of the "elements":

> *It is curious also, to see this large building, capable of housing several hundred guests, exposing its broad sides boldly to the violent winds without the chains with which the Mount Washington Hotel has had to be anchored to the stones. The roof of Cloudland has twice been carried away, but is now safely moored with heavy rocks.*

Mr. Finck shared his experiences in an editorial in the *New York Evening Post* shortly after his visit. No doubt he was completely impressed for he described the dampness of the air as "never depressing, but rather exhilarating." An obviously well-traveled man, he went on to say:

> *Just below and behind the hotel is a gulch from which often arises mists on which the setting sun paints perfect circular rainbows. Less brilliant as those under Niagara or the Vernal Falls in the Yosemite, but very beautiful nonetheless; and within the circle the spectator sometimes sees his own shadow with a halo around it.*

Visitors enjoyed the novel geography and the atmosphere of merriment. They liked to sit on the wide porches running the length of the south and east sides of the hotel and watch the sun bathe the mountaintop. But even the Cloudland Hotel could not conquer human nature—that is to say, it couldn't please everyone. One guest who left Roan Mountain with decidedly mixed feelings was Mr. Finck, who had visited earlier in 1898 and had so enjoyed the place that he returned. Unfortunately, his second trip grated on his nerves from start to finish. The source of Finck's dissatisfaction was a song called "A Hot Time in the Old Town," as revealed in an article he wrote for the *Brooklyn Citizen* in 1900. Perhaps Cloudland should not bear the blame for a guest who arrived on the Roan already carrying excess baggage. Finck's elaborate complaint went as follows:

> *One afternoon, when I was watering flowers in the backyard, a boy in the street whistled a tune that I had not heard before. Had he been within reach I should certainly have turned the hose on him, for the infliction of that tune on my unwilling ears seemed as great an outrage as if he had thrown a rotten potato in my face. It made me, to use a colloquial phrase, "mad as a hornet," not only because of its offensive vulgarity, but because there was something in the nature of that mephitic air that made me feel certain I should hear it a thousand times during the summer. And by prophetic soul divined the truth. In the course of a week or two every boy in town was*

> *whistling that tune, every other man humming it, and every tenth woman playing it on the piano. I fled from New York and buried myself in the Mammoth Cave in Kentucky. In course of the ten-hour trip, a young man in our party whistled that tune half a dozen times, amid the sublimities of subterranean rivers, vaulting domes, and bottomless abysses. I went to the highest habitation east of the Rocky Mountains, the Cloudland Hotel, on the border of North Carolina and Tennessee. For several days there was peace, and life once more seemed worth living; but ere long a young woman arrived to take charge of the piano, and every other piece she played was an arrangement of that detestable song. I changed my room from North Carolina to the wing in Tennessee, plugged my ears with wax, and continued my literary task. In September I went to the mountains of Maine and took a room in a farmhouse. There was a cottage opposite, with a piano and a young lady, and—but why continue this harassing* [sic] *tale? The song, I may add, was "A Hot Time on the Old Town," which May Irwin, I believe, was the first to perpetrate in this country, though I don't pretend to be an expert in criminal history.*
>
> *What is there in the nature of that song that made it thus ravage the country like an epidemic from East to West, from South to North? In other words, what makes a vulgar song popular or gives a popular song its circulation? Or, to put the question in a still more comprehensive form, How can we account for the surprising vogue of certain songs and pieces that are not a bit better than a thousand others of their class not successful, and vastly inferior to many gems of the great masters that are neglected except by a chosen few?*

It is a pity that the Cloudland's register is lost because we can probably never know whether Henry T. Finck ever returned to Roan Mountain in a better frame of mind.

The Cloudland's light may have been bright, but it burned out rather quickly. Even the patronage of European royalty could not support what must have been a very expensive operation. Paul Fink, author of *Backpacking Was the Only Way*, noted that the Cloudland "was never a great financial success," and it is easy to guess why. The cost of shipping in foodstuffs and other products was high. The vacation season in the mountains was short—not much more than ninety days—yet the building had to be maintained year-round. Fires had to be burned all night every night during the summertime. The skeleton staff that remained through the winter could attest to the harsh conditions—mail deliveries often had to be passed through the windows, as the snow sometimes drifted so high that the doors were entirely blocked, and even when that was not the case, the wind might be blowing so hard that the doors could not be pushed open against it. Anyone who has spent much time on the Roan knows the kind of wear and tear that is caused by the wind. Upkeep on the hotel must have been enormous.

General Wilder was the moving force behind the Cloudland, and perhaps the most telling factor in the hotel's decline was his decision to turn his boundless energy to other projects and leave the day-to-day operations on the top of the Roan in the hands of others. Even though the Cloudland continued to thrive, the Panic of 1893 took quite a toll on Wilder's finances, particularly in regards to his Carnegie properties in Johnson City. Three years later, in 1896, he nearly lost the Cloudland Hotel, as he had not paid $11,615 in delinquent property taxes to Carter County—a tax burden twice that of any other delinquent Carter County resident.

Cloudland passed through several managers, who ran it in accordance with lease agreements. The first of them was Frank Stratton. Next came W.E. Ragsdale of Chattanooga and then N.L. Murrell and a man named Wagoner, who operated the hotel in partnership for a time.

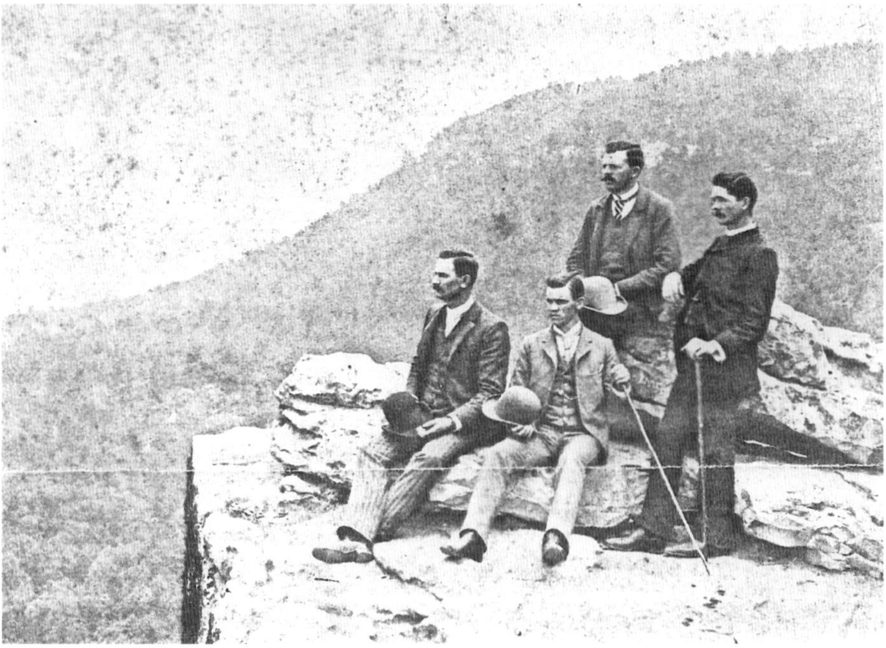

N.L. Murrell, in the striped tie, managed the hotel for ten years beginning in 1897. *Courtesy of the Archives of Appalachia. East Tennessee State University. Murrell Family Collection.*

Murrell was the last to run the Cloudland under lease. In fact, as Murrell's daughter, Pauline Stone, reported, General Wilder "offered him the hotel at Cloudland and considerable acreage for $20,000, nothing down and pay for it as he could. My father did not take it." Running the Cloudland was a family affair for the Murrells. Mrs. Murrell was still speaking fondly of the experience when she was well into her eighties. When a newspaper reporter once asked her what kind of dancing was practiced at the hotel in the old days, she replied spiritedly, "Why my dear, it wasn't the Dark Ages. We waltzed, enjoyed square and ballroom dancing." While she grudgingly admitted that Mount Mitchell was higher than the Roan, she took special pride in pointing out that "it was not inhabited."

After N.L. Murrell's lease ran out in 1905, the Cloudland passed into the hands of John Gouge, who had helped build Wilder's original twenty-room structure on Roan Mountain and was an employee for thirty years. In later years, Gouge was employed as caretaker, and his salary was forty dollars per year plus whatever profit he could turn from summer guests. He and his family lived in the hotel twelve months of the year; his children recalled terrible winters where it was so cold they were nearly snowbound for weeks.

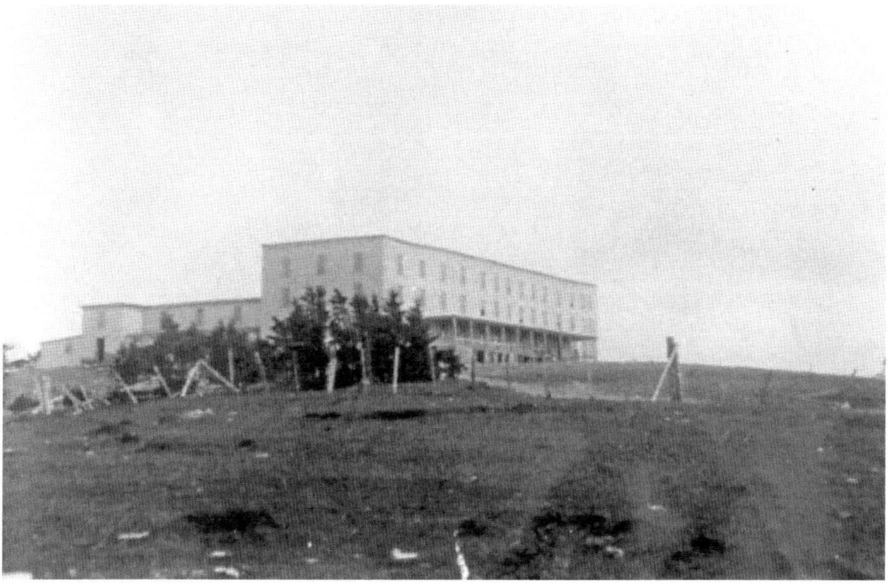

The final year the hotel was open, D.R. Beeson Sr. photographed it in September 1913. On this trip, Beeson enjoyed a fine meal prepared by Mrs. Gouge, one of the caretakers of the hotel. *Courtesy of the Archives of Appalachia. East Tennessee State University. D.R. Beeson Collection.*

Funding was not forthcoming from Wilder, not even after lightning hit the hotel. Before long, the Cloudland was headed downhill. The year 1914 was the final year that the hotel remained open for business; in 1915, the Cloudland Hotel came to the end of its era.

Once abandoned, local folks would come in and ransack the remains, throwing fragile objects from the windows and breaking them to pieces. Paul Fink passed through the area on one of his backpacking trips in 1915 and noted that "the ravages of wind and weather were already evident—glassless windows, leaking roofs, sagging floors and a general atmosphere of decay."

Two years after Wilder's death, in 1919, his heirs sold the remnants of Wilder's paradise to Holden Garland, who in turn sold off what was left of the hotel room by room. People would arrange to purchase one or more rooms and then take whatever they could find—basically the lumber, doors and window frames. A popular stop on the way to the Roan, Jack's Grocery in Burbank, was originally built from Cloudland Hotel lumber.

For years afterward, it was not unusual to find homes and businesses in the area built entirely from Cloudland lumber. On rare occasions, people used a hotel room door—complete with room number—as the front door to their residences. I once happened upon an abandoned house constructed of Cloudland lumber when I was out hiking. It felt like I was stepping back to the days just following the hotel's closing, as the furnishings and possessions of the long-departed inhabitants—cast-iron stove, canned food on the

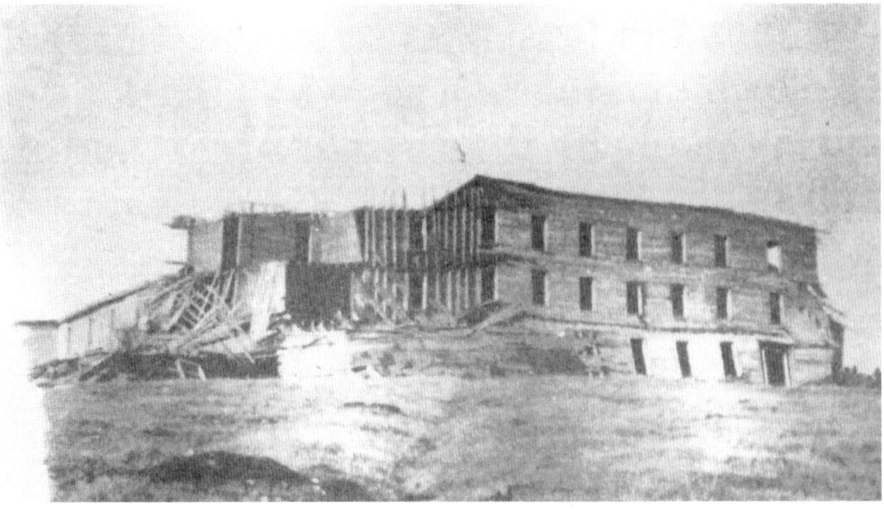

The rapid effects of the elements on man-made structures are quite evident in 1918, when Paul Fink discovers the old hotel nearly lying on the ground.

shelves, clothing hanging in place, corn-shuck mattresses—were completely intact, as if the owners would return at any minute.

Cloudland's fine furniture was scattered throughout Tennessee and North Carolina, but such items as washstands, trunks, dressers and beautiful hand-pegged cherry beds become available only rarely today. Collectors have long since located and bought what they could, while other pieces remain in the possession of the families who have held them through the years.

And we mustn't forget the Roan Mountain Depot Hotel in the village of Roan Mountain. It was sold in 1905 to S.B. Wood, a pharmacist and physician for the Forge Mining Company. He ran the hotel for ten years, but it also suffered from neglect, as did its sister Cloudland Hotel. After some renovation, it reopened briefly in 1949 and then permanently closed its doors in the early 1950s.

I once visited the home of a fascinating gentleman who had spent the first twelve years of his life in the Cloudland Hotel, as his parents were employed there. He told me many wonderful tales of his experiences on top of the Roan, but what I found especially interesting was his account of what had become of the hundred or two hundred rooms full of furniture. It was his parents, he said, who at the closing of the hotel brought down much of the furniture and distributed it among their neighbors and friends.

The famous banquet table immediately came to mind, and I asked whether he knew what had happened to it. "Oh, that," he responded. "It's right here in the kitchen. Would you like to see it?" My heart nearly dropped, as I'd long assumed that the table had been destroyed. We went into the kitchen, and there before me was a narrow, six-foot-long table with pale green planks for its top and flaking remnants of that legendary white line roughly painted right down the center. But it was so short! How could that tiny table possibly have accommodated all the guests at the Cloudland Hotel? If a six-foot table could be exaggerated to grand proportions, then how accurate were all the other stories I'd heard about the hotel? My host was quick to dispel my doubts. He said that the table had been so big that he couldn't hope to fit it into his house, so he had cut it down to its present size and burned the rest as firewood. I was both relieved that the table had once been as big as reported and disappointed that most of it had gone up in smoke.

With both the Cloudland Hotel and Roan Mountain, it is sometimes difficult to tell where fact ends and legend begins. One prominent and ancient local legend concerns the so-called mountain music of the Roan. Herdsmen in the area occasionally heard a strange sound when the wind blew. Some judged it to be perfectly natural, merely the amplification of normal

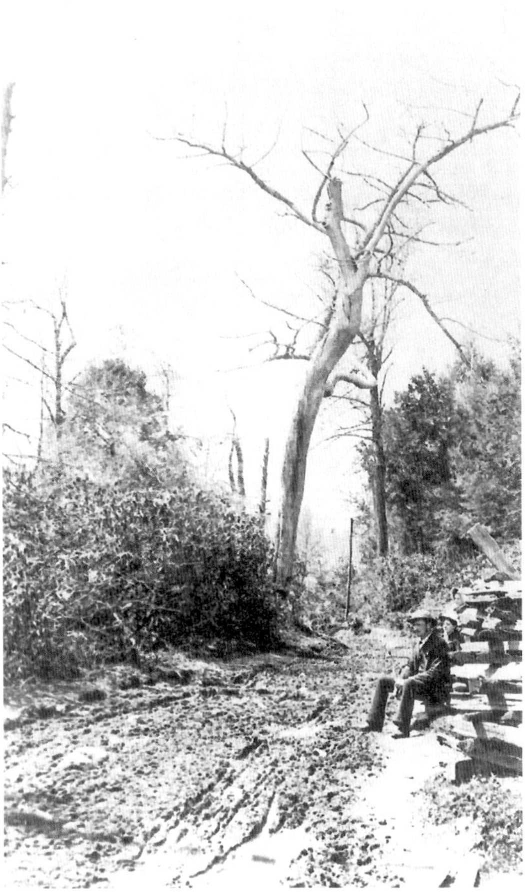

The road to the Cloudland Hotel. 1880s. *Courtesy of Thomas O. Maher.*

wind noises caused by the configuration of rocks on the Roan. Others offered more colorful explanations. One story that arose claimed that the mountain was actually talking. Another said that it was the devil's wind that set clouds to whirling around the mountain in a circular pattern and caused the eerie sound. Still another took the completely opposite approach and ascribed the noise to angels singing in the air over the Roan, perhaps even practicing for Judgment Day; according to that version, the mountain was blessed. It was said that mountain music could only be heard when the air at the peak was clear and the sky blue but thunderstorms raged in the valleys below.

The legend was still kicking around in the days when General Wilder's twenty-room log structure stood atop the Roan, but the popular view by then was that mountain music sounded like the buzzing of a thick swarm of bees. In 1878, Knoxville scientist Henry E. Colton, for whom Colton's Cliff is named, traveled to Roan Mountain to witness the phenomenon. Colton had also visited the Roan as a young man at about the age of twenty-two, publishing in 1859, *Mountain Scenery*. In this early publication, he wrote poetic descriptions of the Roan long before the hotel days:

> *After something over an hour's climbing, we stood upon the top of the Roan. A single glance compensated for all the fatigue of getting there.*

> *The eye swept over a comparatively level prairie, several miles in extent, covered with grass, with huge rocks and patches of the balsam fir tree at intervals diversifying the scenery. Over this broad expanse many cattle graze during the summer months. Viewed from a distance, this bald summit presents an appearance from which it takes its name—the Roan. Of all the mountains I have ever seen this is the most beautiful. Others are grander, more sublime, and more impressive; but none are so pleasing, so romantic, and so charming...*
>
> *One leaves the top of the Roan with feelings of love, an appreciation of beauty, a glow of romance warming the soul with ideas of unutterable poetry; but he quits the Black with a wild sense of strife, an impression of the sublime and rugged, the tremendous reality of life. The lover may stand on the Roan and sigh forth sentimental sonnets; but the soldier may stand on the Black and feel the kindlings of his soul for the din of battle. Could I see but one of them, I would prefer the Roan.*

On this particular visit in 1878, Colton happened to be present on a night when the sound was particularly loud. General Wilder had often heard and spoken of mountain music himself, and he and two other men accompanied Colton out onto the mountain that evening. Colton subsequently returned home and wrote an account of his experience for a Knoxville newspaper. Like many of the scientific explanations that attempted to account for the origin of the balds, Colton's article was a model of convoluted thinking:

> *The sound was very plain to the ear, and was not at all as described—like the humming of thousands of bees—but like the incessant, continuous and combined snap of two Leyden jars (devices for storing electrical charges) positively and negatively charged. I tried to account for it on the theory of bees or flies but the mountain people said it frequently occurred after the bees or flies had gone to their winter homes or before they came out. It was always loudest and most prolonged just before there would be a thunderstorm in either valley, or one passing over the mountain. I used every argument I could to persuade myself that it was simply a result of some common cause and to shake the faith of the country people in its mysterious origin but I only convinced myself that it was the result from two currents of air meeting each other in the suck between the two peaks where there was no obstruction of trees, one containing a greater, the other a less amount of electricity, or that the two currents coming together in the open plateau on the high elevation, by their friction and being of different*

> *temperatures, generated electricity. The "mountain music" was simply the snapping caused by this friction and this generation of electricity.*

Perhaps we should be thankful that the scientific community never pursued the question of mountain music as vigorously as it did explanations of the balds.

Some people deny the existence of mountain music altogether. One correspondent of mine, who now lives in the desert Southwest, claims that neither she nor her family heard the noise during their many years on the Roan. If others have heard it, she suspects they were merely witnessing the same sort of sound she has heard in the desert when the wind sings through the wire fences that surround many ranches—an interesting noise, perhaps, but hardly a fitting subject for legend and mystery. Still, a good many of the old-timers I spoke with were confident in remembering strains of mountain music from the days of their youth.

Another well-known Roan Mountain legend is loosely tied to mountain music—or to the conditions that bring on mountain music, at least. When the valley storms associated with the buzzing or snapping sound eventually clear away, it is said that people standing high on the mountain can look down upon a rainbow that forms a compete circle. Legend has it that the rainbow is God's halo or a halo left by God's angels to protect the Roan and its visitors from all that is evil.

Witnesses to the circular rainbow are harder to come by than are people who have heard mountain music. In fact, I had such bad luck locating *anyone* who had seen the rainbow that I was skeptical of the legend, until one particularly blustery day when I was planning a full moon hike to the highlands of the Roan for a group of visitors to the state park. Close to fifty people had signed up for the trip, so needless to say I grew quite concerned when thick storm clouds rolled in and completely covered the top of the mountain that afternoon. Since I didn't want to lead the group into a torrent of rain later that night, I decided I ought to make an early jaunt to the top and check out the conditions there.

As I drove up the mountainside with a friend, the fog grew thicker and thicker. Convinced that the weather was not going to give way, I was about to turn back and cancel the hike when the cloud cover abruptly fell away. It seemed as if the whole world had opened up before us. We found ourselves under clear blue skies with the storms rolling below us in the valleys. Then, looking to the right, I saw the most unbelievable phenomenon I have ever witnessed. A rainbow began to materialize at eye level, and as it developed, it took the form of a complete circle. And then a *second* rainbow formed within the circle of the first! I can't say how long we stood there. It seemed like a short eternity before the elusive rainbow faded from view. I reaffirmed my faith in legends on the spot.

It is not known whether General Wilder or any of his guests on Roan Mountain ever witnessed the circular rainbow, though some guests alluded to rainbows in their writings. The general and some of the others *did* hear mountain music. All things being equal, it would figure to be easier to witness mountain music today than it was in Wilder's time, since things are considerably quieter on top of the Roan now than they were during the heyday of the Cloudland Hotel.

All that remains of the Cloudland is the stone foundation. Spruce and fir trees grow among the ruins. Yet with a good imagination, you can walk through the kitchen, rock on one of the porches, straddle the state line or dance in the main hall. You can almost hear the music that once echoed from the Cloudland Hotel across the surrounding highlands. Though the building has nearly disappeared, a visit to the site will convince you that its spirit still lives.

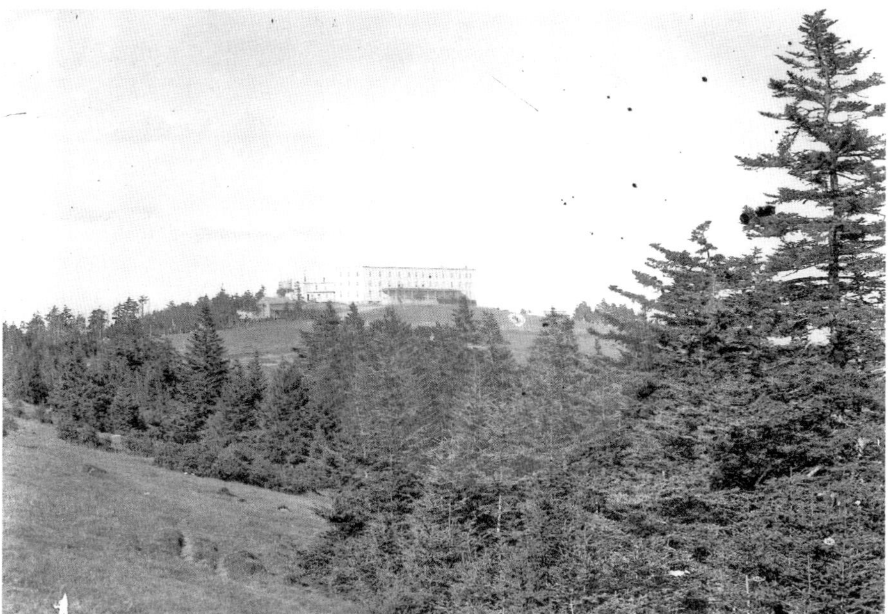

Though the building ultimately disappeared, the memories and stories of the Cloudland Hotel will always remain. Early 1880s.

JOHN MUIR

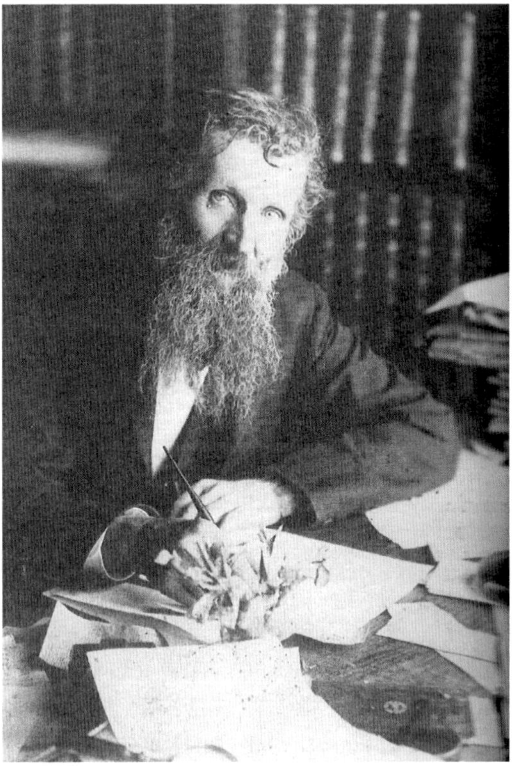

Naturalist and traveler John Muir was a noted visitor to the Cloudland Hotel. *Courtesy of the John Muir Papers, Holt-Atherton Department of Special Collections, University of the Pacific Libraries. Muire-Hanna Trust.*

On a search for new information regarding the Roan, Bob Fulcher, regional interpretive specialist for Tennessee State Parks, came upon the find of a lifetime. As part of his search, he contacted universities across the nation that acted as depositories of documents and recollections of famous American and European botanists. It was during this search that he uncovered one of the most exciting pieces of information regarding Roan Mountain's history.

John Muir, a Scotsman who immigrated to the United States, has long been known throughout history for being an outstanding naturalist. His contributions include the founding of the Sierra Club and the preservation of wild lands across the United States. In California, the University of the Pacific recently placed thousands of items from John Muir's journals and personal letters on microfilm, putting this collection in a retrievable format for the first time.

Historically, it was known that Muir had indeed traveled in the Appalachian Mountains, but there was no evidence showing that he had visited the Roan. The University of the Pacific sent Mr. Fulcher a roll of microfilm to review, containing correspondence dated from 1897 to 1898. After considerable reading of the films, he discovered a letter that John Muir had written to his wife, Louise, from the Cloudland Hotel on September 25, 1898. What a thrilling discovery to find that one of the world's greatest naturalists had spent time on Roan Mountain!

The trip ensued after Muir had taken botanists William Canby and Charles Sprague Sargent on a trip through Alaska in 1897. Wanting to take Muir back to areas in the East that he had not visited since 1867, Canby and Sargent planned a trip to the eastern United States. Muir was anxious to make the trip, writing to Sargent, "I don't want to die without once more saluting the grand, godly, round-headed trees of the east side of America that I first learned to love and beneath which I used to weep for joy when nobody knew me."

Canby planned the trip around some of his favorite botanical areas, which included Luray Caverns, Natural Bridge, Salt Pond Mountain in Virginia and Roan Mountain in North Carolina. Muir's only request of the trip was to "avoid cities and dinners as much as possible and travel light and free."

Unfortunately, the trip to the East was quite hard on him, as the miles of riding and jolting on trains and wagons and eating poor food made him very sick. Upon arriving at the Cloudland, he was quite under the weather, complaining of dizziness and the grippe. Yet before long, the high, clear air of the Roan healed him, as evidenced in his letter to his wife:

> *Dear Louise,*
> *We drove here from Cranberry yesterday, a distance of about 18 miles through the most beautiful deciduous forest I ever saw. All the landscapes in every direction are made up of mountains, a billowing sea of them without bounds as far as one can look, and every mountain hill and ridge and hollow is densely forested with so many kinds of trees their mere names would fill this sheet. & now they are beginning to put on their purple & gold. Liriodendron. Nyssa. Sassafras. Oxydendron. Mountain ash. Tilia birch beech hickory ash Magnolia 3 species. Chestnut etc & maples. I wish I could hand you a bouquet of these leaves their beauty is perfectly enchanting.*
>
> *After lunch yesterday we walked 5 miles along the mountain top to where the storms of winter prevent trees from growing here. The open broad ridge top for miles is covered with rhododendron about 5 ft high which in flower must make a glorious show. Around the base of the rhododendron clumps there is a rich bossy growth of* Leiophyllum buxifolia *a charming heathwort. The temp. is distinctly alpine & for the first time since leaving home feel like my old self. I have been quite miserable but this air has healed me…*
> *Wanda Helen love to all—*
> *From Your Loving Husband John Muir*

Including pressed and fresh flowers within personal letters was quite common in Muir's time, and based on the context of a letter of reply from his wife, it is possible that he did send her a sampling of the Roan's flora. They discussed the beauty of the sand myrtle, a flower that was similar to the heather of his native Scotland, in such a way that it appeared as though his wife had received a sprig of the plant from him.

The men spent at least a month roaming around the mountains and through the southern forests, with Muir being especially impressed with Cranberry, Cloudland and Grandfather Mountain in North Carolina. Upon leaving Roan Mountain, they traveled in carriage to Lenoir, North Carolina, on a trip Muir deemed "the finest drive of its kind in America."

Up to the present day, people of all walks of life have found their way to the Roan for myriad personal and professional reasons. For all of us who admire the early explorers, scientists and naturalists for their hard work and dedication to the discovery of new information about our world, knowing that John Muir also visited Roan Mountain is, without a doubt, exceptionally inspirational. Mr. Fulcher's thoughts perfectly describe the profound importance of Muir's visit as he states, "There was no greater voice for wilderness in American literature than John Muir. He endows Roan Mountain further as a great piece of American wilderness."

IV
Protecting a Resource

The Southern Appalachian National Park Commission

After the devastating floods of May 1901, President Theodore Roosevelt reported to the Senate and House of Representatives the importance of preservation of the southern forests. His letter of transmittal in the secretary of agriculture's report on the conditions of the southern Appalachian region indicated his wholehearted support of the recommendation to save these lands before the damage to them was irreparable. He noted the violent and frequent flooding then occurring over the entire area, the heavy rainfall common to the mountains, the extensive clearing of the land for agriculture the associated erosion problems, the economic value of the forests and the need for a national forest reserve.

It was not until 1923 that direct action was taken to begin investigation into the formation of a national park in the Southeast. It was in the "Seventh Annual Report of the National Park Service" that former parks director Stephen T. Mather indicated his desire to see additional national parks established east of the Mississippi River. His interests were quickly taken to heart, and a committee was appointed on February 16, 1924, for the purpose of investigating the possibilities of acquiring sufficient wild lands for national park status in the East. Several prestigious businessmen were invited and subsequently accepted the opportunity to serve on the committee, which first met on March 26, 1924, naming itself the Southern Appalachian National Park Commission. With no funds available on which to operate, members decided to personally fund their expenses in addition to using three donations of $500 from Mr. Gregg, $500 from Mr. John D. Rockefeller Jr. and an additional $250 from Director Mather of the National Park Service.

It goes without saying that they were inundated with requests from southern states, all of which wanted their lands to become national parks. Overwhelmed, the commission decided to send out a questionnaire to all interested communities in Tennessee, Kentucky, Virginia, West Virginia, Georgia and North Carolina.

With so many choices, the commission decided that a trip through the Appalachian region would be necessary to eliminate many of the requests. Their first travels took the members to Gainesville, Georgia; the North Carolina mountains in the vicinity of Highlands, Asheville, Linville Gorge and Grandfather Mountain; Roan Mountain; and the Great Smoky Mountains area in Tennessee. It was impressive to see that Roan Mountain was amongst the first considered for national park status. Little was said about the Roan in the first reports, only that

> *after spending the night at Bakersville, the committee members were taken on horseback by a delegation composed of local men to the top of Roan Mountain, where they made a careful inspection of the area in that vicinity and returned that evening to Bakersville to spend the night.*

Of course, this was only the beginning, as the commission eventually broke into smaller groups so more areas could be visited. Wherever commission members went, they were greeted with large parties of representatives, dinners, meetings in their honor and even a musical greeting at one location. Their warm welcomes were indications that our country was interested in slowing down industrial progress and setting aside land for preservation.

During these preliminary visits, several areas were quickly eliminated, some with major problems and others with minor. In Alabama, the examined area contained large numbers of valuable coal seams and other mineral deposits, which made it impractical for consideration. Other areas were heavily settled with lands that were cultivated and disturbed. The Cumberland Gap area was also eliminated because of large numbers of mineral deposits.

On December 12, 1924, the committee met and reported on the results of its investigations during its first eight months of existence. The call for wild lands was evident in its report:

> *Nature calls us all and the response of the American people has been expressed in the creation, so far, of 19 national parks…The two-thirds*

> *of our population living east of the Mississippi has contented itself with a few State Parks, not knowing that in the southern Appalachian Range there are several areas which fill the definition of a national park, because of beauty and grandeur of scenery, presence of a wonderful variety of trees and plant life, and possibilities of harboring and developing the animal life common in the pre-colonial days but now nearly extinct...All that has saved these near-by regions from spoliation for so long a time has been their inaccessibility and the difficulty of profitability exploiting the wealth that mantles the steep mountain slopes...we face the immediate danger that the last remnants of our primeval forests will be destroyed, however remote on steep mountain side or hidden away in deep lonely cove they may be.*

Therefore, in an effort to define the most appropriate lands for this last effort to save our dwindling forests and wildlife, the commission set forth a list of requirements needed for its project to be successful and worthwhile to the American people:

> *It would benefit the greatest number, and it should be of sufficient size to meet the needs as a recreational ground for the people not only of to-day but of the coming generations. The committee therefore decided that no site covering less than 500 square miles would be considered.*

With that thought in mind, Roan Mountain's consideration as a site ended. The area around the Roan was already extensively settled, with great amounts of land being used for agricultural purposes. Up until this point, the Roan had been a frontrunner in acquiring national park status; however, the Roan received one of the highest compliments from the commission members when they reported, "We responded to the call of the poet—to see Roan Mountain if we would really see the southern Appalachians."

The majestic Roan was set above all others as the one place that represented the southern Appalachians. Though no longer considered a prospective site, the Roan still shone brightly in the crowd.

On December 12, 1924, the committee made its recommendations to the chairman based on its travels and outlined the requirements that a national park must meet to be recommended to Congress.

It recommended two areas for national park status. The first was the Great Smoky Mountains area, considered the best due to "the heights of the mountains, depth of valleys, ruggedness of the area, and the unexampled variety of trees, shrubs, and plants." A few problems were pointed out,

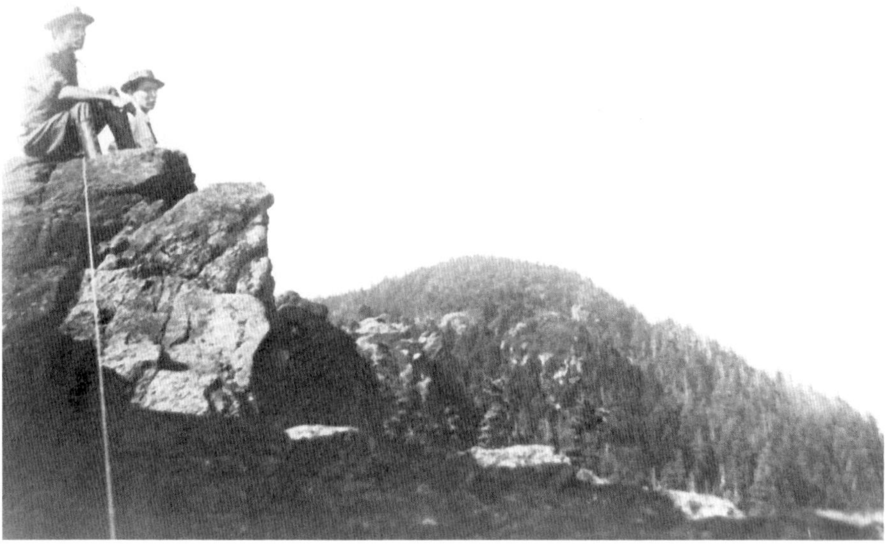

Later, after the 1913 visit of D.R. Beeson Sr., the Southern Appalachian National Park Commission learned of the incredible beauty of Roan Mountain and added it to its list of considerations for national park status. *Courtesy of the Archives of Appalachia. East Tennessee State University. D.R. Beeson Collection.*

particularly the ruggedness and heights that would make road and park development quite difficult and incur great expense and time. The committee also considered the excessive rainfall a possible problem, though it was quick to point out that this factor had not been carefully studied.

The second area of high interest was the Shenandoah Valley in Virginia. Its appeal was due to the easy three-hour ride the park would be from Washington, D.C., and to it being just a day's ride for 40,000,000 people. Its attributes included primeval forests, cascading streams, canyons, gorges and beautiful caverns. It also lent itself well to historical interests, boasting Civil War and Revolutionary War battlefields, as well as the birthplaces of several American presidents. The suggested prospect of developing a skyline drive along the mountaintop quickly caught the attention of the committee.

The Mammoth Cave region of Kentucky was also being considered simultaneously with the Smoky Mountain and Shenandoah regions. All three of these areas were felt to possess their own unique features, making them ideal candidates for the first three national parks in the East.

On January 27, 1925, a bill was introduced that provided for securing lands in the southern Appalachian Mountains and the Mammoth Cave region of

Kentucky for preservation as national parks. The bill passed the Senate on February 12 and the House on February 16 and was approved by the president on February 21, 1925 (Public No. 437, 68th Congress). The bill ordered the secretary of the interior to determine the boundaries of these areas and to "receive definite offers of donations of lands and moneys, and to secure such options as in his judgment may be considered reasonable and just."

Thus, a long and arduous process took place as the committee tried to negotiate, buy land, fund purchases and work around the many problems that quickly arose in trying to make such large acquisitions. The passing of the above bill also encouraged an additional interest in the acquiring of state lands for park status. At the Fifth National Conference on State Parks at Skyland, Secretary Work addressed attendees with the following comments:

> *We have gradually established an artificial life dependent upon the indoors, until now to complete the cycle we are turning back to the simpler pleasures found in the woods, in contact with nature...we are attempting after a fashion to complete a cycle begun by the forebears of those in this region who struggled to overcome the forests and wild life we now seek to conserve.*

He also commented frequently on the need for more state parks, reminding everyone that "a State Park every 100 miles" would be an ideal situation for the traveling motorist, breaking the distance between the upcoming national parks. Works considered the entire movement a wonderful opportunity for each state to take action in reserving their smaller parcels of land for state park status. He continued by saying:

> *To further the State Park idea, which is the inspiration of this gathering, I hope it is unnecessary for me to reiterate my desire to support your efforts along these lines. In doing so let us not overlook the underlying purpose of the outdoor movement, which is to give us a momentary glimpse of the simpler things of life, to increase our appreciation and understanding of nature, to bring us closer to the scheme of the creation, and educate our children "through Nature up to Nature's God."*

Following this inspirational meeting, the committee resumed its work of acquiring lands, but it was often faced with problems and pressures. Around the Smokies there were huge, working lumber operations that were not willing to stop without injunction proceedings or condemnation. Commission members visited lumber company officials, hoping to convince them that any further cutting of timber would injure the chances of the Smokies being purchased as a national park site. Unfortunately, they gained little sympathy from the lumber companies. In addition, private landowners were offering opposition and were not in favor of selling their land. These pressing issues prompted the third meeting of the Southern Appalachian National Park Commission on July 18, 1925. The following statements were issued as a result of that meeting:

> *The commission may find it necessary to modify its boundary as originally contemplated and consider the advisability of the creation of a national park which will lie largely in the State of Tennessee...about one-half of the North Carolina project originally designated seems available, but the holdings of two or three of the largest timber corporations are difficult to acquire as virgin areas; if they are not secured until after the timber is cut off, they will not be fit for a national park for recreational use.*
>
> *The companies referred to are at the present time engaged in active operations on some of the higher elevations and are removing the spruce and balsam forests in their entirety. The spruce and balsam areas, which have been cut over, do not reforest themselves and immediately become covered with an almost impenetrable thicket of blackberry and other undesirable growths peculiarly susceptible to forest fires.*

The committee members immediately decided that it was imperative that they acquire as much of the designated territory at once, before any more damage could be wrought upon this pristine area. Rapid fundraising became a sudden issue, and individuals were appointed to obtain land options. Their appointments quickly ended, as it was too expensive—not to mention, their results were unsatisfactory.

A new meeting was called that brought together all of the associations in each state that had been operating independently of one another up to this point. They came together in a new association called the Appalachian National Park Association (Inc.), composed of representatives from each state in addition to one member of the Southern Appalachian National Park Commission. Their major purpose was to move forward on a national effort to acquire lands for the proposed parks. They developed a plan of cooperation in which they could act as one unit with a common cause.

On March 26, 1926 (Public. No. 268, 69th Congress), the president approved a bill that provided for the establishment of the Shenandoah National Park and the Great Smoky Mountains National Park. The acreage designated was 521,000 acres for Shenandoah and 704,000 acres for the Smokies, which was recommended by the secretary of the interior. Then, on May 8, 1926, a bill was introduced to the House to provide for the establishment of the Mammoth Cave National Park in Kentucky with a designation of 7,618 acres and was approved by the president on May 25, 1926 (Public, No. 283, 69th Congress).

Finally, on February 6, 1930, seven years after the initial work in 1923, the Great Smoky Mountains National Park was formally presented. The governors of North Carolina and Tennessee gave presentation speeches to the federal government. North Carolina governor O. Max Gardner presented 58,622.58 acres in his state:

> *We are presenting to you "the most massive uplift" in the East containing 18 peaks towering about 6,000 feet...lying in almost equal portions in North Carolina and Tennessee...and contains 1,000,000 acres of virgin forests, some of which were full grown when Columbus discovered America.*

Immediately following Governor Gardner's speech, Governor Henry H. Horton of Tennessee presented his state's deeds to 100,176.63 acres. He gave praise to those who had worked so hard to make this day a reality and concluded with the following words, which suggested a hot race ensuing between the two neighboring states:

> *Let me add that Tennessee is interested in bringing this accomplishment to a successful close as speedily as possible. We now have contracted for 40,000 acres more than was delivered to you to-day, and suits are pending in court for condemnation proceedings to 37,000 acres more.*
>
> *We are running a race with North Carolina as to which can first deliver the entire amount necessary for the park to the Government of the United States.*

Not long after the February 1930 presentation of the Great Smoky Mountains National Park, final work was underway to complete the creation of the Shenandoah National Park and Mammoth Cave National Park. On December 30, 1930, the chairman of the Southern Appalachian National Park Commission called a meeting to ask for the dissolution of the committee. The final arrangements for the Virginia and Kentucky lands were now in the hands of the National Park Service. Their mission—to select and devise a plan for acquiring parklands—had been fulfilled.

On June 1, 1931, the commission issued its final report to the secretary of the interior and was thus dissolved on June 30, 1931. It was a most satisfying and gratifying end to an incredible accomplishment made by these individuals over the course of eight years:

> *United States Department of the Interior*
> *June 12, 1931*
> *Order No. 515*
> *It is ordered and directed that the Southern Appalachian National Park Commission, authorized by an act of Congress Approved February 21, 1925, is hereby dissolved, effective at the close of business on June 30, 1931, said commission having completed the duties contemplated under said law. All files and records of said commission are hereby transferred to The National Park Service at the close of business on June 30 next.*
> *Ray Lyman Wilbur, Secretary*

THE CIVILIAN CONSERVATION CORPS AND THE U.S. FOREST SERVICE

One of the first governmental efforts to protect Roan Mountain's resources came in 1933, when the Civilian Conservation Corps (CCC), a Depression-era agency that put the unemployed to work in building public works projects, constructed a fire tower and cabin at Roan High Knob. It was a well-intentioned venture but also a fruitless one. For one thing, the magnificent forests that the tower was supposed to protect from fire were in the process of being consumed by logging interests, so there was little to guard except brush. And furthermore, a typical day in the tower frequently yielded a twenty-four hour view of thick banks of clouds. The fog was so dense at "Cloudland" that a fire could probably have been spotted from the CCC tower only if the structure itself were ablaze. The tower was used for only a few years, and it was torn down after about ten years. Concrete pilings still mark its former site.

A popular spot among treasure hunters has long been a sizable dump located below the road near the tower site. It contains trash left by the old CCC crew, and for years it has yielded antique bottles and other forgotten artifacts from Depression days. A shelter for hikers on the Appalachian Trail now stands near the foundation of the fire tower on the former site of an old shelter used by CCC workers.

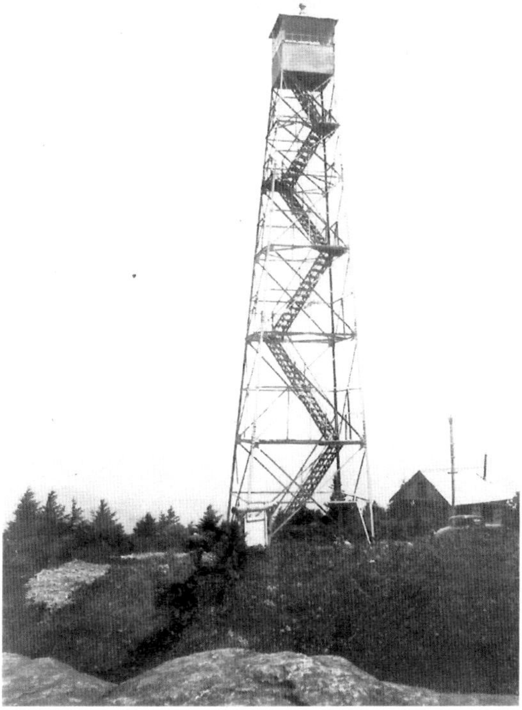

Right: The Civilian Conservation Corps fire tower at Roan High Knob in the 1930s. *D.M. Brown Collection.*

Below: The cabin by the fire tower, now an Appalachian Trail shelter. 1938. *Courtesy of the Tennessee State Library and Archives.*

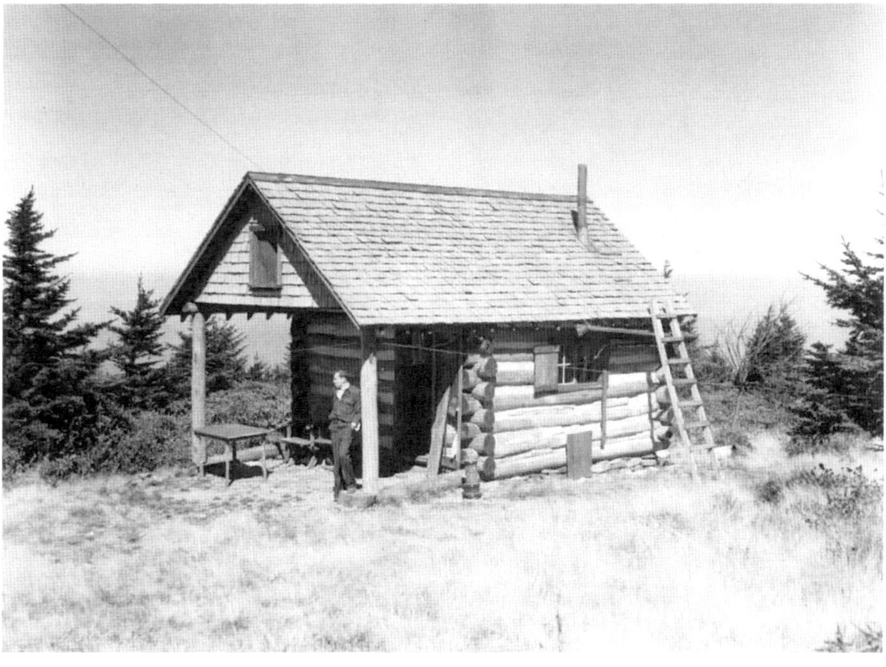

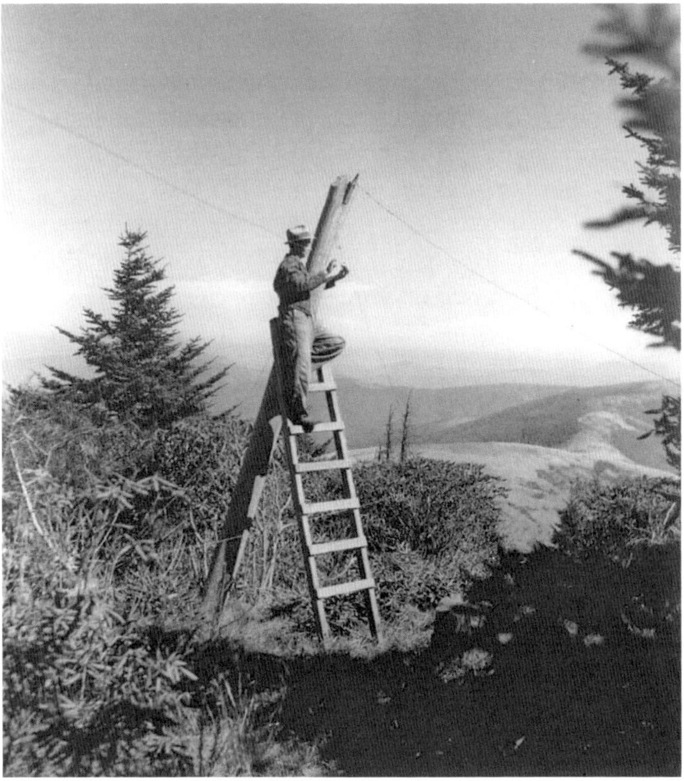

Left: Running a telephone line to the fire tower. 1938. *Courtesy of the Tennessee State Library and Archives.*

Below: When the air is clear, the views from Roan are amazing, especially from the top of the fire tower, as seen in 1938. *Courtesy of the Tennessee State Library and Archives.*

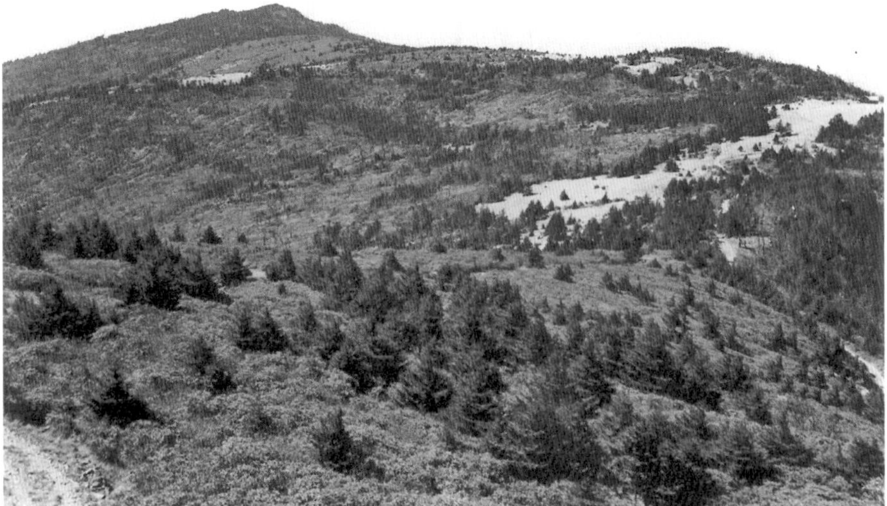

A more effective effort at protecting the mountain from logging came in 1941, when the United States Forest Service purchased approximately seven thousand acres along the top and sides of the Roan. This put the Roan under the oversight of the Cherokee National Forest in Tennessee and Pisgah National Forest in North Carolina.

It was hoped that putting a significant portion of the mountain in the public domain would reduce the risk of future abuse and allow the Roan to heal its wounds and reforest its slopes. The initial plans were unexpectedly put on hold, for later that year on December 7, the Japanese attacked Pearl Harbor, moving America toward another world war.

Building the Roads

After the end of World War II, it didn't take long before residents in Tennessee came together with a very intriguing plan. Though a popular destination, the top of Roan Mountain was difficult to scale via the single-lane dirt road. To rectify this problem, the concept of connecting Tennessee, North Carolina and a Forest Service road at Carver's Gap was born. And

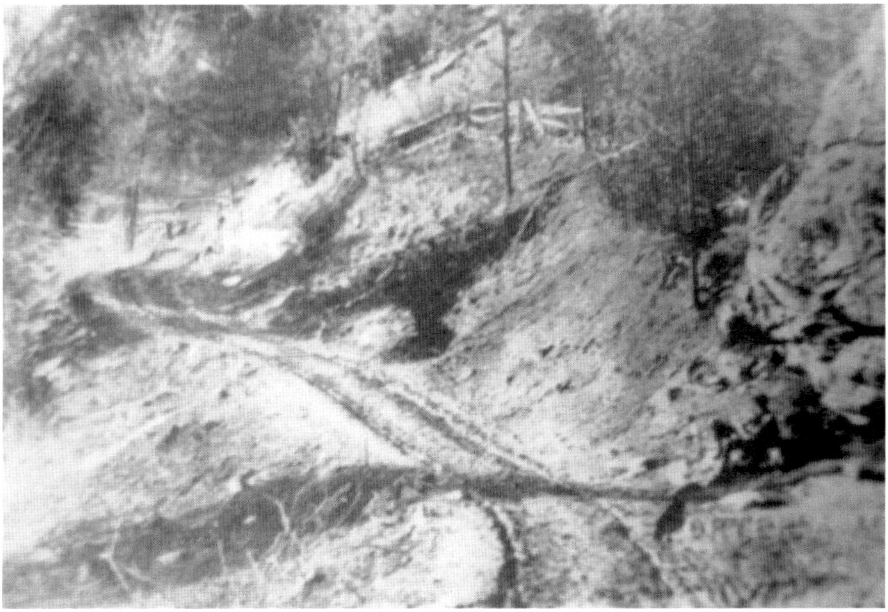

The extraordinary need for good roads is evident in this early 1900s look at the rugged, dirt track in front of the Sheltering Rock. *Courtesy of Mel McKay.*

this was by no means an idea without passion—quite the contrary. The individuals involved in completing this mission were completely devoted to a positive outcome. So in 1946, the Roan Mountain Citizens Club was formed with the funding and completion of a road to the top of the Roan its sole intent.

There are a lot of ways a community could go about requesting funding for costly endeavors. In the case of the highlands of Roan, the answer was obvious. In many ways, the mountain spoke for itself; all one would have to do was get people up there. And if you are reading this now and you have been on the Roan, you most likely totally understand this concept.

So in 1947, the very first Rhododendron Festival was planned for June 22 on top of Roan Mountain; this quickly morphed into a huge community project with attention paid to transportation, a great program and lots of good music and food. "We hand-worked that road for the first festival," stated Paul Cates, club member. At that time, the road to the gardens was just an old wagon trail.

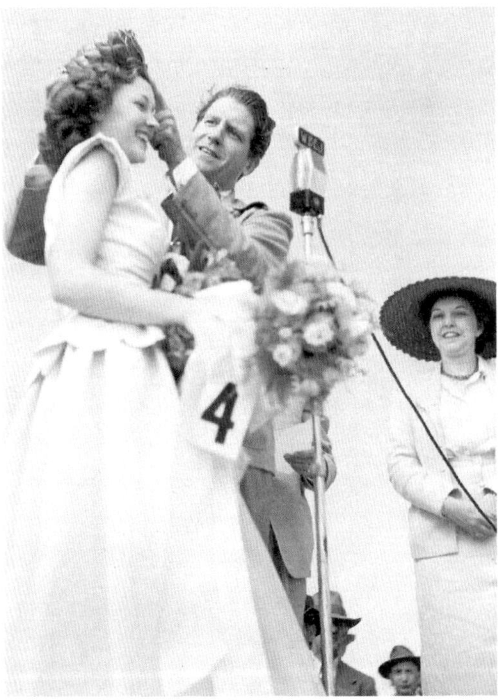

Betty Peoples, crowned the first Rhododendron Queen in history, in 1948 on top of the Roan. *Courtesy of the family of Betty Peoples.*

When the day arrived, distinguished guests Tennessee senator Tom Stewart and North Carolina governor Gregg Cherry joined the entourage headed to the top of the mountain. It was quite a celebration, with speeches and excitement fueled by the possibility of a better future.

When Sunday, June 20, 1948, arrived, the second annual Rhododendron Festival had grown immensely. This became the first year of the Rhododendron Queen contest, whose winners, in later years, could go on and compete for Miss America. Miss Betty Peoples, an eighteen-year-old senior from Elizabethton High School, garnered the honor of being the very first festival queen.

Governor Jim McCord of Tennessee and Lieutenant Governor L.Y. Ballantine of North Carolina were guests of the event and traveled together from the village of Roan Mountain up to the top. Along the route, guests were entertained by a host of vignettes, which included the Overmountain Men at the Sheltering Rock, Little Boy Blue, milkmaids, bear hunters and oxen doing farm work.

As they climbed to the top, many cars were lost to overheating, causing occasional backups in the procession. Ultimately, upon reaching Carver's Gap, girls dressed in Scottish costumes pinned heather on the dignitaries before their final ascent to the gardens.

In one of many speeches, Governor McCord addressed the crowd. "I'm coming back some day, and when I do I hope we will have an oil road," he stated, giving a great deal of optimism to the event.

The road was not here yet, but that did not extinguish the flame that kept community members actively working toward their goal. The 1949 festival welcomed the visit of a new governor of Tennessee, Gordon Browning. The scenario was similar, with vignettes along the road to the top, good food, fellowship and promising speeches.

Finally, in 1950, both Tennessee and North Carolina prepared contracts for the building of roads from both approaches. The Tennessee contract was let on April 14, 1950, for a road priced at $389,000.00 and ran for 7.6 miles from Burbank. At a cost of $470,080.76, the North Carolina road would cover 12.8 miles from the town of Bakersville.

The U.S. Forest Service opened bids on its planned road from Carver's Gap out toward the gardens in 1951, but it rejected all the bids, as they were too high. Instead, it decided to build the road itself. Forest Supervisor D.J. Morris pulled in funds from a half dozen sources to make the project

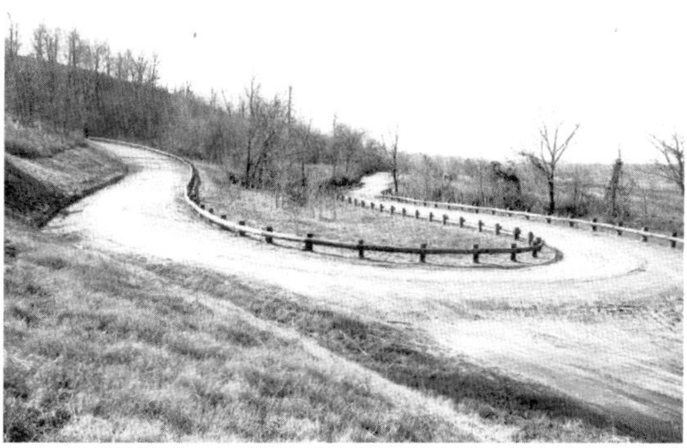

After several years of hard work, the new "oil road" to the top of the Roan was dedicated. 1952. *Courtesy of the Tennessee State Library and Archives.*

a reality, with the cost for blasting alone estimated at $117,000. The initial plans included a 350-car parking area at the old Cloudland Hotel site, in addition to a loop road through the gardens.

The culmination of all of this work came to fruition in 1952, when the three roads were dedicated; the Tennessee, North Carolina and Forest Service roads all linked at Carver's Gap. This long-awaited event saw the biggest crowd ever, with at least twenty thousand people gathered for the official ribbon cutting.

As the years rolled on, the festivals continued on top of the Roan, with many great reasons to attend. In September 1956, Knoxville resident and festival visitor Nancy Tanner told the *Toe Valley News*:

> *That weekend…hundreds of people came to see the magnificent displays of wild rhododendron, acres and acres blooming in a setting of blue spruce against a background of mountains rolling to the horizon. When I returned to the hot, dusty parking area, crowded with cars from many states, I was struck by the rapt expression of a local woman. "Beautiful sight, isn't it,"*

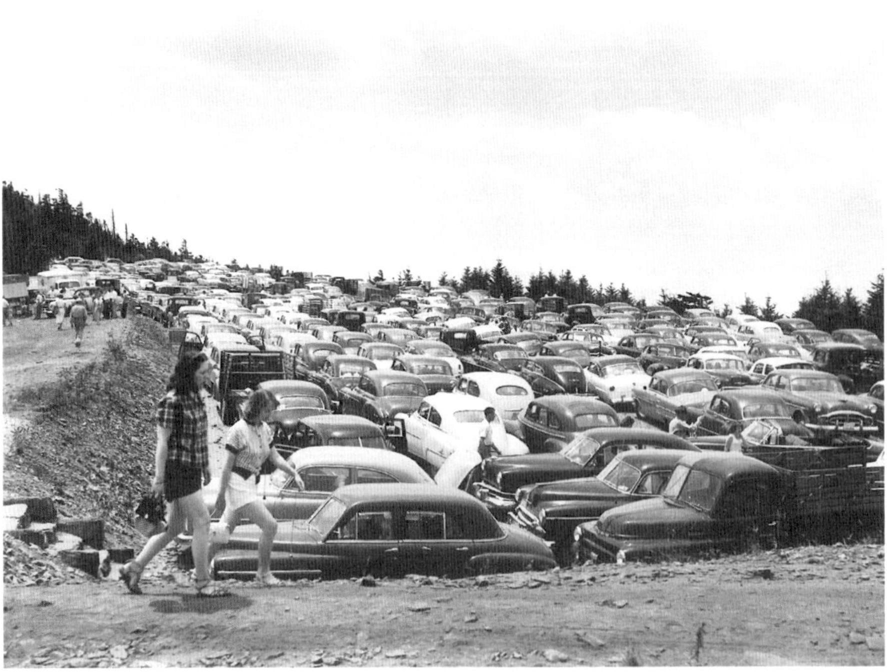

The year after the dedication of the new road, the Rhododendron Festival attracted an enormous number of guests. 1953. *Courtesy of the Tennessee State Library and Archives.*

> *I said. "Shore is purty," she agreed. "All them beautiful cars. Every year I come up here just to see them."*

Eventually, North Carolina and Tennessee went their own ways and began hosting separate events in each state. The extreme efforts necessary to organize a festival on top of the mountain ended, along with the stress of negotiating unknown weather conditions, travel and parking.

Even though the Citizens Club accomplished its first mission, it was not its last. The club continued to engage in projects that would bring modern services to the people of Roan Mountain. Acquiring phone service for residents and securing the presence of a bank, a fire truck, stage curtains for the new school and a Tennessee State Park are examples of its successful endeavors.

Members continue to be active in community service, particularly in the field of education. Each year, the club gives $1,000 to Cloudland Elementary and Cloudland High School to be used for academic needs. Its continuing Support a Student scholarship has been in place for many years to help a Cloudland High graduate successfully complete his or her college career. Its most noticed event continues to be the highly attended annual Rhododendron Festival, which takes place each June in Roan Mountain State Park. Though the Roan Mountain Citizens Club met the goals of its initial mission many years ago, the organization is still a viable and active community group.

Roan Mountain State Park

The efforts that ended in the successful construction of a new road to the top of the Roan had also served to introduce legislators to the remarkable beauty and recreational opportunities available in the East Tennessee mountains. Just seven years after the dedication of what is now Highway 143, the Tennessee legislature passed Senate Bill #17 on January 15, 1959, making Roan Mountain State Park a reality. It was a memorable moment for local residents, many of whom had worked long and hard for the creation of a park.

To the present date, the majority of the parkland has been acquired through the purchase of private tracts. The first 90 acres came courtesy of a $50,000 grant from the state. The bulk of the land was acquired between 1970 and 1974, when twenty-two tracts totaling 1,947 acres were purchased. The park now stands at a little more than 2,000 acres. Between 1959 and 1974, the only facilities in the park were a small primitive campground and

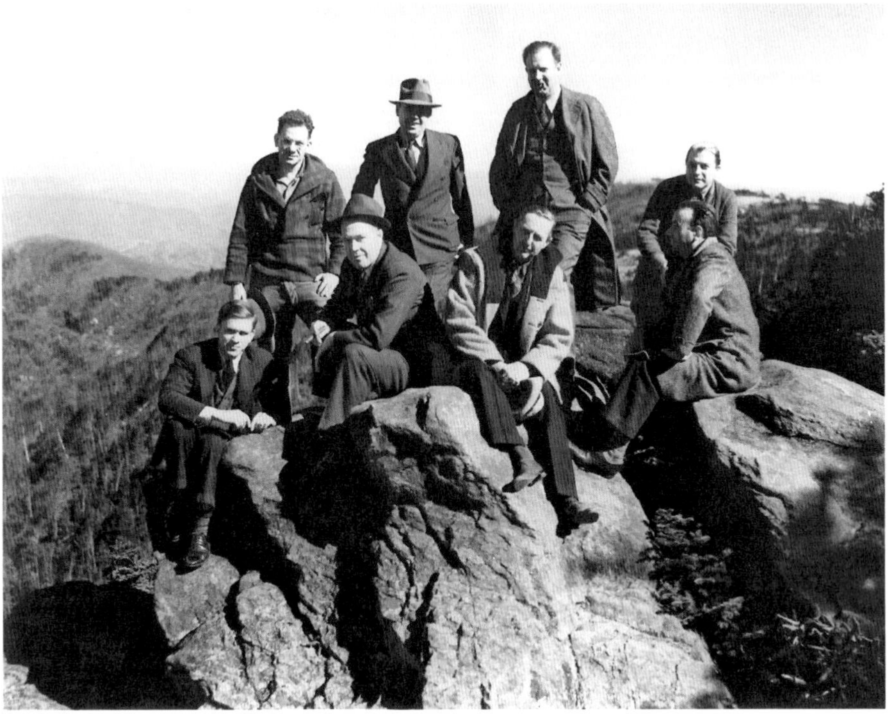

Almost twenty years before legislation was signed creating Roan Mountain State Park, folks from the Tennessee Conservation Department were checking out the area. 1938. *Courtesy of the Tennessee State Library and Archives.*

maintenance area located on the site of the present campground. Once the acquisition of land was completed, however, the park changed rapidly. As a result of development in the late 1970s, it now boasts an impressive array of facilities that contributes greatly to the Roan Mountain experience.

On June 21, 1980, Governor Lamar Alexander presided over the dedication ceremony of the $1.5 million improvements, which included twenty cabins, twenty additional campsites, a twenty-five-meter pool, two tennis courts, a restaurant and a recreation area. Congressman Jimmy Quillen was in attendance and brought attention to the sense of pride and satisfaction the completed project had given to the community.

The park entrance is about four miles from the village of Roan Mountain on Tennessee Highway 143. The visitors' center is immediately to the left; the attractive, rustic building provides park information, in addition to an Interpretive Museum, a Gift Shop and a Nature Center. While the building was under construction, an old water wheel from the local lumbermill was donated to the state. It was split in half for transport and brought to the new site, where it became a permanent and distinctive part of the building.

For those interested in the area's mining history, a trail leads from the visitors' center back into a hemlock forest to the site of the Peg Leg Mine. Peg Leg is an offshoot of the famous Cranberry vein, once considered among the most remarkable deposits of iron ore in the United States. The Cranberry vein stretches for twenty-two miles and crosses the Tennessee/North Carolina line at Hump Mountain to the north. Neither Cranberry nor Peg Leg is mined any longer.

From the visitors' center, if traveling up the mountain, you will drive three miles up Tennessee Highway 143 before reaching the Miller Homeplace. The drive prior to reaching the right turn to the homestead is beautiful, with the Doe River on your left and mountains stretching up to your right. Along the way, the park trail system crosses the highway at Cate's Hole, one of the most colorful walks during the early spring wildflower bloom.

The Miller Homeplace is definitely a must-see stop whenever you visit the park. In 1872, Dave and Louise Miller came to this secluded mountain holler and set up housekeeping on land they were renting from General John T. Wilder. In 1904, Dave and his son, Nathaniel, bought this land from Wilder; now it was his own.

A second log house was built by 1910 that became Dave and Louise's abode, while Nathaniel and his wife made their home in the white-sided house. In 1924, Nathaniel died, and his son, Frank, took over the farm. Later, Frank Miller became an on-site interpreter at Roan Mountain State Park from 1983 to 1995.

Those who knew Frank were eager to hear his tales of living in the holler without electricity and having to walk a pretty piece to get out to a real road. Everything they needed to survive was made right there, including their beds, which were made by stuffing cloth ticking with corn shucks and straw. Milk and taters were kept cold in the root cellar, and clothes were washed with lye soap in a kettle over a fire. The challenge of keeping warm during cold winters was met by covering the walls in the house with newspapers; those same papers now provide a glimpse into days gone by.

The property was covered with acres of orchards and numerous American chestnut trees. Frank often spoke of the days when the nuts were so thick on the forest floor that it was difficult to walk. On a positive note, their herd of hogs absolutely loved the never-ending supply of food.

Today, Beth Ann Jarrett, a member of the family, follows in Frank's footsteps and continues the tradition of sharing the remarkable stories of their family's life in this cozy holler just off the beaten path. You'll be entertained by more than stories, as her gardening skills have brought color to the land—so much color that the site is now certified as a monarch way station by the North American Butterfly Association. And we must not forget Beth Ann's animal friends that delight young and old visitors over and over again.

A right turn on Highway 143 as you exit the Miller Homeplace will take you to the cabin area. The first twenty rustic cabins, constructed in the late 1970s, are nestled comfortably in the woods. Each comes equipped with an array of conveniences: a full kitchen, a wood stove, a modern bathroom, a private bedroom downstairs, a loft with two single beds, supplementary electric heat and linens. The cabins are designed to sleep six. In 1997, ten additional cabins were built that were similar in structure to the first twenty but include two full beds in the loft, an additional bathroom and phone service. There is not a finer experience than to spend a night, or a week, nestled in the woods enjoying the peaceful beauty of this environment.

Just past the cabin area you will find a large swimming pool, tennis courts, playgrounds and a volleyball court. Behind the pool is the park's amphitheater, the site of many special events and programs.

The right turn past the pool area leads to the campground that provides private sites draped in mountain laurel. The mountain forests that surround Tennessee Highway 143 constitute the majority of the parkland. Twenty-five miles of foot trails give access to the more remote sections of the park. In addition, a mountain bike trail begins behind the first picnic shelter.

In its early days, Roan Mountain State Park seemed to be Tennessee's best-kept secret. Word of the beautiful new facilities was slow in reaching the rest of the world. However, once people did learn of the park and its facilities, festivals and educational programs, they came to visit. Roan Mountain State Park no longer qualifies as a well-kept secret; it has been discovered by people from all parts of the globe.

The Roan once had to attract visitors solely on its own merits, but now, with the park, it has a support staff resting at its feet. Park personnel seek to encourage the intelligent use of resources and to enhance the experience of those who have come to see the mountain's main attractions. The hard use the mountain receives during the peak season is regrettable, and every effort is made to keep it at a minimum, but even at its worst, it is a far cry from the wholesale abuses of past generations. Roan Mountain today is in as good condition as it has enjoyed in many years.

The Southern Appalachian Highlands Conservancy

In 1952, the new "oil roads" were dedicated to taking travelers to the top of Roan Mountain from both North Carolina and Tennessee. Beginning this same year, Stanley Murray, chairman of the Appalachian Trail Conference, spearheaded an effort to relocate the Appalachian Trail. In Roan Mountain, the old course traversed along twenty-four miles of roadways—not a pleasant walk. Working with the Tennessee Eastman Hiking Club, Stanley planned and led the seventy-two-mile relocation of the trail across the Roan massif.

Stanley Murray was a man with a vision that could not be stopped. He, along with other dedicated individuals, realized that there was more land to protect on Roan Mountain than the U.S. Forest Service could possibly fund. So in 1966, Stanley led the Roan Mountain Preservation Committee in efforts to identify and make contact with landowners who held land that was in need of preservation. It was not long until the need for funding arose; as a result, the Southern Appalachian Highlands Conservancy (SAHC) was created in 1974 from the early Preservation Committee.

SAHC now had the ability to raise the funds necessary to secure available land, either through ownership or easement. It wasn't looking for just any land; rather, it was seeking areas that had been identified as in need of conservation to provide sustainability of the ecosystem and view shed protection.

Today, its mission is to conserve the unique plant and animal habitat, clean water, local farmland and scenic beauty of the mountains of North Carolina and East Tennessee for the benefit of present and future generations. And it is well on its way to upholding its mission; just on the Roan Highlands, it has protected over fifteen thousand acres acquired in fifty-one separate tracts. Overall, this nonprofit land trust organization has safeguarded nearly fifty thousand acres of important lands in western North Carolina and East Tennessee.

In 2011, the Southern Appalachian Highlands Conservancy celebrated forty-five years of land protection efforts on Roan Mountain—quite an honor to so many who have worked diligently and stayed true to their goals.

FRIENDS OF ROAN MOUNTAIN

With a mission of "fostering great awareness and understanding of the natural, historical, and cultural significance of Roan Mountain," the Friends of Roan Mountain (FORM) was created. Chartered in March 2000, this 501c3 organization is moving forward at a rapid rate.

The primary goals of FORM are sponsorship and support of four naturalists rallies in Roan Mountain each year. At its inception, Friends of Roan sponsored two long-standing rallies: the spring and fall Roan Mountain Naturalists Rallies. In 2011, the spring rally celebrated its fifty-third year and the fall rally, its forty-ninth year. Fred Behrend, who came to America from Germany in 1896, first implemented both of these events.

Behrend found his way to Elizabethton when the Bemberg Corporation was looking for a German-English stenographer—a perfect fit. He quickly fell in love with the natural side of East Tennessee and was inspired to begin an event that would take people into the forests to learn about nature.

Now, over fifty-three years later, Friends of Roan continues two additional naturalist-oriented events: a winter rally and an event especially for young people called Xtreme Roan Adventures.

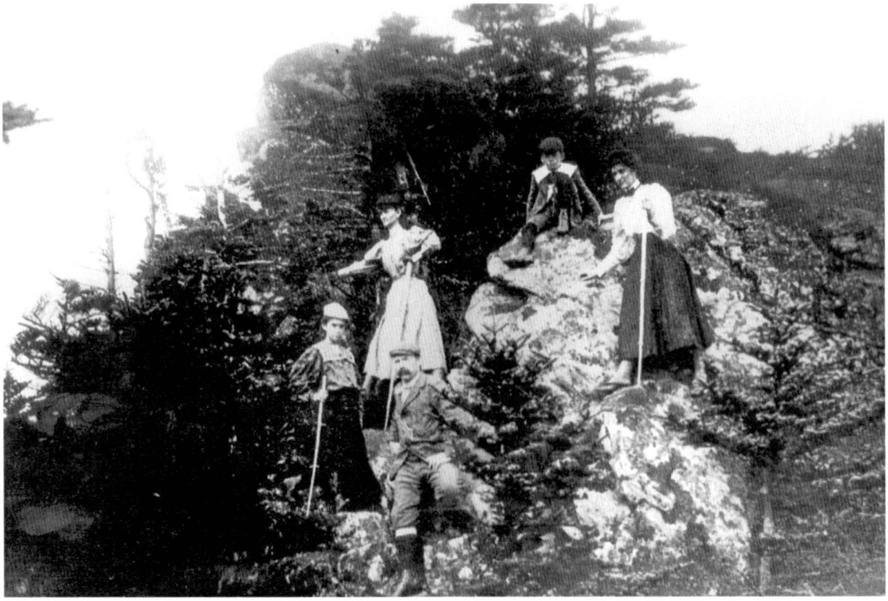

Guided nature excursions were provided for Cloudland Hotel guests in the 1880s and continue today, with thanks to active conservation organizations. *Courtesy of Thomas O. Maher.*

These rallies are a huge part of the efforts of Friends of Roan, but there is more. Of equal importance is the group's dedication to environmental education, financial sponsorship of scientific research on Roan Mountain and support of Roan Mountain State Park in its naturalist and environmental mission.

With a large membership, a hardworking board of directors and many projects constantly in the works, Friends of Roan Mountain will continue its growth and dedication to environmental education and protection in the Roan Mountain area.

A Historical Gathering

September 25, 1998

The wind was howling through Carver's Gap at 9:00 a.m., but the sky was clear, promising to be an extraordinary day for an extraordinary gathering. Aside from the vegetation rustling in the wind and the flurry of migratory birds chattering and moving from tree to tree, it was impressively quiet. Not a soul had yet arrived at the gap. I reflected for a moment on what was soon to take place. The thought was exciting and inspirational, for today was Friday, September 25, 1998, exactly one hundred years since John Muir had sat at the historic Cloudland Hotel and written a letter to his wife. The air that had "healed" Muir in 1898 was soon to bring together an incredible group of individuals who had made the Roan an important part of their lives. Bob Fulcher, regional interpretive specialist for Tennessee State Parks, perfectly described the probable scene when Muir arose one hundred years ago to this day, breathing the clear Roan Mountain air:

> *A hundred years ago today John Muir woke up on Roan Mountain. He ran among the clumps of rhododendron; he puzzled over the balds. When he wrote that letter to his wife, he named the genuses of the plants he found here like he was in heaven, naming the saints. Whenever we walk on this mountain, we put our feet down in the tracks of great people, people like Muir, Fraser, Michaux, and Asa Gray.*

It was a very humbling and soulful thought—one that perfectly framed this unforgettable day. At noon, Tennessee State Parks was preparing to document the enormous number of folks who had worked with and for Roan

Mountain in a very special photograph. These unique individuals had made a special contribution to the Roan and its understanding, just as John Muir had in the past, and thus were to be the subjects of a historic photograph.

Through the use of a camera made in 1905, a 360-degree, five-foot-long, panoramic photograph would be made of the group standing in a circle atop Round Bald. The historical significance of this undertaking was profound, as those present for the photograph would soon find their images a component of the new exhibits and Interpretive Center at Roan Mountain State Park. Even greater was the knowledge that all of these folks had devoted a good portion of their lives to the Roan.

Before long, folks began to arrive; first one car and then several. Everyone had until noon to make the trek up the side of Round Bald. Some wanted a head start so they could take their time and soak up the beauty of the day; others, driving a great distance, found themselves having to rush to the top. There were people from the U.S. Forest Service, the

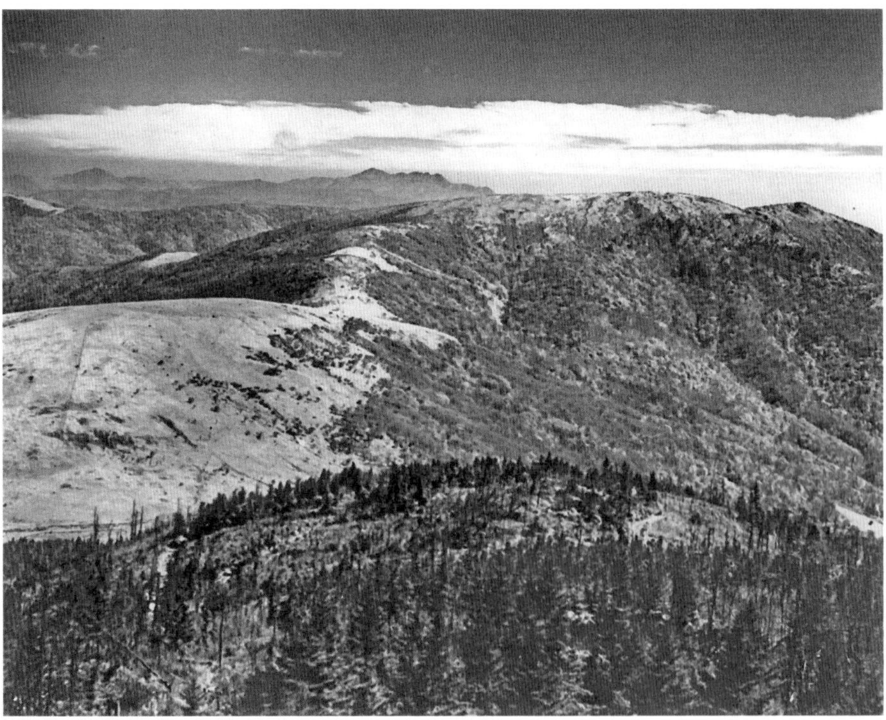

This incredible view of Round Bald, continuing out to Jane and Grassy, was the site of the gathering for a commemorative five-foot-long photo. 1947. *Courtesy of the Tennessee State Library and Archives.*

Tennessee Wildlife Resources Agency, Tennessee State Parks, the Southern Appalachian Highlands Conservancy, the U.S. Fish and Wildlife Service and the Appalachian Trail Conference; professors from East Tennessee State University, Appalachian State University, Western Carolina University and Mars Hill College; members of the Tennessee Conservation Commission, Friends of Roan Mountain and the Roan Mountain Naturalists Rally; General John T. Wilder's great-grandson; and teachers, high school conservation clubs, geologists and naturalists, both professional and amateur.

There were many significant individuals who were not documented in the photograph yet were remembered for their commitment and love of the Roan. Some were unable to make the steep climb; others had schedule conflicts. But the spirit of all could be felt on top of Round Bald that day as 103 representatives of those who considered the Roan a significant and biologically diverse mountain formed a circle in preparation for the long-anticipated event.

L. Edward St. Johns, a photographer from Morrison, Tennessee, had flown into the Elizabethton airport at 10:00 a.m. Bob Fulcher, who was the catalyst of this event, had left the park earlier to pick him up and get him to the top of the mountain on time. Students from the Elizabethton High School Ecology Club waited anxiously at Carver's Gap for his arrival, as they had graciously volunteered to carry all of his equipment to the top of the mountain. As they completed their mission, the rest of the group waited patiently on the bald, visiting old friends and sharing tales with those they may not have seen in years. Of the 103 persons present, almost everyone was already acquainted. Looking around this varied group of people, it was thrilling to see so many who attached such importance to Roan Mountain and so many who would alter their busy schedules to be here for this moment.

As the time arrived for the actual photograph to be taken, everyone became quiet and listened to instructions: how to stand, signing in and becoming a part of a video documentation. Thanks were offered, and a few special people were introduced. The fog that had blown in was beginning to dissipate, promising a clear image. "Is everyone ready?" Mr. St. Johns called out. "Here we go!" And with that, the ninety-three-year-old camera began to rotate slowly on its axis as the film inside advanced in synchronization with the rotation. Within approximately forty seconds, everyone's image was recorded on a five-foot-long strip of film. This process was repeated another time as photographs were made in color and black and white. As the camera scanned slowly around the circle, those at the start of the photograph had the opportunity to sit back and watch the others waiting their turn. At the beginning of the circle, Tom Gatti, Judy Murray and Thomas Maher quickly ran to the end of the circle so they would appear twice in the final image—on the far left and on the far right.

Once the deed was done, everyone slowly began to work their way off the bald. Reporters meandered around talking to folks and preparing television and newspaper interviews, while students remained to help carry the equipment back to Carver's Gap. You could sense a humbling satisfaction in the group as their mission was completed and successful.

By 5:00 p.m., all was quiet on Roan Mountain. Folks had left for the day but not forever. We all left knowing that the special places of our earth must be cared for, and most importantly, that there were numerous individuals who would give of their time and talents to protect Roan Mountain and other natural areas of the world.

EPILOGUE

It is a pleasure to say that the sense of discovery that prevails on the mountain has remained intact since the days when hay fever sufferers at the Cloudland Hotel could be seen combing the mountain looking for exotic plant life or even since the great botanist-explorers came to search for their place in scientific history. Visitors today still catch the excitement, still feel pangs of curiosity and still sense an air of exploration.

Many a metal detector has been carried through the woods in hopes that it would unearth valuable information about the hotel and its guests. A dump associated with the hotel has proven quite elusive, as has the famous guest register. Some treasure hunters have found success, though the possibility of opening another door into the Roan's past keeps people searching. "For some reason I just felt I should pick up this rock," said one gentleman who was moved to explore the hotel site years ago. "There's a million rocks there; it was real weird. And there, stuck between these two rocks, was this gold coin. Guess it's been there a long, long time."

New forest growth quickly covers the works of man, so there is always the chance that something special waits just beneath the heavy plant cover. It is easy to catch the spirit. I've been prone to it myself. On one occasion, some friends caught my interest with a wild and woolly tale about an important artifact from the Cloudland era that they'd discovered on the mountain. I was eager to see it, of course, and they agreed to take me. The only catch was that they wanted to go at night to add a touch of excitement to the trip.

That day had been crisp and clear, but as night approached, a thick fog rolled up the mountain and unfolded on its crest. By the time I met my friends on top of the Roan, we could barely see to walk or drive. I began to feel foolish for agreeing to walk blindly into a forest in a pea soup fog. Off we went, looking for something that had never been spelled out for me, but my friends tried to reassure me by saying that what we were going to see was well worth any minor discomforts we'd have to suffer along the way. It was a rough walk in our rain gear through the trees, rocks, moss and holes, with nothing to guide us but our flashlights. I felt doubly gullible when no one seemed to know exactly where this "thing" was supposed to be; they only knew the general direction. I was beginning to wonder if we were on a "snipe" hunt. We looked high and low as the fog grew thicker, heavier and wetter. My hair was dripping from the dampness, and my feet were beginning to grow heavy. I was becoming convinced that I was the victim of a bad joke.

Then someone yelled, "Over here!" We hurried around the back of a big gray rock and concentrated our flashlights on a spot where a large, square shape seemed to be growing straight out of the ground. I stood staring for a moment, but I couldn't hope to identify the object in the fog and the shadows. "It's an old coffin, an old grave from the hotel," one of my friends explained. "It must have worked its way back up out of the ground. I bet they're all over this mountain!" No one knew quite what to make of our discovery, but it was obvious we'd stumbled upon a significant part of the Roan's history, perhaps even a mysterious graveyard. I wanted to look more closely in the light of day, so I took a moment that night to mark the spot where we exited the woods. Then we stumbled back out onto the trail and down toward our cars.

The fog lifted the next day, and I wasted no time in heading back up the mountain. The route we had traveled the previous night was part of the Appalachian Trail; back in the days of Cloudland, it was also the old road by which visitors would make their way up to the hotel. It was still in good shape considering its many years of service, and I found the going much easier in the daytime. Locating my marked spot was relatively simple; the little pile of rocks I'd made stood out to the left of the trail as I crested a small hill. I turned left into the woods and started climbing.

I walked a good distance without spotting anything familiar, and I was on the verge of turning back when I saw the big gray rock up ahead. Behind it, half buried and half exposed, was a large wooden box that did in fact seem to be trying to wedge its way out of the earth. It was about seven or eight feet long and three feet wide, and it was divided by a partition inside. The part above ground had a large wooden lid. It looked terribly odd to be a casket, so I began to consider other possibilities. My best guess was that the structure was an old toolbox remaining from the days the original road was being constructed. It would have made a great shelter, providing ready access to the equipment needed for maintenance. Later, local residents confirmed my guess.

I was unsure whether to be disappointed in the discovery or pleased with my detective skills. If there is a lesson to be learned from this story, it is that things are not always what they appear at night, especially high on a mountain in a thick fog—or that friends who seem to be pulling your leg probably are. From another point of view, I prefer to remember that night as an affirmation of the need to keep digging for information. A forgotten toolbox may not be of the same importance as a graveyard, but it is nonetheless a valuable window into the past. It made me want to learn more.

Roan Mountain has that effect on people. It seems to breed an air of optimism and possibility. I still remember my first visits, when I was trying to come to decisions about my future, how sinking into that wonderful carpet of bald grass on top of the Roan seemed to make my problems somewhat lighter. I thought back then that everyone should have such a place to go to get back in tune with his or her heart and soul. Since I have become a full-time resident of the area, I feel it much more strongly.

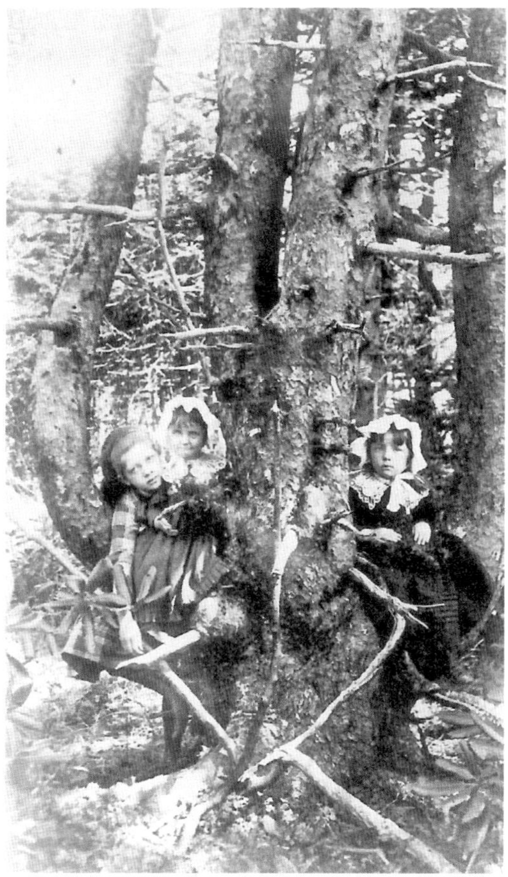

Wilder kin in the "lyre" tree, named for its harp-like shape. 1880s. *Courtesy of Thomas O. Maher.*

It will take the care and understanding of all who visit Roan Mountain to maintain its integrity and preserve its unique natural features. The Roan is a special mountain, and a fragile one, too. Yet within that fragility is strength with the power to refresh the spirit and open the way to discovery. With a little help from its friends, Roan Mountain will be able to experience a future every bit as illustrious as it's past.

Bibliography

Amman, G.D., and C.F. Speers. "Balsam Woolly Aphid in the Southern Appalachians." *Journal of Forestry* 63 (1965): 18–20.

Amman, Gene D., and Robert L. Talerico. "Symptoms of infestation by the balsam woolly aphid." U.S. Forest Service, Res. Note SE-85. Southeastern For.Exp.Sta., USDA.For.Ser. 1967.

Arthur, John Preston. *A History of Watauga County, North Carolina*. Richmond, VA: Everett Waddy Company. 1915.

———. *Western North Carolina: A History from 1730 to 1913*. Raleigh, N.C: Edwards and Broughton Printing Company, 1914.

Arthur, John Preston, and William F. Bade. *The Life and Letters of John Muir.* Vol. 2. Boston: Houghton Mifflin Company, 1924

Bakuzis, E.V., and H.L. Hansen. *Balsam Fir.* Minneapolis: University of Minnesota Press, 1965.

Barb, Mark A. "Natural History of the Northern Saw-Whet Owl (*Aegolius acadicus*) in Southern Appalachian Mountains." Master's thesis, East Tennessee State University, 1995.

Barnhart, John Hendley. *Biographical Notes upon Botanists*. Boston: G.K. Hall, 1965.

Barry, Patrick J., and Theodore M. Oprean III. *Evaluation of Balsam Woolly Aphid on Roan Mountain*. USDA For. Ser., Report No. 79-1-12. Toecane Ranger District, Pisgah National Forest, April 1979.

Bartram, William. *Travels through North and South Carolina, Georgia, East and West Florida: The Cherokee Country, &c.* Philadelphia: James and Johnson, 1791.

Bayley, W.S. *General Features of the Magnetite Ores of Western North Carolina and East Tennessee*. Washington, D.C.: Department of the Interior, U.S. Government Printing Office, 1922.

———. *Magnetic Iron Ores of East Tennessee and Western North Carolina.* Washington, D.C.: Bureau of Mines, 1923.

Beetham, Nellie. "Pollen Studies on Roan Mountain." Master's thesis, Duke University, 1950.

Behrend, Fred W. "Evening Grosbeaks and Snow Buntings on Roan Mountain and Big Bald Mountains, Tennessee-North Carolina." *Migrant* 26 (1955): 14–16.

Billings, W.D., and A.F. Mark. "Factors Involved in the Persistence of Montane Treeless Balds." Ecology 38 (1957): 140–42.

Blackmun, Ora. *Western North Carolina: Its Mountains and Its People to 1880.* Boone, NC: Appalachian Consortium Press, 1977.

Bowlick, C.A. "A Study of the Cranberry Ore Belt." Master's thesis, Appalachian State Teachers College, 1955.

Britton, E.G. "Botanical Notes in the Great Valley of Virginia and in the Southern Alleghenies." *Bulletin of the Torrey Botanical Club* 13, no. 5 (May 1886).

Brown, D.M. "Conifer Transplants to a Grassy Bald on Roan Mountain." *Ecology* 34 (1953): 614–17.

———. "Vegetation of Roan Mountain: A Phytosociological and Successional Study." *Ecological Monographs* 11 (1941): 61–97.

Bruner, S.C., and A.L. Field. "Notes on the Birds Observed on a Trip through the Mountains of Western North Carolina". *Auk* 29 (1912): 368–77.

Buehler, D.A., et al. *Status Assessment and Conservation Plan for the Golden-winged Warbler,* Vermivora chrysoptera, *in the United States.* Golden-Winged Warbler Working Group. U.S. Department of the Interior. Fish and Wildlife Service Biological Technical Publication, FWS/BTP-R6XXX-2006. http://www.gwwa.org/ecology.html.

Cain, S.A. "An Ecological Study of the Heath Balds of the Great Smoky Mountains." *Butler University Botany Study* 1 (1930): 177–208.

Camp, W.H. "The Grass Balds of the Great Smoky Mountains of Tennessee and North Carolina." *Ohio Journal of Science* 31 (1931): 157–64.

Campbell, E.T. *Tweetsie Tales.* Vol. 1. Blowing Rock, NC: New River Publishing Company, 1989.

Carney, C. B. *Weather and Climate in North Carolina.* Agricultural Expt. Stat., North Carolina State College, Bull. 396, Raleigh, 1955.

Carolina Kids Conservancy. "Meet Your Endangered Neighbor: Spruce-Fir Moss Spider." *Carolina Kids for Critters* (Fall 1998): 12.

———. "Roan Mountain Celebration." *Carolina Kids for Critters* (Fall 1998): 10–11.

———. "Why Preserve the Highlands of Roan?" *Carolina Kids for Critters* (Summer 1998): 10–12.

Carter, Barbara E. "A Survey of the Tree Layer of the Spruce Fir Forest on Roan Mountain: Carter County, Tennessee, and Mitchell County, North Carolina." Master's thesis, East Tennessee State University, 1979.

Castro, Philip K. "A Quantitative Study of the Subalpine Forest of Roan and Bald Mountains in the Southern Appalachians." Master's thesis, East Tennessee State University, 1969.

Chamberlain, Morrow. *A Brief History of the Pig Iron Industry in East Tennessee.* Chattanooga, TN, 1942.

Chickering, J.W. "A Summer on Roan Mountain." *Botanical Gazette* 5, no. 12 (1880).

Church, S.A., and D.R. Taylor. "Speciation and Hybridization among Houstonia (*Rubiaceae*) Species: The Influence of Polyploidy on Reticulate Evolution." *American Journal of Botany* 92 (2005): 1372–80.

Coates, Ruth Allison. *Great American Naturalists.* Minneapolis, MN: Lerner Publications Company, 1974.

Cockerel, Bennie Lee, Jr. "Prey Preferences of the Northern Saw-Whet Owl (*Aegolius acadicus*) in the Southern Appalachian Mountains." Master's thesis, Appalachian State University, 1997

Colton, Henry E. *Guide Book to the Scenery of Western North Carolina.* Asheville, NC: Western Advocate, 1860.

———. *Mountain Scenery. The Scenery of the Mountains of Western North Carolina and Northwestern South Carolina.* Raleigh, NC: W.L. Pomeroy, 1859.

Committee for Tennessee Rare Plants. "The Rare Vascular Plants of Tennessee." *Journal for the Tennessee Academy of Science* 53, no 4 (October 1978).

Cooper, Horton. *History of Avery County.* Asheville, NC: Biltmore Press, 1964.

Corbett, Sherry. "Roan Park Dedicated." Elizabethton Star, June 22, 1980.

Coyle, Frederick A. "The Mygalomorgh Spider Genus Microhexura (*Araneae, Dipluridae*)." *Bulletin of the American Museum of Natural History* 170, no. 1 (1988).

Davis, John H., Jr. "Vegetation of the Black Mountains of North Carolina: An Ecological Study." *Elisha Mitchell Scientific Society Journal* 45, no. 2 (May 1930).

Dellinger, Clyde J. *Tweetsie and the Clinchfield Railroads: Crossing the Blue Ridge Mountains.* Morganton, NC: News Herald Press, 1975.

Dellinger and Associates, Clyde J. *The Roots of Tweetsie.* Charlotte, NC: Clyde J. Dellinger, 1983.

Dull, C.W., J.D. Ward, H.D. Brown, G.W. Ryan, W.H. Clerke and R.J. Uhler. *Evaluation of Spruce and Fir Mortality in the Southern Appalachian Mountains.* Protect. Rep. R8-PR. U.S. Department of Agriculture, 1989.

East Tennessee State University. "Harvesting the Hardwoods." Archives of Appalachia. http://www.etsu.edu/cass/Archives/Subjects/Hardwoods/intro.htm.

Eller, Glen, and Gary Wallace. *Birds of Roan Mountain and Vicinity*. Elizabethton, TN: Lee R. Herndon Chapter, Tennessee Ornithological Society, 1984.

Fanslow, Mary F. *Resorts in Southern Appalachia: A Microcosm of American Resorts in the Nineteenth and Early Twentieth Centuries.* Johnson City: East Tennessee State University, 2004.

Ferrell, Mallory Hope. *Tweetsie Country*. Boulder, CO: Pruett Publishing Company, 1976.

———. *Tweetsie Country*. Johnson City, TN: Overmountain Press, 1971 and 1991.

Finck, H.T. "Mammoth Cave and Cloudland." *New York Evening Post*, August 27, 1898.

Forsaith, C.C. "Anatomical Reduction in Some Alpine Plants." *Ecology* 1 (1920): 124–35.

Friends of Roan Mountain. www.friendsofroanmtn.org.

Frome, Michael. *Strangers in High Places*. New York: Doubleday and Company, 1966.

Fulcher, Bob. "Hack Line Road: The Route to the Roan." *Tennessee Conservationist* (May/June 2001).

———. "Muir, Michaux, and Gray, on the Roan." *Tennessee Conservationist* (September/October 1998): 14–20.

Ganier, A.F. "Summer Birds of Roan Mountain." *Migrant* 7 (1936): 83–86.

Gates, William H. *Observations on the Possible Origin of the Balds of the Southern Appalachians*. Baton Rouge: Louisiana State University Press. 1941.

Gray, Asa. "Notes on a Botanical Excursion into the Mountains of North Carolina." *American Journal of Science and Arts* 42, no. 1 (1892).

Gray, J.L., ed. *Letters of Asa Gray*. 2 vols. New York: Houghton Mifflin Company, 1893.

Gray, Ralph, W.E. Garrett and R.F. Sisson. "Rhododendron Time on Roan Mountain." *National Geographic* 61, no. 6 (May 1957): 819.

Guidetti, Roberto. "Two New Species of *Macrobiotidae (Tardigrada: Eutardigrada)* from the United State of America, and Some Taxonomic Considerations of the Genus Murrayon." *Proceedings of the Biological Society of Washington* 111, no. 3 (1998): 663–73.

Hardin, Mike. *Cy Crumley Speaks to the Nation on We the People.* Transcribed by Mary McCown. www.johnsonsdepot.com.

Hardy, A.V., C.B. Carney and H.V. Marshall Jr. *Climate of North Carolina Research Stations.* Agricultural Expt. Stat., North Carolina State University, Bull. 433, Raleigh, NC.

Harshberger, J.W. "An Ecological Study of the Mountainous North Carolina." *Botanical Gazette* 36 (1903): 241–58, 368–83.

Hendrick, Elizabeth, ed. *The Selected Letters of William James.* New York: Doubleday, Anchor Books, 1961.

Herndon, Lee R. "Birds of Carter County, Tennessee." *Migrant* 21 (1950): 57–68.

———. "Summer Visitors on Roan Mountain." *Migrant* 48 (1977): 13–14.

Holmes, J.S. *Forest Conditions in Western North Carolina.* North Carolina Geological and Economic Survey, Bull. 23, 1911.

"John Strother's Survey Diary." *The State* 33, no. 23 (1966): 10–14.

Johnson, Kristine D., Hoover L. Lambert and Patrick J. Barry. *Status and Post Suppression Evaluation of Balsam Woolly Aphid Infestations on Roan Mountain.* Toecane Ranger District. Pisgah National Forest, May 1980.

Joslin, Michael. "Jane Bald." *Johnson City Press Chronicle*, March 29, 1999.

Keith, Arthur. *Geological Atlas. Cranberry Folio.* Washington, D.C.: U.S. Division of Geology, 1903.

Kenney, Tom. A *Place Called Roan Highlands.* Southern Appalachians Highlands Conservancy, July 1999.

Knight, Richard L. *The Birds of Northeast Tennessee: An Annotated Checklist.* 2nd ed. Bristol, TN: Bristol Bird Club, Bristol, 2008.

———. "Evidence of Probable Breeding by the Hermit Thrush on Roan Mountain, Tennessee/North Carolina." *Migrant* 68 (1997): 123.

———. "Golden-Crowned Kinglet Nest on Roan Mountain, North Carolina/Tennessee." *Migrant* 58 (1987): 48–49.

———. "Pine Siskin Nest on Roan Mountain, North Carolina." *Chat* 58 (1994): 119–20.

———. "Summer Birds of the Roan Mountain Highlands." *Migrant* 81 (2010): 1–28.

Korstian, C.I. "Perpetuation of Spruce on Cut-Over Lands." *Ecological Monographs* 7 (1937): 125–67.

Lanman, Charles. *Letters from the Alleghany Mountains.* New York: G.P. Putnam, 1849.

Lee, W.D. *The Soils of North Carolina, Their Formation, Identification, and Use.* Agricultural Expt. Stat., North Carolina State College, Tech. Bull. 115, Raleigh, NC.

Lindsay, Mary M., and Susan Power Bratton. *Grassy Balds of the Great Smoky Mountains: Their History and Flora in Relation to Potential Management.* Department of the Interior, National Park Service. *Environmental Management* 3, no. 5 (n.d.): 417–30.

———. "The Vegetation of Grassy Balds and Other High Elevation Disturbed Areas in the Great Smoky Mountains National Park." *Bulletin of the Torrey Botanical Club* 106, no. 4 (October–December 1979): 264–75.

Lura, Richard, Ed Schell and Gary Wallace. "Nesting Alder Flycatchers in Tennessee." *Migrant* 50 (1979): 34–36.

Lyle, Robert B., and Bruce P. Tyler. "The Nesting Birds of Northeastern Tennessee." *Migrant* 5 (1934): 49–57.

Mark, A.F. "The Ecology of the Southern Appalachian Grass Balds." *Ecological Monographs* 28 (1858): 293–338.

———. "The Flora of the Grass Balds and Fields of the Southern Appalachian Grass Balds." *Southern Appalachian Botanical Club Journal (Castanea)* 24 (1959): 1–21.

Merritt, Frank. *An Early History of Carter County, 1760–1861.* Kingsport, TN: Kingsport Press, 1950.

———. *A Later History of Carter County, 1865–1980.* Kingsport, TN: Arcata Graphics, 1978.

Miall, Louis Compton. *The Early Naturalists.* London: Macmillan & Co., 1912.

Milling, T.C., M.P. Rowe, B.L. Cockerel, T.A. Dellinger, J.B. Gailes and C.E. Hill. *Population Densities of Northern Saw-Whet Owls (*Aegolius acadicus*) in Degraded Boreal Forests of the Southern Appalachians.* USDA Forest Service. General Technical Report, 1997.

Morley, Margaret. *The Carolina Mountains.* Boston: Houghton, Mifflin and Company, 1913.

Nelson, Diane R. "Tardigrada." In *Ecology and Classification of North American Freshwater Invertebrates.* N.p.: Academic Press, Inc., 1991.

Nelson, Diane R, and Karen L. McGlothlin. "A New Species of *Calohypsibius* (phylum *Tardigrada, Eutardigrada*) from Roan Mountain, Tennessee-North Carolina, U.S.A." *Zoological Journal of the Linnean Society* 116 (1996): 167–74.

———. "A New Species of Hypsibius (phylum Tardigrada) from Roan Mountain, Tennessee, U.S.A." *American Microscopical Society, Inc.* 112, no. 2 (1993): 140–44.

Nitze, H.B.C. *Iron Ores of North Carolina.* Raleigh: North Carolina Division of Geology, 1893.

North American Rayon Corporation. "First Rhododendron Festival." *Watauga Spinnerette* (July 1947): 14–15.

———. "Fourth Annual Rhododendron Festival." *Watauga Spinnerette* (September 1950): 35–37.

———. "Roan Mountain Rhododendron Festival, June 20–21." *Watauga Spinnerette* (June 1953).

———. "Sixth Annual Rhododendron Festival." Watauga Spinnerette (August 1952): 14–17.

Noss, Reed F., and Robert L. Peters. *Endangered Ecosystems: A Status Report on America's Vanishing Habitat and Wildlife. Defenders of Wildlife.* N.p., 1995.

Noss, Reed F, Edward T. LaRoe III and J. Michael Scott. *Endangered Ecosystems of the United States: A Preliminary Assessment of Loss and Degradation.* N.p.: National Biological Service, 1995.

Oosting, H.J., and W.D. Billings. "A Comparison of Virgin Spruce Fir Forest in the Northern and Southern Appalachian System." *Ecology* 32 (1951): 84–103.

Petranek, Art, and Keith Minnick. *In Search of Tweetsie.* United States Geological Survey Maps. Linville, NC: Trane Publications, n.d.

———. *In Search of Tweetsie.* DVD. Linville, NC: Trane Publications, n.d.

Pielke, Robert A. "The Distribution of Spruce in West-Central Virginia before Lumbering." *Castanea* 46 (1981): 201–16.

Powell, Joseph. *Impacts of Goat Browsing and Disease on Lilium Grayi, Gray's Lily, on Roan Mountain.* Johnston City: Eastern Tennessee State University, April 2011.

Pulliam, H.R. "Sources, Sinks, and Population Regulation." *American Naturalist* 132 (1988): 652–61.

Rabenold, K. "Birds of Appalachian Spruce-Fir Forests: Dynamics of Habitat Island Communities." In *The Southern Appalachian Spruce-Fir Ecosystem: Its Biology and Threats.* Edited by P.S. White. National Park Service Research/Resources Management Report SER-71, 1984.

Ramseur, G.S. "The Vascular Flora of High Mountain Communities of the Southern Appalachians." *Elisha Mitchell Scientific Society Journal* 76 (1959): 82–112.

Redfield, J.H. "Notes on a Botanical Excursion into North Carolina." *Bulletin of the Torrey Botanical Club* 6 (1879): 331–39.

Reiger, George. "$25 Will Save a Rhododendron." *Audubon* 78, no. 3 (May 1976): 46.

Rhoads, S.N. "Contributions to the Zoology of Tennessee No. 2, Birds." *Proceedings of the Academy of Natural Sciences of Philadelphia* 47 (1895): 463–501.

Russell, N.H. "The Beech Gaps of the Great Smoky Mountains." *Ecology* 34 (1953): 366–74.

Scribner, F. Lamson. "The Grasses of Roan Mountain." *Botanical Gazette* 14 (1889).

Sennett, G.B. "Observations in Western North Carolina Mountains in 1886." *Auk* 4 (1887): 240–45.

Sheppard, Muriel Earley. *Cabins in the Laurel.* Chapel Hill, NC: Chapel Hill Books, 1935, 1991.

Smith, T.W., and M.J. Waterway. "Evaluating the Taxonomic Status of the Globally Rare *Carex roanensis* (*Cyperaceae*) and Allied Species Using Morphology and Amplified Fragment Length Polymorphisms." *Systematic Botany* 33 (2008): 525–35.

Smith, T.W., J.T. Donaldson, T.F. Wieboldt, G.L. Kauffman and M.J. Waterway. "The Geographic and Ecological Distribution of the Roan Mountain Sedge, *Carex roanensis* (*Cyperaceae*)." *Castanea* 71, no. 1 (2006): 45–53.

Southern Appalachian Highlands Conservancy. www.appalachian.org.

Stuckey, J.L. *North Carolina, Its Geology and Mineral Resources.* Raleigh: N.C. State University Print Shop, 1965.

Tamashiro, Dana Ann A. *Genetic and Morphological Variation in Northern Saw-Whet Owl Populations in Eastern North America.* Master's thesis, Appalachian State University, Boone, NC, 1996.

Tanner, James T. "Woodcock Nesting on Roan Mountain." *Migrant* 13 (1942): 49.

University of Tennessee Knoxville. The Golden-Winged Warbler Working Group. http://gwwa.utk.edu.

U.S. Congress, Senate. *Message from the President of the United States Transmitting a Report of the Secretary of Agriculture in Relation to the Forests, Rivers, and Mountains of the Southern Appalachian Region.* 57th Cong., 1st sess., Document No. 84. 1902.

U.S. Department of Agriculture., N.C. Agricultural Expt. Stat., and TVA. *Soil Survey Reports for Mitchell County, North Carolina.* Washington, D.C.: U.S. Government Printing Office, n.d.

U.S. Department of the Interior. *Final Report of the Southern Appalachian National Park Commission to the Secretary of the Interior.* Washington., D.C.: U.S. Government Printing Office, 1931.

———. *Report of Investigations: Cranberry Magnetite Deposits: Avery County, N.C. , and Carter County, Tenn.* Bureau of Mines, R.I. 4274, 1948.

U.S. Geological Survey. *Cranberry Folio.* No. 90. Washington, D.C.: U.S. Government Printing Office, 1903.

———. *Roan Mountain Folio*. No. 151. Washington, D.C.: U.S. Government Printing Office. 1907.

Ward, J.D. *Status of Balsam Woolly Aphid,* Adelges piceae *(*Ratz.*) on Roan Mountain*. USDA For. Ser., Report No. 75-1-3. Toecane Ranger District, Pisgah National Forest, 1974.

Ward, J.D., and E.T. Wilson. *Status of Balsam Woolly Aphid,* Adelges piceae *(*Ratz.*) on Roan Mountain.* USDA For. Ser., Report No. 73-1-34. Toecane Ranger District, Pisgah National Forest, 1973.

Warden, J.C. "Changes in the Spruce-Fir Forest of Roan Mountain in Tennessee over the Past Fifty Years as a Result of Logging." *Journal of the Tennessee Academy of Science* 64 (1989): 194–95.

Warner, Charles Dudley. *On Horseback: A Tour in Virginia, North Carolina, and Tennessee*. Boston: Houghton, Mifflin and Company, 1889.

Weigl, Peter D., Travis W. Knowles and Allen C. Boynton. "The Distribution and Ecology of the Northern Flying Squirrel, Glaucomys sabrinus coloratus, in the Southern Appalachians." Department of Biology, Wake Forest University, Winston-Salem, NC, 1999.

Wells, B.W. "Andrews Bald: The Problem of Its Origin." *Castanea* 1 (1936): 59–62. 1936.

———. *Major Plant Communities of North Carolina*. Agricultural Expt. Stat., N.C. State College, Bull. 25. Raleigh, NC, 1924.

———. *The Natural Gardens of North Carolina*. Chapel Hill: University of North Carolina Press, 1932.

———. "Origin of Southern Appalachian Grass Balds." *Ecology* 37 (1956): 592.

———. "Southern Appalachian Grass Balds." *Elisha Mitchell Scientific Society Journal* 53 (1937): 1–26.

Wells, B.W., and B.S. Wells. *Origin of the southern Appalachian grass balds*. Science 83: 283. 1936

Wetmore, A. "Notes on the Birds of Tennessee." *Proceedings of the United States National Museum* 86 (1939): 175–243.

White, P.S., E.R. Buckner, J.D. Pittillo and C.V. Cogbill. "High-Elevation Forests: Spruce-Fir Forests, Northern Hardwood Forests, and Associated Communities." In *Biodiversity of the Southeastern United States.* Vol. 2, *Upland Terrestrial Communities*. Edited by W.H. Martin, S.C. Boyce and A.C. Echternacht. New York: John Wiley & Sons, Inc., 1993.

White, Philip. "Decadal-Scale Trends in Forest Succession and Climatic Sensitivity in a Red Spruce-Fraser Fir Forest at Roan Mountain, Pisgah and Cherokee National Forests." Master's thesis, Appalachian State University, Department of Geography and Planning, August 2010.

Wilkins, Kay. "The Cloudland Once Catered to Elegant Guests atop Roan." *Johnson City Press-Chronicle*, July 4, 1976.

———. "Cy Crumley: A Railroading Man." *Johnson City Press-Chronicle*, July 4, 1976.

Williams, Samuel Cole. *General John T. Wilder: Commander of the Lightning Brigade*. Bloomington: Indiana University Press, 1936.

Zeigler, Wilbur G., and Ben S. Grosscup. *The Heart of the Alleghenies or Western North Carolina*. Raleigh. NC: Alfred Williams and Company, 1883.

Index

C

M

N

S

T

About the Author

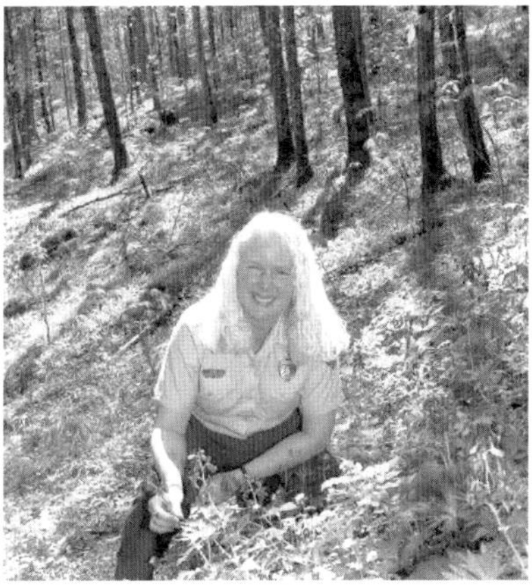

Though a native of Maryland, the upper East Tennessee mountains have long been Jennifer Bauer's home. She is a three-time graduate of East Tennessee State University with degrees in biology, art, teaching and science education. Employed as a park manager at Sycamore Shoals State Historic Area in Elizabethton, she began her career in the role of park interpretive specialist at Roan Mountain State Park for twenty-one years prior to promotion. Of utmost importance in her professional and personal life is becoming a good environmental and cultural educator, coupled with a strong belief in the importance of conservation and preservation. In 2007, Jennifer wrote *Wildlife, Wildflowers and Wild Activities: Exploring Southern Appalachia*, a collection of creative ways friends and families can explore the outdoors. She has two beautiful daughters and two granddaughters who are the joy of her life. Hiking, nature study, clogging, weaving, natural dyeing, spinning, watercolor painting and music are but a few pastimes of interest to her.